Pete and Sean Taylor (Photo courtesy of Pedro Taylor)

GOING FULL SPEED

The Sean Taylor Stories

AS TOLD BY:
PEDRO "PETE" TAYLOR

with Family - Friends - Teammates - Coaches and a Team Owner

STEVEN M. ROSENBERG

authorHOUSE®

AuthorHouse™
1663 Liberty Drive
Bloomington, IN 47403
www.authorhouse.com
Phone: 1-800-839-8640

Published by AuthorHouse 05/07/2015

ISBN: 978-1-4969-6080-1 (sc)
ISBN: 978-1-4969-6079-5 (e)

Print information available on the last page.

Book covers designed by Steven M. Rosenberg

Due to the dynamic nature of the NFL and collegiate sports, players and or coaches affiliated with teams mentioned herein may have changed affiliations or may no longer be under contract with any team. The authors have made every effort to provide accurate information at the time of publication.

This book is printed on acid-free paper.

To fans of Sean Taylor everywhere

Contents

Included interviews

(In order of appearance)

1. Sean's Father: Pedro Taylor
2. Sean's Grandmother: Connie Dingle
3. Sean's Stepmother: Josephine Taylor
4. Teammate: Antrel Rolle
5. Family Friend: Coach Marcus Jones
6. Half Brother: Joseph Taylor
7. Half Sister: Jazmin Taylor
8. Richmond Heights Middle School Teacher and Track Coach: Timothy Blount
9. Teammate: Marcus Hudson
10. Killian HS Head JV Football Coach: James Bryant
11. Killian HS Basketball Coach: Saul Weissman
12. Killian HS Basketball Teammate: Darren Weissman
13. Friend: T. J. Holten
14. Friend: Mike McFarlane
15. Gulliver Prep Head of Schools: John Krutulis
16. Gulliver Prep Football Teammate: Buck Ortega
17. Gulliver Prep Head Football Coach: Steve Howey
18. Gulliver Prep Assistant Coach: Ralph Ortega
19. Gulliver Prep Assistant Coach: John McCloskey
20. Univ. of Miami Head Football Coach: Larry Coker
21. Univ. of Miami Assistant Coach: Don Soldinger UMSHoF
22. Univ. of Miami Coach: Curtis Johnson
23. Univ. of Miami Teammate: Jonathan Vilma
24. Sean's NFL Agent: Drew Rosenhaus
25. Washington Redskins Team Owner: Daniel Snyder
26. Washington Redskins Defensive Coordinator: Gregg Williams
27. Washington Redskins Teammate: Clinton Portis
28. Washington Redskins Teammate: Renaldo Wynn
29. Washington Redskins Coach: Steve Jackson

Prologue: A Chance Encounter

Do you believe in predestination? I ask because the number one question posed about the writing of this book is how I met Sean Taylor's father, Pedro "Pete" Taylor, in the first place. I can only describe it as a chance meeting, one of destiny, as though it were supposed to happen.

The story actually begins on Thursday, November 10, 2011, three days before the Washington Redskins were to play the Miami Dolphins at Sun Life Stadium in Miami. My son the Dolphins fan and I were shopping in one of his favorite South Florida sports apparel stores, Canes Wear of Davie, Florida, owned by my friend Brett.

Canes Wear features a huge assortment of team apparel, fan wear, and goodies from the Miami Hurricanes (the Canes), other assorted Florida university teams, and pro teams, such as the Miami Heat, Miami Dolphins, and Miami Marlins.

There are baseball caps, T- and polo shirts, jerseys, slippers, ties, etc. There's also a massive amount of signed memorabilia and tchotchkes, such as banners, key chains, watches, charms, bobbleheads, dog sweaters and loads of other assorted sports stuff.

On one of the apparel racks in the back of the store, my son spotted a Sean Taylor #26 Miami Hurricanes jersey, and being the big Sean T. fan that he is, he had to have it.

"Dad, Dad, Dad, Dad, Dad," he excitedly proclaimed.

"What, what, what, what?" I responded.

"Looooook," he said, and held up the jersey so I could see it. He followed with, "Can I have it?"

In actuality, he asked me to extend him some "Dad credit" so he could buy it—with Dad's cash. Before I spoke to my friend about a deal, I asked my son to try it on. What do you know? It fit.

So I asked Brett, "How much for the Taylor jersey?"

My buddy gave me the "friends and family" discount, so I agreed to make the purchase. (Mention my name for your discount … wink, wink.)

Fast-forward to Sunday, November 13, 2011: Game day—a day on which I hosted ten Redskins fans who flew in for the game from Washington, DC, Asheville, North Carolina, and Long Island, New York. Through internal Dolphin team connections, I was able to finagle pregame warm-up field passes for our small group. So there we were on the sidelines, watching the teams stretching, running, punting, and tossing warm-up passes before the game. Both of my sons were on the field with me, and my younger son wore the Canes #26 Taylor jersey.

About halfway through warm-ups, my younger son tapped me on the shoulder and pointed toward a guy standing about fifty feet away from us. "Dad," my son said, "Do you know who that guy is?"

"No," I replied. "Should I?"

"That's Sean Taylor's father," he said.

"How do you know?" I asked.

He replied, "Look at him. He looks just like Sean!"

People who know me know I'd speak to a lamppost if I knew it would respond, and that day was no exception. "Do you want to meet him?" I asked.

"Yeahhh!" was his animated response.

"Would you like to have your picture taken with him?" I continued.

"Yeahhhhh!" my son answered with even more enthusiasm.

So I said, "Hang on a minute," and I walked over to the man my son believed to be Sean Taylor's father.

"Excuse me, sir," I said. "Are you Mr. Taylor?"

"Why, yes, I am," replied the man.

"Do you see that young guy standing over there? The one with the Hurricanes jersey on?" I continued.

"Yes, I do. That's great," replied the elder Taylor. And then he said something like, "Nice jersey."

"Well, would you mind taking a picture with my son? He is such a huge Sean Taylor fan."

"No problem. Of course," he said.

Pedro "Pete" Taylor, a well-built, 5'10½" gentleman, called out to his son Gabriel Taylor, who was ten years old at the time and also on the field, flanked by his entire Pop Warner football team (Pop Warner is the football equivalent of Babe Ruth or Little League baseball). They were guests of the Dolphins, who were going to honor Gabe and his team, the Florida City Razorbacks, at halftime as the Miami Pop Warner player and team of the week for that age and weight class. Pete Taylor was the team's coach, and he was joined by the rest of his coaching staff.

"Come here, Gaby. We're going to take a picture," Pete shouted to the diminutive Taylor—who, by the way, looks exactly like Sean and his father and who sports the same smile. And with that, Gabe and his teammate Ralph Williams V raced over to take a picture with his dad and my son.

After I took the picture, I thought about how very impressed I was with the elder Taylor's willingness to engage with us, and I asked if he had a few moments to chat. He did. "Do you have *any* idea how much your son Sean still means to Redskins Nation and to the city of Washington, DC?" I asked him.

The ever-so-humble Mr. Taylor hemmed and hawed and finally said, "Yes, well, um, maybe."

"In that case, sir, you really have no idea," I said.

The Redskins hadn't exactly set the world on fire over the past twenty or so years, so the fans had few superstar players to glom on to. Among the Redskins fans attending games at FedEx Field, in Washington, DC, there were legions still wearing the jerseys of their perennial favorites, such as Sonny Jurgensen, John Riggins, Clinton Portis, Chris Cooley, and Santana Moss; not to mention the thousands who still wore the Sean Taylor number 21 Redskins jersey.

It wasn't until 2012 that something amazing happened: drafting second, the Washington Redskins chose a young man who was born in Okinawa, Japan, and played quarterback at Baylor University—Mr. Robert Griffin III, also known as "the Savior" and "the New Face of the Franchise." He became an instant fan favorite, and before long, his jerseys started selling like hotcakes.

🏈

Sean Taylor's death affected me and thousands more like me in a very profound way. All of those feelings came storming back in the midst of my conversation with Mr. Taylor, and before I knew it—I swear—I was crying like a baby. It wasn't a mere whimper; it was honest-to-goodness bawling. That never happens to me, but what happened next was even more amazing. Pete Taylor hugged me and patted my back like a baby.

"There, there," Pete said. "It'll be okay."

Okay? Okay? Are you kidding? I thought. It was a very emotional moment, and at the same time I was truly embarrassed. To tell you the truth, I'd had no idea that was going to happen.

When I finally settled down, I nearly commanded Mr. Taylor to wait right where he was. "I want to show you something," I said. He agreed to stay put.

In my group was a gentleman who goes by the moniker Skins Superfan, the de facto leader of an überfanatical group of Redskins fans called ZeRedskins. I walked over to Skins, who had not seen field warm-ups since the glory days of RFK Stadium.

I asked how he was enjoying himself.

"Having a great time," he said.

Frankly I think he was blown away. I pointed to Mr. Taylor just as my son had done to me and asked Skins, "Do you know who that guy over there is?"

"Yes, I do," he responded. "That's Sean Taylor's father, right?"

"That's right," I said.

"Holy crap!" Skins exclaimed. "Are you kidding me? That's amazing."

"No, I'm not kidding. I met him, and it's really him," I said. "Would you like to meet him?"

"Haaaiiiil yes," he said, giving the standard Redskins exclamatory response.

So we both walked over to Mr. Taylor so I could introduce the two of them. Trust me when I tell you that another emotional moment ensued.

"I have been a fan of your son forever," Skins gushed. "Look at my wrist. I never take this wristband off."

He showed it to Mr. Taylor. It read, "RIP Sean Taylor, HTST #21."

"Mr. Taylor," said Skins, "I rep your son twenty-four seven, three sixty-five," and at that he flashed the 21 sign by holding up his index, middle, and pinky fingers on his hand and pointing them to the heavens. Pete Taylor followed suit, and he too threw his 21 up to the heavens. That moment was very emotional for Skins, and a tear rolled down his cheek. "I head a group of loyal New York City-based Redskins fans called ZeRedskins and wo. love to induct you into our group one day," Skins announced.

Skins's son Garrett, also known as the G-Man, was there too. He was proudly wearing his Sean Taylor Redskins #21 jersey, and when he came over, he got to meet Mr. Taylor as well. After a brief chat and some picture-taking, Mr. Taylor told Skins that if he ever came up to DC for a game and Skins's group attended the same one, he would be honored to be inducted into the group. At that they hugged and said their good-byes.

"Do you see what I mean?" I asked Mr. Taylor. Before he could respond, I said, "Hold on. Let's try it again." He agreed to stay put for a moment, and I walked over to a complete stranger who happened to be wearing a burgundy Redskins Taylor #21 road jersey. I walked up behind the guy and asked, "Big fan of Sean Taylor are you?"

"Yes, I am," said the man.

I pulled the "do you know who that guy over there is?" routine.

"No, I don't," the man responded.

"That's Sean Taylor's father," I said.

"Are you f'n kidding me?" he blurted out. "How do you know?"

"Trust me. It is. Would you like to meet him?" I asked once again, pretending I had known Sean's dad forever.

"Hail yes," he said, giving the exact same response Skins Superfan had given. "Do you think I can get a picture with him?" the stranger asked.

"I don't see why not," I answered. I asked what his name was. He told me it was Bob. So Bob and I walked over to where Mr. Taylor was standing. I said, "Mr. Taylor, this is my friend Bob. He would like to know if he could have a picture taken with you."

"Of course," Mr. Taylor responded.

So I took their picture with Bob's cell phone and off walked one happy Sean Taylor fan. Incidentally, I think Bob instantly texted the pic to everyone he knew. But it wasn't enough. I had to do it one more time, and I did.

When the last guy walked off completely blown away after meeting the father of his idol, I asked Mr. Taylor if he was starting to get the picture. He said he did.

It was time to tell Mr. Taylor a little bit about me, such as how I had owned and operated a Washington, DC-based PR/ad agency for the past twenty-four years and how I had written and directed many radio and TV commercials featuring many local sports celebrities, including Redskins Chris Cooley, Darrell Green, Mark Brunell, and Stephen Davis. I also coached former Redskin Ken Harvey in his first radio spot, but I never had the pleasure of working with Sean Taylor. Then I told him who some of my clients were.

By that time we were being ushered off the field, so I thanked him for taking the picture with my son, exchanged contact information with him, and agreed to speak with him again.

◆

After a year of much discussion concerning how we could work together, we decided to begin by writing a book on Mr. Taylor's life with his son Sean and what it was like to raise and coach a superstar only to have him taken away at such an early age.

I do a lot of bouncing back and forth between DC and South Florida. At the end of November 2012, I returned to my Palm Beach County condo, and by early December we had our first of many storytelling sessions. What followed were dozens more interviews with Pete's family members, coaches, football players, roommates, teammates, an agent, and even one very heartbroken owner of the Washington Redskins.

Through their words, written just as they said them, sometimes in the harsh, X-rated language they used, you will learn all about Sean Taylor—Sean T, the Meast, S dot 21—and according to Pete Taylor, "You'll get the good, the bad, and the ugly."

Also included in this book are what we call:

- revelations—stories you've probably never heard about Sean before,
- life lessons—things that would serve Sean—or frankly anyone—well in life, and
- training tips—the things Pete taught to Sean in order to get his body and his mind ready for athletic competition.

◆

I had the privilege of seeing Sean play many times and was endlessly impressed with his passion and prowess on the field. I must admit, however, that I was also one of those gullible individuals who believed the negative press surrounding the sometimes controversial and mostly media-silent player. My new take on the matter? Don't believe most of what you hear or read in the media (more on this later).

So, according to many—including Washington Redskins owner Daniel Snyder—this is a story that should have been written years ago. I believe I was chosen to be a part of this project because it was prescribed in the heavens. Yes, I do believe in predestination.

Steven M. Rosenberg, January 2015

PART 1

1

The Break-In

On Monday, November 26, 2007, at approximately 1:30 a.m., Sean Taylor awoke to loud noises emanating from somewhere in his four-bedroom, four-bath home with private fenced-in pool, sitting on three-fourths of an acre on Old Cutler Road in Palmetto Bay, Florida.

"Jackie ... wake up! I think I hear noises, and there may be someone in the house," Sean Taylor said to Jackie Garcia, his then girlfriend and mother of their eighteen-month-old baby daughter, also named Jackie. "Jackie, where's the machete?"

Half asleep, Jackie responded, "By the bed."

"I want you and Baby Jackie to stay hidden under the covers while I check this out," Sean said urgently. Jackie agreed and pulled the bed sheets over her and their child's head.

Sean found the machete he used mostly as a gardening tool and "for protection [as his girlfriend Jackie stated at the trial of convicted killer Eric Rivera, Jr.]." He picked it up and headed for the locked bedroom door so he could survey the house and quite possibly use it to defend his family.

As Sean approached the door, seventeen-year-old Eric Rivera, Jr., kicked it open. Rivera and three accomplices (Jason Mitchell, who was convicted of second-degree murder and masterminding the burglary, and two alleged cohorts, Charles Wardlow and Timothy Brown, who still await trial) were rummaging through the house. They were searching for what they believed was a large sum of cash they had heard Taylor kept in his safe, sometimes upwards of one hundred thousand dollars. Why so much cash? One of Sean's half sisters testified during the trial that it was easily accessible gambling money.

The fourth accomplice, Venjah Hunte, who was the proverbial "getaway driver," remained inside the vehicle just outside of Sean's home. Hunte eventually plea-bargained for a twenty-nine-year sentence in exchange for his testimony against the others. So far his testimony has not been needed.

So when the bedroom door flew open from the force of Rivera's kick and Eric saw the massive 6'2", 212-pound Sean Taylor standing there, he panicked and shot Sean in the upper leg. The bullet hit the femoral artery, and with a loud grunt, gasping for air, Sean Taylor collapsed, falling face first to the floor.

As Taylor lay there in a pool of his own blood, Eric Rivera likely screamed for his companions in the house to abort the heist and quickly make their exit.

According to the report filed by the Miami-Dade Police, when Rivera got to the rear glass patio door, he shot at it so he and his cohorts could escape unimpeded.

When they emerged, they ran toward the front of the home and scaled the cement-and-iron fence, racing for their rented black Toyota Highlander SUV with coconspirator Venjah Hunte waiting inside.

The five then sped off into the wee hours of the morning, heading northwest toward Alligator Alley and eventually ending up in Ft. Myers, Florida, where they all lived.

●

There's a lot more to this story, so let's flash back to the beginning.

2

How Sean Taylor's Father Pedro "Pete" Taylor Met Sean Taylor's Mother (and Sean)

It was mid-1982 when Pedro "Pete" Taylor joined the Homestead Police Department. "I was coming out of church in Homestead when I saw a very attractive young woman standing outside her mother's house," said Pete Taylor. "The young lady was Donna Junor. We struck up a conversation, one thing led to another, and we started dating."

It didn't take long for Donna and Pete to realize they had very little in common and were not a match. "The communication just wasn't there," Taylor said. "So after several months, we broke up."

What happened next is nearly unbelievable.

🏈

April 1, 1983 was a beautiful spring South Florida day. It was cool enough in generally warm and humid Miami for a little shoot-around on the basketball court near Pete Taylor's home. "I'm shooting baskets and see my uncle Joseph walking toward the court," Taylor said. "He's walking and yelling, 'Hey Pete. Come here. I have to talk to you.'

"'Joe, what's up?'

"'Hey man, you're a new father!' my uncle said with that 'you ain't gonna believe this' voice. 'You just had a new baby girl.'

"I thought he was kidding, and all I could muster was, '*What?*'

"'Yeah man, you a daddy!' my uncle said.

"Totally thrown for a loop, I said, 'Maaan, I know it's April Fool's Day, so quit playin'!'

"As we walked back to the house, Joe says, 'Hey, man. I was just kidding. You didn't have a baby girl. You had a baby boy!'

"Playing along, I asked, 'If I'm a new daddy, where's my baby at?'

"He said, 'Connecticut.'

"'Connecticut? I don't know anyone in Connecticut!'

"'Yes, you do,' my uncle said. 'I got a number for you, and I suggest you call it.'

"So I did. Well, he was right. I had fathered a new baby boy. It was Sean Michael Maurice Taylor, who was born on April 1, 1983. Turns out that the woman I met in Homestead, Donna Junor, who I had dated for about six months, had family in Hartford, Connecticut."

There was one time during their short relationship that Donna thought she was pregnant. Pete was told about the pregnancy, and it turned out to be a false alarm. So when she found out she was pregnant with Sean, Donna once again informed Pete, but since she wasn't showing, he didn't believe her. The next thing that happened was, "she moved to her grandmother's house, except she didn't tell me she was leaving."

Pete Taylor described Donna in this way: "She was not a bitter person. When it came to the two of us, we just couldn't communicate. I'm not one to have a lot of drama in my life, so we stopped dating and never got back together."

After the breakup, Pete and Donna did not communicate, which is why he was in the dark about her move to New England. Nevertheless, after Sean was born, their line of communication was reopened. Sort of.

"I had just completed the police academy, and what's more, I knew my life was about to be turned upside down. So when I found out Sean was born, I contacted Donna's family and made arrangements to fly up to Hartford, Connecticut, to see my new baby boy the next day."

They made arrangements for the new daddy to stay at Donna's aunt's home. By the time Pete got up there, Sean had already come home from the hospital. "I was up there for a week, and with Donna's permission, I picked up Sean in the evening and he stayed with me each night during my visit. In the mornings, I got Sean up and ready to go back to his mom's, because she was doing the feedings and stuff." According to Taylor, "Sean never cried and went right to sleep at night. That was the beginning of our bond, which I thought would never be broken.

"I must admit, it was very difficult leaving Sean after seeing him for the first time, but I had to return to Miami," Pete said. For a while, Donna traveled back and forth between Hartford and Miami, making the new dad very happy because he got to see Sean a lot more than he would have if he had been living exclusively in Connecticut.

Approximately five months after Sean was born, Donna moved to Miami. Upon occasion, Pete's mom or Pete would drive to Homestead to get Sean and bring him to the house. "I loved that boy right from the get-go!" Pete Taylor said.

Sean was not Donna's only child. He had an older half sister, named Monika. The following Christmas, Pete got Sean clothes and presents. Not only that, but he also got Sean's sister presents so she wouldn't feel slighted. "I did everything a father could do during the holiday season and then some for the kids. Remember, no drama."

Donna eventually had another boy and girl, Jamal and Sasha. When Pete's son was a little older and got picked up for visits, any time he and his father went to the store, Sean always asked if he could bring something home for Donna's other children. "If I got Sean a little toy, he would ask if he could bring home some candy for them." And of course, Pete agreed. Sean always had a big heart; according to Pete, "My son didn't have a selfish bone in his body.

"Some say I could have just given up on Sean. After all, so many kids grow up never knowing who their dad is. I didn't want that for my child. In fact, I wanted to be the best dad I could be. To understand why, you have to know a little more about me and how I grew up."

3

Pete Taylor's Humble Beginnings

PEDRO "PETE" TAYLOR WAS BORN IN FLORIDA CITY, FLORIDA, A SUBURB OF Miami in the southernmost part of Dade County, in February 1961. Florida City was a migrant farm community with a multiracial base. There were descendants of the Spaniards, Mexicans, Cubans, Italians, and African Americans in the area. According to Pete, it was actually called Little Detroit before it was called Florida City. It became the incorporated town of Florida City in 1914.

As a young man, Pete grew up with, as he put it, "two loving parents," his father Pedro Taylor, for whom he was named, and his mother, Constance "Connie" Mackey Dingle. Pete had one older brother named Eddie George Taylor, who was born eleven months earlier.

The brothers were essentially raised by their father and his extended family in Florida City, while their mom studied nursing at Florida A&M University (FAMU), located in Tallahassee, Florida..

"While my mom was going back and forth to college, my grandparents Harold and Gertrude Mackey helped my father raise my brother and me with the help of my aunt Merleane. They were the ones responsible for getting us to the A. L. Lewis Elementary School every day. That wasn't so difficult, since it was right across the street from where we lived.

"I really admired my mom for coming home every other weekend to make sure we had clean clothes and to perform her other motherly duties," said Taylor.

This continued for four years until she graduated and became a registered nurse (RN). As part of her four-year program, she ended up going to Jacksonville, Florida, to do her internship. When she completed it, she returned home to Miami. According to Pete, "She was very dedicated, and her career lasted thirty-three years. She was an inspiration to us all."

Pete's mom is his buddy, his pal. He calls her that because when Sean played college football, she became his traveling partner. "Even when we hit the road with the whole family to see Sean play in various cities and especially championships, she was the one who helped me drive and was always supportive.

"You can't ask for a better person than that, someone you can call at the last minute and say, 'Mom, we have to go see Sean tomorrow.' And her response was, 'That's okay. I'm ready.'"

⬤

Pete's father, Pedro Taylor, was born in the Bahamas and grew up in Jamaica, attending school through the sixth grade. Pedro's mother gave up trying to raise him and eventually relinquished him to the Lee family, where he would be better taken care of. Mr. Lee was a wealthy architect and agreed to take care of Pedro.

Pete's father eventually relocated to Florida. Pete's parents made a point of taking the boys on an annual family trip to Jamaica to be with their "extended family," the ones who were so nice and raised Pedro Taylor. "For me it turned out to be a beautiful, rewarding getaway," Pete Taylor said of his time on the island.

As Pete and Eddie grew up, their father told them stories about the kind and generous people who raised him. Pete said, "He was trying to constantly remind us that even though he wasn't raised by his birth parents, he still grew up in a loving, caring home."

Pete's dad, Pedro, had a dream of becoming an architect, just like the man who raised him. "However, he had little education and a big heart filled with determination," Pete said of his father. He began to draw, and after getting his GED, he went to college at Miami-Dade to follow his dream and became an architect.

"My dad even became a pilot and eventually got his own plane," recounted Pete. "When I was old enough, my dad shared his pilot knowledge and skills with me, and I learned to fly single-engine Cessnas.

"After many hours in the air, the day of my last lesson had arrived. I was with a licensed instructor that day and performed all the routine maneuvers. On the last maneuver—one in which I was to put the plane into a stall—when I tried to get out of the climb, I pushed the yoke [which controls the plane's upward and downward movement] in just a little too far, and the plane went into a nosedive. I was with a very experienced private instructor, and thank God for that, because guess what … we lived. Trust me; that was the last time I decided to get behind the yoke, and if it wasn't for that brilliant trainer, I wouldn't be here telling this story today. I would have crashed and burned. In the end, I never did solo."

●

In 1966 Pete and his brother Eddie spent a lot of time on their granddaddy's farm in Homestead, Florida. "He used to pick up farm workers who would help plant okra, beans, squash, etc.," recalled Pete. And it was on the farm that he and his brother were introduced to football by their uncle Willy. There was lots of room to play, and early on, all they did was toss the ball back and forth among the three of them. Eventually they moved on to catch, touch, and tag. It turned out that the boys were very gifted and very fast.

A short while later Eddie and Pete joined a neighborhood sandlot football league. "My brother was the quarterback [QB], and I was the receiver," Pete said. "We played with no helmets or pads, but it wasn't flag football either. It was 'bring your *A* game' and just play.

"Not only did we play on the farm, but we were expected to work there too. With Uncle Willy running off to the football field to play or practice, my granddad ended up taking my brother and me to the fields to make us work for him, and all for twenty-five cents per basket of whatever it was we were harvesting. I thought that wasn't enough for even a five-year-old, so I said to my granddaddy, 'You really need to pay us more money than this.' He agreed. But he never did.

"By the way, Granddaddy recently passed away at ninety-seven years old, but that never stopped me from reminding him until right before he passed that he still owed me money for working on his farm!"

Pete's wide-receiver and punt-returning uncle Willy Mackey went on to play for Florida A&M, which today is a Mid-Eastern Athletic Conference (MEAC) Division I college. The MEAC is a historically black college division that also includes Bethune-Cookman, Norfolk State, North Carolina A&T, and Hampton, just to name a few. It was in this division that Uncle Willy played and won the conference's football national championship.

●

As the boys grew, their passion for football also grew. But since local games were mostly on Friday nights and Saturdays, they couldn't play, for religious reasons. The family were Seventh-Day Adventists, and Friday nights and Saturdays were their Sabbath.

"It was a little frustrating trying out for football, making the team, and then finding out we couldn't play," Taylor said. "Don't get me wrong. I am grateful for my religion and its teachings, and I didn't miss what I couldn't do." Or so Pete told himself.

●

When Pete was just eight years old, he and his responsible brother learned how to run the family's general store, which featured a soda fountain and a lunch counter. They also sold meat, canned goods, dry goods, etc.

Since the boys were so young, there were always those who came in trying to take advantage of them. They would say things like, "Hey, didn't I just give you a ten?" expecting Pete or his brother to give out more change than they were due. Needless to say, no one got away with that trick.

With so much on their plates, including schoolwork, chores, and running the store, there wasn't any time for playing ball or even just running around outside. But the boys did get their workouts in.

"We got our physical activity from boxing," Pete recalled. "Our dad was into it, so he taught us both how to defend ourselves. Sometimes our lessons took place inside the store, so we had to be careful not to break anything. The bottom line was, we learned early about working hard and playing hard and at the same time, how to use our brains. We also figured out nothing was going to come easy for us."

In addition to owning the general store, Pedro Taylor began building and repairing homes from top to bottom. So not only could he draw the plans, but he could then build whatever the plans called for. It started simply enough with additions to the Taylor home and then other neighborhood homes.

Pete Taylor remembered, "After we got done at the store, we'd work for our father as a carpenter's and/or construction apprentice. We called it a 'helpmate.' We learned life lessons, such as how to properly use wrenches, screwdrivers, hammers, and sledgehammers. Can you picture us little kids lifting and then whacking a wall with a sledgehammer? Man, that was a sight." If that wasn't enough, the boys learned to pour concrete. "In today's world many kids never even get to hold a hammer. We became adept at handling tools, and in the long run it saved us a lot of money, because later on we could fix our own homes, something 'professionals' charge an arm and a leg for."

Something tells me this would have made a great HGTV reality TV show.

◆

In school, Pete was the class clown. Despite his clowning around, he still got Bs in his classes. "It was my conduct in class teachers had a problem with. So the words I needed to learn were 'self-control.'" That reminder showed up on every report card.

Looking back at those times, Pete realized he had the capability to do better, but being the class clown was so much more fun. "Maybe it was my way of acting out because I spent so much time working for my father and very little time having fun in the streets and playgrounds."

Pete wanted to play basketball, football, or any kind of ball for that matter, but couldn't. There wasn't any time except for a little after church on Saturday. "Speaking of the Church, one of the things I loved about my parents was they instilled upon us how to be godly kids. Sadly ... in my opinion, that's missing from many homes today."

◆

Life went on for the Taylors. Eventually Pete's parents divorced after twelve years of marriage.

In 1971, Pete was ten years old and really wanted to play football. "So I asked my dad if I could try out. He said, 'Go. Try out. Play football.' So I tried out for the Pop Warner Homestead League in Dade County, and I made a team in the 110–115-pound class.

"After exactly one week of conditioning and running, the coach began passing out the equipment. When they got to me, I got my helmet but the team ran out of shoulder pads. The coach tells me to hold on, that he'd have more pads in a day or two. In that conversation I said, 'Okay, okay, Coach, but I really want you to get those shoulder pads as soon as possible.' That was because I was eager to take the field and show him what I could do. So here I am on the sidelines watching everyone go through the drills and tackling and having fun. Me? I'm getting frustrated. I really wanted to go out and hit somebody, but of course the coach prevented me from doing so."

The next day—still no pads. So instead of running around on the field, Pete was told to "go knock the fence down," meaning he was to do the slide move where you jam your hands with one guy, move, and then jam your hands with the next guy, and so forth.

"So we all go through more drills; then it's hitting time again, but I can't participate because my shoulder pads hadn't come in. I noticed some of the guys had taken off their shirts, so I grabbed a couple and balled them up and stuffed them under my jersey, making it look like I had shoulder pads on. All of a sudden Coach says, 'I need another player,' so I run out on the field. Yes! Here's my chance to go hit somebody, but Coach blows the whistle! He realizes I don't have real pads on and he screams at me, 'Get off the field; you ain't got pads on. Get out of there.' I said, 'Man, just let me hit somebody, and don't worry about the pads.'"

Nothing doing. As a consequence, the coach made Pete run. The bad news was that it was the last day he went to practice before being forbidden to play on Fridays and Saturdays by his father once again for religious reasons. "I never did get the chance to show the coach what I had," Pete said. Unfortunately that was the end of Pete's brief Pop Warner experience. He had to wait another year before he got his chance to play again.

🏈

In 1972 the boys found themselves in Houston with their dad. Houston was a booming city in the early seventies. Since their father was in the construction business and Houston was where the money was, that's where his father thought they should be.

When it came to sports, Pete and his brother began playing baseball. However, in Texas football is the king of sports. It's almost a religion. But they don't let kids play until the sixth grade. Prior to sixth grade, kids in Texas are relegated to baseball, basketball, or track.

"In Houston I eventually tried out for the football team at Miller Junior High," Pete Taylor said. "I made the team and played safety. Those games were played after school, so there was no religious conflict. I also tried out for and made the basketball team."

After about three years, everyone in the Texas oil town started talking about a massive oil pipeline project way up north. It was the next great moneymaking frontier.

As it turned out, there was even more steady money to be made than anyone could imagine, and Pete's father wanted in, so he began preparing the boys for a move to Anchorage, Alaska. He decided to go to the "Great American Icebox" and work on the Alaska pipeline.

Maybe he felt trepidation about the prospect of taking his children even farther away from their mother, or perhaps he thought they couldn't handle the severe cold. Whatever the reason, just when he was ready to move, he informed his boys they weren't going with him and instead sent them back to Miami to live with their mother.

Being in Miami and living with their mother once again prevented the Taylor boys from playing football because of the Friday night religious ban. Disappointment set in—hard. It turned out that wrestling proved to be an interesting and enjoyable alternative. Pete Taylor said, "The matches were on Tuesday, Wednesday, and Friday nights, so I got to participate in sports but only on Tuesdays and Wednesdays. I tried out at the brand-new Southridge High School in Miami and made the inaugural team."

Done with Alaska, Pete's father returned to Florida City when Pete was in eleventh grade, and per his wishes, the boys moved back in with him. "That's when we transferred to South Dade Senior High," Pete Taylor said. "Once again I tried out for the football team and made it, but once again I didn't get to play because the games were on Friday nights." It was frustrating.

4

The Tragedy of '79

Revelation

In 1979, Pete's father Pedro was piloting his own plane back and forth from Nassau and Freeport in the Bahamas to the Turks and Caicos. He used to do mercy runs with food and clothing for the poor. On one of those trips there was a terrible storm. Somewhere in between the Turks and Caicos and Nassau, Pedro Taylor encountered bad weather, and the little prop plane he was flying went down, crashing and killing him.

Pete's father meant a great deal to him, and losing him right after his eighteenth birthday was a devastating blow. However, it had everything to do with why he wanted to stay in Sean's life. He knew what it was like to basically grow up without a father, and that was the last thing he wanted for his newborn son.

"It took me almost twenty years to get over his death," Pete said. "I had a great life with my parents. They lived for us. They loved us. They took care of us. They fed us and, most of all, made sure we got a good religious upbringing. Therefore, I did everything I could to stay in Sean's life and have a relationship with him."

Being only eighteen years old when his father passed away meant Pete's turbulent childhood continued as he moved back in with his mother and reentered Southridge High. He eventually graduated from South Dade because of the difference in their graduation policies and the transferring of credits.

5

Pete's College Years

AFTER HIGH SCHOOL, PETE TAYLOR ENROLLED AT FAMU IN Tallahassee, where his mother had attended nursing school. At one point during his two years there, he tried out for the football team as a walk-on despite not having gotten much playing time in high school. Pete's brother Eddie went to FAMU first, but when their dad died, he didn't get the opportunity to finish out that year and came home.

"When it came time for me to try out for the football team, I already knew the coach," Pete said. "It was Rudy Hubbard, the coach my uncle played for. My roommate was also going to walk on." So the two of them began training on their own. "We ran: ran steps, did the 110 and the 200, ran up and down the hills of Tallahassee." They did every conditioning exercise they could think of so they would have a shot at making the team. Then came tryout day.

"We had to run five 40s, ten 110s, etc. I passed the first milestones," recalled Taylor. Some of the other gridiron hopefuls didn't make the cut, as they ended up falling by the wayside. In fact, when they fell, some fell into piles of red ants! "I remember this one guy named Tank. He fell in the dirt and into an anthill. He couldn't get up. The ants were all over his body. We had to grab him and pour water all over him. The problem was, he passed out. Despite all this, Tank ended up making the team." Go figure.

"There was also this guy named Burnside—maybe 6'2", 6'3" —and I don't mind saying this, but I was a better athlete than him as well as a lot of the other guys. But guess what, I got cut! Perhaps it was because I was only

16

5'10½". On the other hand Tank, at 5'8", made it as a running back. We had some good players back then, and one or two of them even got drafted by the NFL. It turns out they kept Tank around mostly as a punching bag, so I was glad that wasn't me."

FAMU was a good sports school. Through the years, many notable players have gone there, including Olympic runner turned NFL player Bob "Bullet" Hayes, who went on to play for the Dallas Cowboys in the early sixties. Vince Coleman played there and went on to have a stellar career with the St. Louis Cardinals baseball club.

So Pete Taylor got cut. But wouldn't you know it—one of FAMU's QBs was also named Pete Taylor, and at 6'3" or 6'4", how could anyone possibly get the two confused?

"When I went somewhere and had to give my name, they would say, 'Are you Pete Taylor the QB?' I couldn't lie, so I said, 'No, that's the other Pete Taylor.' In any event, I guess they appreciated my honesty."

To further understand the Sean Taylor story, remember this: Pete got cut, so he didn't really have the opportunity to play college football. "I realized even if you're better than the next man, if you don't work hard and you don't produce, you're not going to be on that field," Taylor said. "I didn't get the chance because back in those days they wanted players with size and height (except for Tank), so it was of the utmost importance to instill upon Sean that determination plus hard work will pay off in the long run."

Life Lesson

"I wanted Sean to understand that a positive attitude brings on positive change, and your attitude determines your aptitude.

"You can assign a numerical value to the letters in ATTITUDE (a=1, t=20, i=9, u=21, d=4, e=5) and when you add them up, the word equals 100.

$$A \quad T \quad T \quad I \quad T \quad U \quad D \quad E$$
$$1 + 20 + 20 + 9 + 20 + 21 + 4 + 5 = 100$$

"You have to check yourself and make sure you are working at 100%.
"Another thing I always told Sean: 'Don't be outworked!'"

Eventually Pete Taylor became discouraged with college, partly because he didn't make the football team and partly because he became homesick. Also, as a result of the tragic loss of his father, he couldn't concentrate on school, as that still weighed heavily on him. "My heart was in the right place, but I knew my mind was not. So I came back to Miami," Taylor said.

At that point Pete should have been reminded of what his mother once told him: "As long as you're going to college, I will pay for it. But the minute you leave, you're on your own."

So Pete was now on his own. When he got back to Miami, he needed money, so he mowed yards, did other lawn maintenance, and washed cars to earn it.

Shortly thereafter, Pete started working full-time for the Homestead Goodyear Tire Company, where he learned how to change tires, do oil changes, and deal with other minor mechanical automotive issues. "Before long I became the service manager, and everything was going well. Or so I thought. One day the manager comes in and says, 'Guess what, Pete. We're downsizing, and I'm afraid you're going back to being a tire guy.'

"'No problem,' I said. Back then I looked at this as a demotion. Today I feel like it's okay to step back, all the while trying to figure out how to move forward.

"The whole time I worked for Goodyear, we were the store where the local police cruisers were serviced, and that's how I first came in contact with the department. After speaking to many of the officers, I became interested in law enforcement. So at twenty-one I got my chance to enter the field of criminal justice."

6

1983

"SO HERE I AM WITH A NEW CAREER AND A BRAND-NEW BABY WHO EARLY on I got to see every once in a while," Pete Taylor reflected.

As previously mentioned, Pete immediately fell in love with his new baby. But he wasn't the only one who immediately fell in love. "Sean meant so much to my mom throughout their lives together as she played an integral role in raising him," Pete added.

❧

So what was Sean like from the time he could crawl, walk, and, yes, even get potty trained? To learn about these details, speaking to Pete's mom, Ms. Connie Dingle, was a great place to start. Here's what Pete Taylor's mother, Sean's grandmother, had to say.

Sean's Grandmother Connie Dingle

"Sean was my first grandchild," said the quiet, thoughtful, and demure Ms. Connie Dingle. "He was a very sweet boy, and I loved him as if he were my own. We traveled together, played together, and prayed together. I even toilet trained him. I was with him one weekend when he was about eighteen months old, and I went and got me one of those potties where you peepee in it and it sings a lullaby. He seemed to take to it quite naturally and was trained in a matter of days.

"When he started learning his ABCs and numbers and stuff, he'd pick it right up. He was a very smart boy. You'd just give him some words to learn how to spell and go over it with him. [You'd] come back in ten to fifteen minutes, [and] he got it. When we traveled to different places, we'd look at different signs, and I would ask him to spell them. These were words like 'STOP,' 'STORE,' names, whatever.

"When Sean was in elementary school, I helped him with his times tables, spelling, and reading."

As for discipline, "You'd speak to him once and he did exactly what you told him to do. I never had to spank him or anything." (Grandma was a little old school.)

❧

According to Ms. Dingle, even as a small child, Sean's favorite thing was participating in sports. He and his dad would toss the ball around in the backyard or play in the park.

When he was a lot older, Sean had football practice in the morning and basketball practice in the evening. "So if his father was busy, I would drop him at practice and pick him up. Sean was not only busy with sports but with his education as well," said Ms. Dingle.

❧

For another female perspective on the youngster, I went to a source that was also very close to Sean, Josephine Taylor, the woman who would later become his stepmom. At first glance, she appeared to be a woman with a certain forcefulness about her, someone who would never take crap from anyone.

We met in the Starbucks inside the Boca Raton Barnes & Noble, and what followed was a candid interview including her recollection of meeting Sean for the first time.

Josephine "Josie" Taylor

"I met Sean when he was just three weeks old when Donna Junor, Sean's mother, brought him from Connecticut to Florida," said Josephine Taylor. When Sean was a little older, "he was a very aggressive, playful kid. He was awesome. He could never sit still from the moment he woke up until the moment he went to sleep. He was always busy, and he always had a ball in his hand."

Josephine also said, "He would do his schoolwork when we could get Sean to sit still long enough." If he ever needed a little extra help, a tutor was provided. It was always education first in the Taylor household, and throughout the years all of the kids got tutors to help facilitate better grades.

Despite his hyperactivity, "Sean was never a discipline problem," said Josie. "Anytime I told Sean what to do, he did it. There was never any talking back from any of my children."

7

Six-Year-Old Sean Wants to Play Football

SOUTH FLORIDA BOYS COULD JOIN ORGANIZED FOOTBALL PROGRAMS AT the age of six, and Sean wanted to play. Pete started tossing the football around with Sean when he first learned to walk in the backyard. But in 1989, when he was six years old, pinning Sean down was hard because he moved around so much.

At his first opportunity Sean began playing Pop Warner football for the Dick Conley League located at Harris Field in Homestead. As a tyke, Sean was in pads and helmet for the first time. To say he was hyperaggressive on the field would be an understatement. He could run, he could hit, and he was taller and lankier than all the other kids.

Pete remembers Pee Wee Sean this way: "On the field, he did something called a wild hit, or what I called an 'I don't give a damn hit.'" Here's another one. "He did an 'I don't care what happens to me, but I'm gonna level you' hit because 'I am going to be okay; you're not.'

"It wasn't a classic solid hit. He'd just run over you. I used to tell him, 'You have to wrap him up and finish.' But he didn't care. He thought he'd just knock them down and maybe if they were lucky they'd get up. And I was like, 'Wow. This kid is crazy!'"

One day Sean asked his dad what a helmet-to-helmet hit was. Pete was stunned. "I said, 'Sean, would you mind repeating yourself?'

"Sean asked again, 'What does "helmet-to-helmet hit" mean?'"

Pete had been coaching other people's kids for a long time, so when Sean asked him that question, he was floored. "I thought he was just out there to have fun. But actually, I freaked out. My first thought was, 'This boy is going to hurt himself or someone else.'

"Sean said, 'Dad, someone told me that when I hit a guy, hit helmet to helmet.'

"I responded with, 'Ooookay.' It was at that moment I decided to get back into coaching him—soon—so I could teach this kid and his team the right way. Someone gave him some very bad information, and it could cause him serious injury. I didn't want that to happen."

Even Josie remembered Sean as being aggressive in football. "I remember him, when he first started playing Pee Wee football at six years old, tackling two kids at the same time. I just thought it was cute. I didn't think, *'Well, he's going somewhere with this.'* I didn't think, *'Wow, this kid is awesome. He can tackle two kids at once.'"*

She also never imagined that Sean would one day play football for the Miami Hurricanes or the NFL's Washington Redskins!

Pete remembered that first season. "Sean's team made the six-year-old playoffs, and they lost! If you know anything about Sean, you know he doesn't like losing. So even at six, when his team lost a game, the boy walked around with a chip on his shoulder and didn't want to speak to anyone for about a day or two. Then he'd come out of it. I always told him to give it everything he had, but win or lose, you have to still have fun."

Sean's Friend and NFL Star Antrel Rolle

Antrel Rocelious Rolle was born and raised in Homestead, Florida. He went to South Dade High School there and, like Sean, years later went on to play at the University of Miami. He was drafted eighth in the first round by the Arizona Cardinals in 2005, the year after Sean was drafted. His first pro jersey number was 21, which was Sean Taylor's last jersey number. At the time of this writing, Antrel was thirty-one years old, the same age Sean would have been had he lived.

Even Antrel, the nine-year NFL veteran currently with the New York Football Giants, who played with Sean on his six-year-old team, saw the intensity of Sean's play early on.

"As youngsters we had a drill called the Oklahoma, which started on our backs. We would turn over and just collide full speed into each other. When we hit, it was like lightning struck. Two little guys coming at each other full force, and we definitely made a ruckus. So after we hit each other, we were on our backs and we both laid there for a while looking at each other, and it was like, damn! [You hit hard!] And that was our introduction to football."

Coach Marcus Jones

Football Coach Marcus Jones is a lifelong friend of Pete Taylor. They grew up together; they both went to Southridge High School and played sports together. He remembers Pete as a tough ballplayer, so watching Sean, that amazing little six-year-old, play football was no surprise to Coach Jones.

Jones considered himself more of an uncle to Sean than a family friend. "When I first got to know Sean, he was a scrappy kid with a lot of energy. Early on I started telling Pete that kid was going to be something special. I didn't know what—sports, acting … in any case, he had that special persona. I just didn't know what that meant until he started playing football."

Being a football coach, Jones had been around lots of child athletes. He said the special ones were easy to spot. So when he was coaching the ninety-pound kids at the Richmond Optimist Program and Pete was coaching at Colonial Park, Marcus said, "It didn't matter how good Sean was. We had a great team at Richmond that could beat his team, or any team for that matter."

Four or five years later, Richmond was still the powerhouse. In the fifth or sixth grade, Sean was playing for a mediocre team. "He was one of their better players," Jones said. "However, Sean never got his props."

That's because he didn't get much of a chance to stand out, as they always put Sean in a position where he couldn't excel. To Jones, that made no sense at all.

"So I remember one game where we were getting ready to play Pete's team. Pete said, 'Marcus, are you ready?'

"I said, 'Yeah.'

"Pete said, 'You know, Sean is pretty tough.'

"I said, 'I know. But you know what you're going against. You're going against the best when you're playing against Richmond.'"

In the four years prior, Marcus's team had no one player rush over twenty yards against Richmond. He kept saying that when it came to Pop Warner, they were the best team in the state of Florida.

"The game started. We kicked off, and Sean returned it ninety yards. That had never happened before," explained Marcus. "So I look across the field, and Pete had this smirk on his face. I know what he was thinking, too. *'I told you I had something special.'* Well, the game wasn't over yet. It was just the beginning. Before long, Sean started doing things. I was the defensive coordinator for our team, and my head coach came to me and asked, 'Marcus, what are you going to do about this?' I told my coach, 'I can't stop him. The only thing I can do is try and contain him.'"

By the end of the game, Sean had rushed for about four hundred yards but had scored only once. "We did manage to keep him out of the end zone," Marcus said. "But I'm telling you, I've never seen anything like that. After the game I said to Pete, 'One day this kid is going to be in the NFL.'"

Marcus continued: "By the way, we won the game by a touchdown [the game actually ended in a tie], but what Sean did—I had never seen anything like that in my life! From that day on, I called him 'Super Taylor.' Anything he touched, he was the best at it."

As the self-proclaimed uncle, Marcus had the chance to speak to Sean off the field. "I used to talk to him all the time about what he can and can't do." Take football, for example. "I said to him, 'Sean, you need to stay down. You're coming up too high.' He had a lot of 'angry' built in, but I didn't understand why until I spoke to him later on about that.

"Finally I realized what it was. Sean was the type of kid that wanted to please everybody. He wanted to make everybody happy. And when you were his friend, he'd do anything for you.

"There was no doubt anytime you had him on your team, you had a chance of winning. That's how I felt. When Sean started becoming a part of the team we had at Gulliver Prep, I didn't care what the score was. I knew we had a chance of winning."

When Marcus's son, also named Marcus, and Sean met up at Gulliver Prep, they became great friends. "However," Marcus said softly, "something was always bothering Sean."

No doubt it was the bouncing back and forth between Pete's and his mother's homes. "He was torn between the two of them. He loved them both equally." But despite that, in Marcus's opinion, Pete was better for Sean. So not only did he not get the stability of the single-family household kids need, but he also didn't get to play football when he returned to his mother's house. He got to play only when he was with Pete.

The bottom line? Sean poured his anxiety into his game. Marcus said that when Sean played on defense, he was a "terror." And what's more, "The way he played at ninety pounds was the same way he played when he went to the NFL. For him it came very easy. Sean was like a missile."

Pete Taylor

"By the next season I was ready to coach again," Pete Taylor said. It was important for him to teach his son the right way to play the game, so he took him to another park. That's where it all broke down. His mom decided to relocate to Broward County and took Sean with her.

"Our communication was so bad, it took a while for me to even know where they relocated to," Taylor said, with those painful memories showing on his usually jovial face. "When I was able to track her down, I asked if I could see Sean so I could spend time with my son and work on his skills. So I'd see him for a day and *poof*—gone. I wouldn't see my boy for three months. Then, just like before, the grandma would call once in a while and say, 'Sean is here. Do you want to see him?' 'Of course' was the answer. It was always yes. This went on until summertime, when Donna left him with me for about two months. This made me very happy.

"This pattern of having him in my life, then having him whisked away, continued for a couple of years until he was about nine. Then, lo and behold, things changed."

8

The Disappearing Act Continues

IT WAS 1992 WHEN PETE TAYLOR GOT A CALL FROM SEAN'S MOTHER, DONNA, who said, "Now that Sean is nine years old, I'm going to let him stay with you."

Pete's reply? "Wow. That would be great." And that's what happened. "Sean moved in with me, and Josie and our children Joseph and baby Jazmin," said Papa Pete.

Side Story

As per routine, Sean would come home after playing football at Colonial-South Dade Park, and Josie would want to wash his dirty uniform every night. Josie would say, "Take your uniform off and put it in the washing machine."

One night Sean said, "Josie, don't wash my uniform."

When Josie asked why, he said, "Because I'm the only one out there with a clean uniform. Every other kid's uniform is scuffed up and dirty, and I want to look like I was playing."

Josie's response to that was, "Well, okay, but every two days I'm going to wash that stinky uniform." That was a schedule they could agree on.

Half Brother Joseph Taylor

Sean grew up in two households. He lived part-time with his mom Donna and part-time with his father Pete and Pete's then-wife Josephine Taylor. In the Taylor household, Sean lived with his half brother Joseph and half sister Jazmin, both younger than he was.

Following in his father's footsteps, Joseph is now a full-time police officer at Miami-Dade.

Joseph can't really remember his earliest interactions with Sean because "it all mashes together. There are too many memories, so it's hard to remember my earliest one," he said.

Joseph did say, "It was a real competitive relationship. There were a lot of fights, but not bad fights—competitive fights, especially when it came to something like wrestling."

Pete Taylor always loved wrestling, and as it turns out, his boys loved it, too. "Starting when I was six, we all wrestled together—me, Sean, and my dad, who became our resident wrestling guru. We tried out the moves Dad taught us on each other, but Sean was bigger and stronger." That said, Joseph held his own, especially when they double-teamed their father.

Pete Taylor

Sean's stay lasted for about a month, and then away he went again. His mom took him back after she changed her mind about his living with the Taylors.

As mentioned, for the month he was with his father, Sean played football for the South Dade Rams. Needless to say, the coach really liked him. But when he vanished, the coach called Pete every day, asking, "Where is that kid? Where is Sean? Are you going to bring him back out?"

Every day, Pete Taylor said to him, "Sean is not here. I don't know where he is, so, no, I can't bring him out.

"Maybe he didn't believe me," Pete said, "but it was fact. So finally I said, 'Would you please stop calling me, because it looks like his mom is going to keep him.' He was not happy. I was not happy."

Donna kept Sean for the next school year and brought him back for the summer. Pete told Sean's mom he would like to keep him, and she told Pete she'd let him stay for a couple of weeks and then take him home.

Sure enough, Sean stayed for about a month before Donna removed him from the Taylor home, just as she had said she would. This series of events was hard on the Taylors and particularly tough on Sean, who at that age was in need of family consistency or at least a more regular visitation schedule.

With Sean gone again, Pete continued to call his son every week to let him know he was thinking about him and to see how he was doing.

◆

One day a few short months later, on a whim, Pete called Donna's house when Sean was supposed to be in school. It was about eleven in the morning, and lo and behold, Sean answered the phone. Pete said, "Sean, what's up? How are you doing? Did you go to school today?"

When Sean answered yes, Pete asked, "Then why are you home?" Sean said he was home because he had to come home. That didn't make any sense to Pete, so he asked Sean what happened.

Sean said his mom was there talking to someone at that moment.

Revelation

That someone was from the Department of Youth Services (DYS), who had come to the house because someone at Sean's school had reported his mother for hitting him upside the head with his own book bag. Sean loved to fish, and he had a little fishhook sticking out of the bag. The fishhook had cut him when she hit him.

While at Donna's, DYS asked where Pete was, and Donna must have said she didn't know. "But when I called in," Pete said, "the mystery was solved. There I was. In reality, Donna didn't want me to know anything about what was going on with Sean, so she pretended not to know where I was."

Sean's maternal grandmother told Pete point blank, "Since you was next of kin, it might be a good idea if Sean came back to live with you."

"The bottom line was, I got permanent custody after the courts deemed it necessary to have him stay with Josie and me under the watchful eye of DYS, who would be checking in from time to time," said Taylor. "So the first thing I had to do was to transfer Sean to Richmond [Heights] Middle School."

Josephine Taylor commented, "When we gained legal custody of ten-year-old Sean, for the first week or so, he had a very hard time adjusting. It's different when someone has to live with you as opposed to just visiting." He did miss his mother very much for those first couple of weeks, making him one miserable little boy. According to Pete, "Sean cried himself to sleep every night for two weeks."

Soon Pete set up a regular visitation schedule, which meant Sean could visit with his mother Donna every other weekend. That certainly helped with the transition. At the time, Donna was living with her grandmother Mrs. Clark in Florida City, so things got easier and easier once Sean was on a regular meeting schedule.

As far as getting along with his brothers and sisters at his dad's house early on, "He had no problem playing with his siblings Joey and Jazmin," Josie said. "In fact, he had no problem playing with any kids. He and Joey would jump on our backyard trampoline and would play basketball." They had fun playing together and with friends in their tree house too.

When did Josie have her first inkling Sean could be a great football player?

"I never did. It never crossed my mind that Sean would be a famous person. I just knew he liked sports. I never really paid attention."

9

The Baby Half Sister

JAZMIN "JAZ" TAYLOR WAS BORN IN 1993, WHICH MAKES HER TEN YEARS younger than Sean. She offers a unique perspective and insight on the love and loss of a big brother. If you've ever lost someone near and dear to your heart, you'll understand.

🏈

"We're ten years apart, so it really wasn't like a brother-sister relationship. It was like, after my dad, it was Sean. I don't want to say he was like a second father. I looked at him more like my protector. If anyone bothered me, they'd have to deal with him.

"When he was home, I wouldn't walk. He would pick me up and carry me anywhere I wanted to go. One time we were in California and UM [University of Miami] just won the Rose Bowl. I was just eight or nine years old. We were all at his hotel. The players were all getting on the bus to go home, and we were in the gift shop buying something. It was a madhouse, really crowded, and the players were signing autographs, and everybody was trying to get to Sean.

"So when he saw me running to him, he just picked me up. I actually have a picture of that hanging on my bedroom wall. According to my mom, I was getting a little old for that sort of thing, and she said, 'No, Sean, you can't keep picking her up. She's getting older, and you're treating her like a baby.' When she said that, Sean just looked at her and said, 'If I don't carry her, how am I supposed to hold on to her forever?'

31

"Sean was also my chauffeur, but the thing is, we all had different things to do. After school, Sean had football practice and I had gymnastics. We were always busy. There was never time to just chill. We always had somewhere to go. It was always something. Then when we'd come home, my dad and Sean would be outside, working out. I was outside with them, playing their little cheerleader.

"Joey was much closer in age to Sean, so they hung out a lot. Like I said before, we didn't have a true brother-sister relationship. He really was more like a parent. So when my parents were too busy, he was the one who took me to cheerleading practice in that little blue car he had. He would also pick me up from school if he had to."

When Jazmin and Sean had their private time, they spoke mainly about boys. Or should we say "no boys." That was it: No boys! He used to ask Jazmin if she had a boyfriend.

"So I looked at him and said, 'No! What are you talking about?'"

"He used to tell me, 'You don't want a boy like me. You don't want a boy like me.' So I guess he was talking about one of those football players."

Sean and Jazmin had a nice, sweet, loving relationship. On the other hand, "With [brothers] Joey and Gabriel, they were beating me up because I was the only girl. It was a house full of boys and me and my mom. There was a lot of testosterone flying around in that house. With Sean it was exactly the opposite. He wouldn't beat me up. He wouldn't yell at me either. What he would do was flick me. With his thumb and his middle finger, he would come up behind me and flick me. They were the worst, most painful flicks ever, and since they were coming from him, I knew he was mad at me. He never yelled or hit, just flicked."

Jazmin talked about a day one summer when just she, Sean, and his girlfriend were at home. "FYI, I didn't like any of his girlfriends. The only ones I liked were Cassie and Jackie, and that was it.

"So Sean and his girlfriend were arguing about one thing or another, and I was being nosey, hiding behind a wall in the house, looking and listening, but he never said a word. Eventually they left. "When he came back, I was in my mom's room watching TV, and he just opened the door to the room, came in, flicked me, and left! That was just to show me he knew what I was doing hiding behind the wall. I was like, 'darn, caught.'"

After thinking for a moment, Jazmin speculated as to why she disliked Sean's girlfriends. Was it the way they looked, the way they sounded, the way they behaved? What was it about them she didn't like?

"I was the only girl I wanted Sean to always be around. I thought I was the only one who could have Sean's heart. Even when I found out Sean was having a little girl, I had an attitude with him for about two weeks. Eventually, when I was out shopping and I saw baby clothes, I would say, 'I want to get this for my niece. I want to get that for my niece.'"

10

Paying for As and Middle School Sports

"In 1994, the year Sean moved in with us, we spoke a lot about grades, grades, grades," Pete Taylor said. "You always had to keep improving—keep getting better. Another thing we spoke about was self-confidence, self-control, and conduct.

"The challenge was to figure out the best tool to keep Sean motivated in a new household and to keep his GPA up. I looked at school like it was a job. So if my kids did a good job, I paid them."

So with all of his children, Pete's tactic was to pay for performance.

"I paid all of my kids ten dollars per grade point. What's more, I always told my kids how much was on the line so they wouldn't settle for just eleven dollars or twenty-two dollars. I wanted them to max out. I wanted them to be the best they could be.

"'How about this?' I said to my kids. 'If you get all As, I'll give you a one-hundred-dollar bonus.' This way Sean and my other two would keep focus on their GPAs. They all wanted to maintain at least a three point five, but on the off chance they hit that four, it cost me one hundred dollars."

Life Lesson

"If you want to see your child's performance increase, offer him or her a bonus. Not a bribe, but a bona fide bonus. Some of you may say you can't afford to do this. And my contention is that twenty or thirty dollars over the course of a semester is not a lot of money. You might throw that much or more away on

cigarettes, a bottle of Jack, or beer. Aren't your kids worth it? Let me tell you, having a little money increases a kid's self-worth and allows him or her to choose what to spend it on. If that kid knows you pay five dollars for an A, and he or she brings home six As (PE not included), that's thirty bucks in that kid's pocket. It's a reward that reaps more rewards in the end. Now if you really can't afford to pay them twenty or thirty dollars, there's got to be a special treat your kids will want so you can save up for it if they 'make the grade.' If there's a light at the end of the tunnel, you'll be surprised what a kid will do."

In 1994, Sean was eleven and ready to play football at South Dade Park. "That's really the first time I can remember Sean making awesome tackles and having a great year," Pete Taylor said. "The team, on the other hand, was not all that good, so he really stood out. That year he played for a coach by the name of Mr. Bruten, who coached the 115-pound team.

"Not knowing if Sean was going to stay or go, I ended up taking him to practice every day, but I didn't coach, because I knew Donna's track record of giving and taking."

A couple of months went by, and Sean had to appear before a judge and report on his progress. He had to discuss how he was doing in school, what his conditions were like at home, etc. DYS was very happy with these reports, because it turned out Sean was doing much better. After their first year together, Sean's grades had improved by a full grade point.

Revelation

"Believe it or not, at age eleven, besides football, Sean wanted to play roller hockey and basketball," recalled Pete. "So what did I do? I started training him to play basketball. It didn't take long until he became a great basketball player.

"As far as roller hockey, it took about half a season until he mastered that game. Not only could he skate, but he could make those skates dance!"

Pete came to the realization that when Sean wasn't playing football, it was good to keep his body loose and mobile in the off-season. So let's just say this was Pete's way of cross-training his son.

Pete Taylor

"When Sean first came to live with me, Donna, his mom, didn't want him to play football because he was so accident prone. All of my kids are quick, but Sean had slow feet. You might say they were 'clumsy fast.' His feet had no form and were all over the place.

"He was always tripping over something or just plain falling down. When she had Sean in Ft. Lauderdale, he got hurt. I didn't know what happened, because as I said, our communication was never that great, but she finally got around to telling me about that injury when Sean came to live with me.

Training Tip

"So I figured I was going to train Sean not to be accident prone. We decided to work on his coordination and his footwork. Remember, he was a tall, lanky kid, clumsy-fast, someone with a fast-moving body but slow-moving legs. He would move a certain way and he'd always trip or something.

"So I began to work on his legs first. We did isolated squats, single-leg squats, and three hundred push-ups. Then we did three hundred sit-ups and an assortment of trampoline work. We also did pull-ups.

"When it came to working out while playing ball, Sean always wanted to get better," Pete said. "So he had a list of things he had to do on a daily basis. Two days a week, we'd run tires." That's when a kid ties a tire to one end of a rope and the other end gets tied to the kid. Then the runner gets the benefit of added resistance, strengthening one's calves, ankles, and feet.

"I can remember vividly this one time with Sean on the side of a road. He was working on strength moves, pulling heavy tires like a sled. His friends and some of his classmates would pass by, and they'd laugh at Sean, saying, 'Oh, Sean, you be running out there with a tire. That's the funniest thing we ever saw.'

"Our big thing was, when we went to the grocery store, Sean, Joey, and Jazmin put the groceries in the car, and my wife would take the car home while the kids and I would jog home. That was our conditioning and stamina exercise.

"When we went out to eat at, say, a mall, we'd all walk the mall before and after dinner. We kept this up as long as I could remember."

According to Sean's half sister Jazmin, her dad made all the kids run home. The only difference was the distance. The younger they were, the less they'd have to run.

Pete noted, "When I was in DC for the Brian Mitchell Redskins Rally the day before the last regular game of the 2012 season, [current 2014 Redskins player] Darrel Young came over to me and said, '[former Redskins player] Mike Sellers told me something about Sean.' He said, 'Did you know Sean would run to his house from the practice facility after a workout? His girlfriend would come by to pick him up, and he told her to go on without him. The rest of the players saw Sean jogging all the way home as they all left the park.'

"Then he told me Mike started calling Sean 'freak of nature' and the rest of the team followed suit. For me, it was a tribute to know the things Sean was accustomed to doing in his younger years, like running the hills and working on his speed, were still carrying over to when he made it to the pros."

When Darrel first got to the Redskins, he chose jersey number 36 because that was Sean's first number as a rookie. "I think that's the ultimate compliment, especially coming from a pro athlete," Taylor said.

Hard work pays off, plain and simple. Sean was always running and trying to improve his speed. He would do extra pull-ups, push-ups, and sit-ups just to get stronger. He got up to eight hundred sets of certain exercises. "This is what molded him into the player he would become starting in middle school, to high school, to college, and then the pros," said Taylor.

Coach Timothy Blount

In 1995, Coach Timothy Blount was both a science teacher and track-and-field coach at Richmond Heights Middle School. It was also the year Coach Blount had an outstanding group of eleven- and twelve-year-old runners. They won many local and regional tournaments and eventually were invited to California to participate in a national track-and-field tournament. But before we get to all of that, what was Sean Taylor the middle school student like? With all he had been through, was he rebellious? Did he misbehave? Did he get good grades?

"I was in my second year of teaching sixth-grade science at Richmond Heights Middle School. Not only that, I was also the track-and-field coach. During that year there was this young man, Sean Taylor, in my classroom who was well mannered, reserved, and very disciplined," recalled Timothy Blount.

At this juncture, Sean had completed his transition from his mom's home to the Taylors' home. Many times under these circumstances you find students who do not adjust well and act up in class and get into a lot of trouble. This was not the case with Sean.

But there was more. "Being fully informed as to Sean's 'situation,' I had to make sure he was accommodated so he would fit well into the system," Blount said.

"As a teacher, my job was to observe and document. I think Sean just took everything in stride. I knew his father Pete Taylor as a very well disciplined individual, and I think that rubbed off on his son. So whatever challenges he had, he accepted them and made the best of his opportunity," added Blount.

"As a student, he did very well. As far as classwork and homework, there were proactive discussions with Sean and Pete so they knew what expectations were.

"Of course, every student has the potential to grow. I also knew he was doing the best he could. Remember, when you're a student athlete, you have to work much harder, as more is thrown your way, and I think Sean did an excellent job maximizing his potential as a student and an athlete."

Prior to track-and-field season, Coach Blount wanted to promote opportunities outside of school for students who were runners. Sean immediately became interested. At first Sean ran the 100, 200, 4 × 100 relay, and 4 × 400 relay, which was no more or less than the standard would allow per school regulations to prevent injuries in young athletes.

Blount made sure Sean was registered for the events that would give him the best results. "So I geared him more toward relays even though he probably could have competed in every event."

Blount knew he had something special with Sean. "Sean possessed what I called the mental fortitude to train and approach each competition with greater passion, autonomy, and confidence. It reminded me of his football skills, but on a track-and-field level."

When it came to the 100- and 200-meter races, Sean blew everybody away. He came in first in nearly every single meet. "At the time, I saw that not only could this kid compete against every school in the district—by the way, we finished in first place in the county—but he could compete against anybody else in the state of Florida. So the 100 and the 200 became his special races."

When asked if Sean had perpetual neck pain from looking behind him at the trailing runners or carrying around all of those heavy medals, the ever-serious Blount replied, "No. He was too humble for that sort of thing."

It was time to move forward with these kids. So when district competitions were over, Mr. Blount took his novice group of eleven- and twelve-year-olds from a middle school track-and-field program to a club track-and-field program registered under the USA Track & Field organization. "I did this so they could compete statewide," Blount said.

It turned out that Sean was his missing piece of the puzzle. Competing alongside Sean were Willy Jackson and Tom and Tony Baker, who were not only teammates but were also just as competitive as Sean Taylor. "His teammates also recognized his skills and gave him the nickname 'Eat-em-up.'

"Sean's talent and his devotion necessitated him running down the competition. I remember in one particular race during the state finals before advancing to the National Junior Olympics, the leader [Bershawn Jackson, who is now an Olympic hurdler] had about a 100-meter gap on Sean. Probably even more, but I'd have to go back and look at the videotape. As the anchor person, Sean got the baton and ran him down to win the race for us."

The competition in California was another story and when speaking about it, Coach Blount began with a big sigh. "Let me just say I registered our team under the name 'Blount Track Club.' We were not supported by any public organization or agency. We had to do everything ourselves. In order for our kids to go, the funds would have to come from within and some other resources we had by connecting with parents.

"It was Pete Taylor who spearheaded the effort to make sure the team had the best shot to try and take our talent as far as it could go. We started doing car washes. Then Pete helped us raise money in the Richmond Heights community so that we had support from our own people and local businesses. Not only that, we had to reach out to parents to make sure they had the opportunity to ask the people they knew for funds.

"Pete gave us his best shot at getting money into the organization so we could not only advance these kids to the state level but all the way to San Jose, California.

"I want to be honest with you," Blount said. "If it weren't for Pete, I don't think we would have made that expedition."

Don't think for a moment it was a luxury trip. This was no charter bus or airplane. "We caught the Greyhound, and it took us a week to get to San Jose, California, so we had to sleep on that bus. There were three parents, not including myself, making the trip. We couldn't wait to see that first decent restroom and a place to lay our heads down, because it felt like that trip took forever!"

The mantra of "Are we there yet?" permeated the ride. "We knew we were going for the gold, but first we had to get there," Blount said. "That weeklong bus trip took a lot out of us. When we arrived, the kids were just completely exhausted, yet relieved," as were the parents.

Was getting there really half the fun?

"I took five kids to the nationals. There was Sean Taylor, Willy Jackson, twins Tom and Tony Baker, and Jeremy Hasty. That was the eleven- [and] twelve-year-old group."

It was amazing. While most of the other teams who came from longer distances flew, those kids went all that way to California by bus and were still able to perform. They were completely fatigued mentally and physically, but they did it. Blount said, "I don't think it really affected them. It was just another summer trip."

There were hundreds of teams from across the United States in different age groups. They all assembled at San Jose College to compete. Only the top three teams in each event could advance from their state to compete in the Junior National Olympics in San Jose.

The kids had to adapt quickly, and when they finally settled in, it was just business as usual. "We had to go back to our routine of practice, then review our strategy. Once they saw their competition, it was like a whole 'nother perspective. They knew from the moment they saw those teams from Florida, California, Mississippi, etc., they had to compete on another level. So they quickly stepped back into reality," Blount explained.

"I knew this relay team was going to be a powerhouse and would get national track-and-field ranking, especially after competing in San Jose and placing first in the semifinals against all ranked teams in the United States. In the finals they placed third overall."

Blount knew that Pete's perspective was that Sean should be involved in an activity to keep him in shape in the off-season, when he wasn't playing football. Pete looked at running as more of a cross-training opportunity than a competition.

When the Washington Redskins took Sean in the first round of the NFL draft in 2004, Blount was delighted. "I was very proud. I [even] bragged to all of my colleagues. I always used Sean as the example for those who thought they could go on and become an exceptional athlete. Here's how I start my talk with my kids: 'Do y'all know Sean Taylor?' After they get over the initial surprise of the question, I'd say, 'I used to coach him.' And they'd say, 'Reeaally?' I'd say 'You see … this is what I'm talking about. You could go on to become whatever you want if you try.'"

Life Lesson

"At an early age, just as my father did with me, I instilled in Sean the notion that you have to work hard to be the best," said Pete. "There's nothing in life that's free. By the way, there's nothing I had my kids do that I wouldn't do myself. So if I told Sean he needs to do seven hundred pushups, I did the seven hundred pushups. I led by example. When it was time to work out on their own, they did it because they knew I could. Sometimes you can tell a kid to do something and they look at you like you're crazy. But if they know you'd do it too, that makes a difference."

In the fall of 1995, Pete moved Sean from Richmond Heights Middle School into Southwood Middle School, located in a somewhat more affluent area of the city. "The reason I transferred him there was, at Richmond, they had something called a 'Zo gang.' Sean was only twelve, but that's when gangs started coming up and recruiting, and we wanted to stay away from that."

Pete was always on top of what was going on at school. "What I used to do was visit the school twice a week. I was one of those concerned parents who would sit in his classroom so Sean would know I was going to stay on him to make sure he got his work done."

Pete recalled the time his children received awards for being meritorious scholars. "It was one of the ladies in the audience that said, 'That's so nice. *These* parents usually see their kids getting awards for being great athletes, but this kid is a scholar, an athlete, and a black kid.' I guess she really wasn't used to seeing that, and I wasn't used to hearing that. You see, paying for As can work wonders."

Life Lesson

"I'd like to send this message out to all the younger kids reading this: You can't just focus on sports. You gotta think about the total package. The big picture. You have to prepare your body and your mind to be ready for the real world. These academic awards meant a lot to me and were actually highlights of raising my kids."

Education was paramount, and it starts with a great attitude. So to get Sean ready for school everyday, ready to learn, one of the things his father did was to make sure he looked his best. "So I made Sean wear a nice shirt and a tie to school," Taylor said.

🏈

Revelation

Some of you may not know that Pete Taylor is the chief of police of Florida City, Florida. As chief, he finds himself speaking to large groups of people, such as at schools and civic associations. Not only that, "I joined a group of dedicated parents and professionals who would speak to the students about black history or my career as a police officer. To this day I work with kids in all kinds of situations. Sometimes it's just throwing the ball around or something as simple as listening.

"I take my job in the community very seriously, and I am out there trying to make a difference. Not that I take away a lot of time from patrolling, but I try and let the kids know they have a friend in the police business. I let them know we care what happens to them. The only time they really see us in action is when we take someone to jail because he or she did something wrong. So I believe in community policing and crime prevention."

◆

"I started coaching football when I was about eighteen or nineteen, before I had kids," Pete said. It's one thing to play football and another thing to coach and instruct. They are different animals. "As a coach, the expectations are higher. You have to reach down and touch and inspire an entire team. You have to touch their inner souls.

"I decided to coach Sean's twelve- [and] thirteen-year-old Florida City football team. It was the last year Sean was eligible to play Pop Warner. The head coach used to get upset with me when I coached the D [the defense]. He asked me, 'Why do you call so many blitzes and different coverages?' My answer to him was, 'When the kids get to high school, that's what they are going to see.'

"They had to buy into the spy [a defense where you take away one of the offense's best players by, for example, double-teaming him, thereby minimizing his impact]. I taught them different coverages, like the 3-4; the 4-3; the 5-3; and the 5-2. These were basic coverages on how to 'spy' or cover a guy—just play man up. That year we didn't get scored on until we played this one team called the South Dade Rams—the very team Sean had come from. Somewhere in the last part of the game, we put our subs in, and sure enough, South Dade made a touchdown, and that was the first time we got scored on the entire season.

"I remember there was this fear of our team. No one wanted to play us. They said we were hitting too hard and putting their players out of games. What can I say? Our team was just physical.

"We had several really good players on the team. There was Antrel Rolle, who plays with the New York Giants; Marcus Hudson, who played for the Carolina Panthers; Jarvis Johnson, who went on to play for Rutgers; and Eric Foster, who played for the Indianapolis Colts. Seven or eight of his teammates went on to play in college, and four went to the pros."

Antrel Rolle & Marcus Hudson

Sean and Antrel played for the Florida City Razorbacks. "We only played together for two years," Rolle said. "However, I played against him almost every year from age seven through thirteen.

"I remember we were about the same height when we were thirteen years old, but when I saw him the following year, I mean, shoot, he was 6'2½", almost 6'3", and I grew to maybe 5'11" at that point. So I asked him, 'What happened to you?' He shot up out of nowhere."

Another one of Sean's teammates early on was Marcus Hudson. He too took note of Sean's growth spurt. "I was taller than him, and he put on size and height all in one summer. That's when he went into beast mode, and ever since then he became the Sean Taylor we all know.

"Out of the four of us that played on that team, I was the tallest, and that summer he reached my height. When I saw him again, I said, 'Sean, is that you?'"

Marcus continued: "He got bigger. He gained a lot more weight, and, of course, he was taller. Like I said, it was a whole transition from eighth to ninth grade. Puberty took its toll on Sean, man. Heavy."

Marcus and Sean spoke mainly about football. If not football, it was another conversation that involved sports, because they were always competing. So if it wasn't football, it was track. If it wasn't track, it was basketball.

"Unfortunately we never faced one another in the NFL," Hudson lamented. "But Sean is one those players I actually looked up to. I loved his intensity. To this day I watch his highlights to get myself motivated. If you want to play football, this is how you play football."

Hudson spoke about why so many great football players came out of South Florida. He said, "It starts in childhood. They all want to be the best. Everybody knows at sixty-five pounds and six years old you watch everybody else out there in the park, and you dream that one day you'll play in the NFL. 'You know what? I'm gonna be the best. No, I'm gonna be the best. Nooo, I'm gonna be the best. That's what I'm talking about; when I get my chance … my big break … I'm gonna play in the NFL.' We breathe football down there in South Florida all the time. It's a history. We have a bunch of hungry kids from the state of Florida who just go out all across the country and show the skills that we have in common and represent South Dade the right way."

When Marcus played with the San Francisco 49ers, he got to play with his longtime friend Frank Gore. "It felt great to be playing with someone I knew from childhood. We related, having played right around the corner from each other. I spent a lot of my time with him.

"The last time I spoke to Sean, I was in Publix in Homestead. He caught me walking out, and he pulled up next to me. We chatted for a while in the parking lot. That was right before he ended up passing away." That was 2007 and Sean was already a Redskin. "That's when we were just caught up in how life was going. We had kids that were arriving at the same time, so we caught up on family. I asked him how his father was doing, stuff like that. We didn't talk too long."

If there was one thing Marcus wanted to convey in his interview, it was this: with a slight chuckle, Hudson stated, "Sean has been a hard hitter since he was a small child. I can remember the first time I saw him; it was like watching a bulldozer. He went through this one kid—and you have to know the park Sean was playing at before he came to Florida City. Well, we were playing the South Dade Rams. They were talking trash to him. He returned a kickoff, and if you can imagine a bulldozer running over a flower, that was him. He ran through this cat, stuck him in the chest, and kept going like it was nothing. The whole park exploded when we saw that hit. I wish I had it on tape, because that should be on his highlight reel.

"I got to put a lot of this on Coach Pete [Taylor] because he brought a level of intensity to eighth graders that I've never seen before. I mean, literally, we gave up maybe three touchdowns that year. I was always on the offensive side of the ball in the later part of the season, and I was like, 'Our defense is for real.' We were doing pretty well with our offense, but when I saw them do the defensive drills, I started understanding why Sean is the way he is, because his dad stepped it up by three hundred and five degrees. He turned up the heat, and when he brings it, he brings it!"

Marcus still misses his buddy Sean, who still lives in his heart. "He motivates me every day. I see him on YouTube all the time. If I'm about to go speak to a group, or if I'm coaching or training someone … before I say anything, I say, 'Go look at the Sean Taylor highlights.' It's all the motivation you need to be the best": http://www.youtube.com/watch?v=KvE3I0A0fek.

Pete Taylor continued

"All together, I have been coaching off and on for twenty-seven years. I coached at Dick Conley Football League Pop Warner, Florida City Razorbacks, Gulliver Prep, South Miami Senior High, and Homestead High School. I even coached for a semi-pro team: the Florida Kings. I never broke through to a higher level though, until 2014, as I became the head coach of the brand-new UIFL [Ultimate Indoor Football League] team called the Miami Inferno which played its games at the University of Miami's BankUnited Center. I really want to use this experience to perhaps get to the next level one day, as I feel I could coach in the D-I college ranks and beyond. I wouldn't even mind being a pro scout because I can spot good talent and I know what it takes to win."

Training Tip

"One thing I concentrated on with Sean was how to properly tackle. Once Sean brought up helmet-to-helmet hits when he was only six, I really wanted to concentrate on tackling. I showed Sean where to make the plant and where to lean and hit. One of the biggest things for me was watching him translate that into actually empowering him. Remember, when tackling, it's all about timing and finishing.

"You know, a lot of kids want to run the ball. Some want to catch the ball. But not a lot of kids want to make a tackle, and that holds true even in the pros. How many times do you see guys just standing around, not engaging or getting in on the play? The thing is, if you can make the tackle and blow them up, you'll get the ball, even take it to the house!"

PART II

11

Killian High School

In the blink of an eye, it was 1997, the year Sean entered Killian Senior High School. In ninth and tenth grade he began to really excel in sports. The hard work was definitely paying off. Those same kids that were laughing at him pulling those tires and working hard were now praising him.

On the Killian Junior Varsity Football Team, Sean played running back and a little safety. He was breaking on the ball, making interceptions, and hitting players—hard. He was making game-winning tackles. And it was in that year Killian had a new JV football coach—Coach James Bryant, a.k.a. "Waterdog."

Coach James Bryant

The Starbucks café within the Barnes and Noble in Kendall, Florida, was a favorite meeting place for our interviews and book-related discussions. This particular wrap-up session between Pete and me was running especially long.

Do you remember in school when it was the last period of the day and you couldn't wait to get out of class and you started packing up your books and things five minutes before the bell rang? That's how I felt the night we met Waterdog. He was running late, and just as I was saying my good-byes to Pete, in he walked. All I can say is that it was worth the wait.

🏈

When Coach Bryant was getting his job at Killian Senior High School in Miami, he had no idea what kind of talent was about to fall into his lap. Bryant inherited a coaching staff that had already been at the school for three or four years. These guys were also the players he had played with when he went to Killian. The coaches kept telling him about this guy named Sean Taylor.

"I was a brand-new teacher at Miami Killian Senior High School, and the brand-new JV coach, coming in with a chip on my shoulder. You know, the next best coach to come through Killian. Since I was an alum as well, it was going to be a foregone conclusion, right?" Coach Bryant began.

"Remember, I was new, so I had no idea who I had on the team and what kind of talent they brought to the table. It's not like high school coaches get to recruit, right?

"My coaches kept saying, 'Wait until you see Sean. Wait until you see Sean.' Apparently they knew all about him from the park system. I didn't."

Having taken a job in Puerto Rico for six years, when Bryant returned to Miami he was a bit out of touch. "So I said, 'Hey, I can't wait to meet this Sean Taylor.'"

Sean's workouts were legendary. Bryant's coaches explained that when Sean was in Pop Warner, his dad used to put him through grueling workouts that they said were "not like when we went to school."

When Bryant finally met Sean, he saw a slightly above-average body—a ninth grader standing 5'9"–5'10". Sean was very well mannered. He was a "yes, sir; no, sir" kind of guy, and Coach liked that, as that's what he demanded from his players. Once practices began, it quickly became evident to Bryant that everything his coaches had said was true.

"I didn't know any better, so as a new coach I put the kids through a punishing four-hour practice. Sean was always the first in line or the first on the field, and so on.

"To me he was just a quiet kid that liked to run. I didn't see him as anything but ordinary, because we had a few kids like him on the team. Those kids were Andre Maddox, Patrick Thomas, and Raymond Murphy, who we called Plantation. There was also a kid by the name of Loren Moss. Those kids were right up there with Sean, so I saw them as the catalyst of my team. I saw them as one.

"I was a big nickname guy," Bryant said. "Raymond Murphy had just transferred into our school from Plantation [a high school in Broward County, Florida]. That's how he got his nickname. They called Sean "Peeto," and I really don't know why. The team gave him that name, not me."

Bryant's ninth graders were fourteen-year-old kids. And as he said, he put them through some hell. They had your typical two-a-days (practice twice a day), and they were pretty tough. Finally the kids were ready to play their first game of the season.

"At that time, another kid, Andre Maddox, was the focal point of the team. Apparently his pedigree was a little deeper than Sean's in the Pop Warner League. Sean was a close second," Bryant said.

In game one, Maddox was thrown out of the game, which meant Sean was thrust into the limelight. According to Coach Bryant, "Maddox got a bum call. He got clipped, and he turned around and threw an elbow at the kid who was on the ground. The refs thought he threw a punch that knocked him down, so they kicked him out. With an ejection comes a one-game suspension, which means he's now out two games.

"All in all, I think Sean performed pretty well. He stepped up.

"So I'm still in the 'who is this Sean Taylor?' mode. All my other coaches were still pretty high on him. The coaches and I struggled with what position to put him at. Sean told me he wanted to be a running back, so I put him at running back. I didn't have anybody else at the time, so I put him there, and he did a good job. My coaches thought he should be playing both ways [on offense and defense]. But at Killian we didn't need to do that. So I fought them on it, and I kept him on offense. I let him play running back, and I wanted to keep it that way because the defense had Maddox and Pat. They had the good players. I had the one good player I thought we could keep [on the offense]."

In game two, Bryant learned something about Sean. "We lost 13–12 to Columbus. There was one instance when they went into the huddle and Sean's eyes appeared to be full of tears. I called him over, and I said, 'What's wrong with you, man? Why are you crying?' He didn't answer me then ... but after the game when I asked him again why he was crying in the huddle, he tells me, 'Coach, I hate to fuck'n' lose.' That's how he said it. 'I hate fucking losing, coach! I don't mean to curse at you. That's not me, but I just hate to lose.' I immediately understood.

"After reviewing the film, I made it a point of becoming a much better coach. I had kids that were really taking the game to heart. I thought, *'I can't pull the wool over these kids' eyes.'* So that's when I knew I really had to step up to the plate."

Killian JV's first game was canceled because of lightning. "We played Coral Reef Senior High School, and they thought they won," Bryant said. They didn't. "We had a bye week after that, so I had a whole two weeks to get my mind right and coach the game like I was a big-time coach. I used to be a big-time player, but a big-time coach? Let's just say I was still learning."

In the two weeks they had off, Bryant's coaches were on him every day. "'We need Sean to play safety. We can't keep giving up these touchdowns like this, blah, blah, blah, blah.' I said, 'No, man. I gave up everybody, and now you want the last good player I have?' They were like, 'Coach, you played safety; you'll know if he's good or not.' I said, 'That's true. That's true.' Well, they finally broke me down."

At first Bryant wasn't listening to his players or his coaches. "They would tell me things about the game, and I would just block them out," he said. "I thought I knew better. New coach. Cocky. Arrogant. That was me. I understood sometimes even the coach has to listen because others may see things you don't.

"So I let Sean go over there and play. I saw some flashes. I said, 'Okay, he's got an idea about what's going on over there.' Let me repeat that I played the position [safety]. I played for four years in high school and two years in college at Kentucky State and one at Florida State.

"In our second game, their quarterback threw into the slant, and I have never seen a kid launch himself at someone the way Sean did. I thought the kid he hit was dead. Then I was like, 'Okay, maybe it was just luck.' But when anything went in the air, Sean had it. I think he had three interceptions and two or three really big hits in the game." Sean played both ways in that game, and he scored twice as a running back. "We beat North Miami 40–0, and that was the start of a snowball effect.

"After the game I tell Pete—and I know Pete won't remember, but I said—'As much as your son wants to play running back, from what I've seen today, he's going to be a safety at the next level and beyond.' Pete was like, 'Nah, man, my son is going to be a running back. He was just born to be a running back.'"

"'I'm sorry,' I said to Pete, 'this guy is going to be a safety.'

"Since I had sixteen-year-old Plantation—two years older than Sean, with better footwork—they shared the running back position."

Sean spent most of the remaining games on defense, and the rest of the season was history. Killian JV went 6–2 and shut out every team they beat with Sean as the X factor. "When he played offense, he was there to basically give Plantation a break. He would even play receiver when we needed him to. In fact, he was the kind of guy that would play anywhere we needed him. He never wanted to come out of the game. He even wanted to run back punts. I said, 'Damn, Sean. We got somebody to run back punts. We got somebody to run back kickoffs, too.' He always wanted to be on the field."

As a position coach, Coach Bryant was in charge of only one area, and that was the defensive backfield: safeties and cornerbacks. "I did such a good job as JV head coach, I kind of bounced with the players who moved up. So when they moved up, I asked the varsity head coach, Sam Miller, 'Why don't you take me with them, man?' I know the kids and I know the plays. Why don't you let me take them under my wing?'" And that's what happened. Coach Bryant got his promotion to varsity.

"I saw a little growth in Sean over the summer. He got to maybe 6' tall, maybe 180 pounds. To me it was just a normal growth spurt. Most of the kids did the same thing. I did see some growth in his legs. I asked him one day, 'Where did you get those legs from, man?' He wasn't a big lifter at the time, so I don't know what happened." He probably got those legs from running.

"When I left JV, I knew this guy was going to be special. It was just a matter of 'let me train him.' I had played the position before. 'Let me work with him, Coach,'" Bryant said to varsity Head Coach Miller. "'I've played the position, and I've seen all the skill sets.' It was unbelievable."

Coach Sam Miller eventually allowed Bryant to work with him.

"Unfortunately the head coach and I didn't see eye-to-eye as far as how he should play the position. He saw defense differently than I did. He was a front seven guy and, in my opinion, knew very little about the backfield. So he kind of left me out there with these young puppies, Maddox and another tenth grader that came up. Plantation was a running back, so he played on the offensive side of the ball.

"So now Sean was exclusively on defense. They didn't want to hear about his offensive skills, because they were loaded on offense.

"We went 7 and 4 and lost in the first round in the playoffs, but we could have been much better. We had a tug-of-war as to how the defense was supposed to be run. In fact, we were very poor against the pass, so I wanted to change some things to make it better. Let me put it to you this way: in my opinion, the head coach's scheme wasn't solid," Bryant stated.

"We came up against Coral Park, the team that beat us four years straight on the same alignment. Their coach was Joseph Montoya. I told our coach that with Sean and Maddox, we could stop them if you give me the things I need. He was like, 'No, no, no, no, no. We're going to run my defense, and it's the only thing that's going to work.'

"I said, 'Sean can't do it by himself. He's good, he's raw, but he can't do it by himself.'

"'No. We'll make it work,' Miller said. 'We'll put pressure on the quarterback, and we'll make it happen.' It didn't happen that way. Sean got toasted for two touchdowns that game. They were pretty long ones, too, one going for sixty yards.

"So then I did something I had never done before. I apologized to Sean. Even though it wasn't my fault, it put me in a pretty bad spot, and I still took the blame. He came to me and said, practically begging, 'Let me do what I do, coach. Just let me do what I do.' So I told him he couldn't do it by himself and we needed a different defense for this game.

"That was a pretty down spot for me, and it took me a while to get it back. We had another couple of games, and … he went on to play well for the rest of the year. He got a couple of big hits in, too."

Coach Bryant said he saw Sean not as a freelancer but as a risk taker. "At safety, you have to take risks," he said. "You can't just sit back there. If you're going to make big plays, you have to take risks."

It turns out that's what Sean was really good at: playing instinctively. He would visualize a play and jump on it. Sometimes it worked, and sometimes it didn't. "It happened with me and as with most safeties. It even happened for Ed Reed. So I hate to say this, but he got into bad graces with our head coach because *he* considered Sean a freelancer," Bryant said.

It soon came time for the championship game against Miami High School. They had *the* Andre Johnson on their side. Bryant's initial thought was, "*Oh, shit! He's a big boy. Is this kid for real?*" So that week they practiced with Sean playing as Johnson's shadow, since Sean was the biggest kid they had.

"In the middle of the game, Sean made a little mistake that Coach Miller saw as a *huge* mistake," Coach Bryant remembered. "Miller started taking Sean off Andre, and Andre went wild on us and scored a couple of touchdowns. We decided to put Sean back on him in a crucial part of the game—like, they needed to score to win. We had practiced putting Sean on the end zone line."

Coach Bryant's gut told him this was going to be a mistake. "So I went to Coach and said, 'You know, Sean isn't ready for this.'"

Miller said, "I want him there."

"The problem is they lined Sean up in the tight-end area, and they wanted to put Maddox on Johnson because Andre was used to playing in the box. For some reason he just wanted Sean on him. Sean didn't know how to play it. I'll put it this way; Sean wasn't ready. So he got caught up in the mix and Andre scored.

"Well, this guy [Head Coach Sam Miller] held grudges. So he felt like Sean was the reason we lost that game. And I'm like, 'Nah, Coach. It's a lot bigger than that, man.' At that point he got on my case. 'Get the fuck out of my office,'" he howled.

"Needless to say, I didn't have the varsity job the next year.

"Coach and I butted heads. But at that point he wrote Sean off. That was it."

Then something unexpected happened. Sean's father decided to transfer Sean to the prestigious Gulliver Prep.

"I didn't think he was gone. I knew he had a rough season, but I told him, 'Look, give us a little more time, man, and I'll get you right. Look, Sean, if you get picks, those are game-changing chances right there.' So we kinda went back and forth on that issue.

"It wasn't until later on that we really talked about what happened."

🏈

Here's what happened next. "I got fired from varsity but stayed at the school," Coach Bryant said. "They demoted me back to JV, and I begged Sean, 'Please! I'll be out there; please don't leave. I heard you thinking about leaving, man, but pleeease, man, please don't leave, maaann.' He told me, 'I just can't work with this guy, man.'" Meaning, of course, Coach Miller.

Revelation

"Turns out him and Miller had a big blowup in the weight room. I wasn't there, but apparently Miller told Sean to 'get the fuck out' because 'you were the reason we lost.'

"Sean said, 'Nah, I think you're wrong about that.' Sean was respectful about it, but Miller busted Sean in front of the whole team. So from what I understand, this was one of the deciding factors as to why Sean left Killian."

Pete Taylor, who had been sitting and listening to the entire conversation with Bryant, at this point said, "Do you know I didn't know any of this? This is the first I heard of Sean being blamed for losing the game, even the blowup in the locker room. The reason this is important is that when I came up with the idea of the transfer to Gulliver, Sean said he was okay with it. And now I know why.

"I'll tell you something else," Pete said. "When I was in the Killian office working out the transfer, I saw Miller and some of the other coaches, but they didn't know what was going on. Ten minutes later, somehow the word got out that I was transferring Sean."

"And they went looking for you," Coach Bryant said, finishing Pete's sentence.

"Yes. They went looking for me," Pete echoed, as he started to laugh.

"Somebody came to get me and asked me if I had seen you, because they heard Sean was transferring out. I was stunned, and all I could say was, 'I hope it ain't true!'" Bryant said.

"It was true. It was true," Pete said, half tongue-in-cheek.

"Well, Sean did come by to tell me he was leaving. You know we were tight because I was the position coach and he wanted to let me know. So I was like, 'Whaaat?'"

"That night I got into it about Sean," Bryant exclaimed.

"With whom? You and Miller?" Pete asked.

"He blamed Sean for the mistake.... I wanted to let him know what's up."

It was a Friday-night home game, and they were the big team to beat. According to Bryant, "Miller said, 'We should have beaten them,' [because]

Sean was D-ing [defending] them up all night." The last play was the only time he failed to do so. So how could the loss have been his fault?

Pete added, "It wasn't the defense that couldn't play; it was the offense that couldn't put up the points. They had playmakers, but they were a team that depended on their defense. Now, if you play that 'just hold on' type of game and leave the defense on the field the entire night, they are going to get tired—get worn down. But they were strong enough to hold up the team. That was the first time in a long time that Killian made the playoffs. They were starting to turn the corner, but I just never knew all those stories."

"He had a pretty good season," added Bryant. "He had five picks and averaged five or six tackles a game; so to me, you can't beat that, man."

"The next time I saw Sean was at a track meet," said Bryant. "When I saw him, I realized—he grew!"

At this point, Sean was in eleventh grade. "He was running track for Gulliver at a University of Miami–sponsored meet," Bryant said. "He walked by me, and I said, 'Sean?' not believing how much he had grown. He said, 'What's up, Coach?' And he gave me a big hug. I was like, 'What da fuck happened to you, boy?' He was like 6'3", and those legs were even bigger than they were [before]. I was like, 'What the hell happened to you?' and he started laughing and very humbly said, 'You know, Coach.' I was like, 'Oh my God!'

"Why couldn't he just have stayed? I had everybody. I had Plantation running track. I had Pat running track. He could have been our missing link, and we could have had a way better team with him. He was running the 100 and 200 at 6'3". I was like, 'I can't believe it, man.' I said to him, 'I hear you're doing some big things over at Gulliver.'

"He said, 'Hey, I gotta do my thing, Coach!'

"I followed him through his senior year in the papers, but I never watched him play in person again. I would see him in Richmond Park, though, and he'd always come over and say hi. He was always very respectful to me, always gave me time, and that's what I loved about him. He never 'big-timed' me. I followed him through the draft, but like I said, we didn't cross paths much. He wasn't a Killian alum, and I was like, 'Damn, Sean, the least you can do is come see your boys play.'

"At the time he signed with UM, Maddox signed with NC State. Plantation had grade issues, so he set up with a junior college. They were all top-level players."

Several Killian players were drafted by NFL teams. "Sean went in the first round to the Redskins. Maddox was drafted in the third round the following year by the Jets. Pat got drafted in the fifth round by the Jaguars. He was there for three years; then he got traded to Kansas City and played there three years, until his contract was up. Plantation is a singer, and I think he's in Arizona. He's rappin' and has a nice little gig goin' on out there," Bryant said. "After Sean left Killian, we kept in contact. When we spoke, we talked about the NFL and so much more."

Pete Taylor

It should be of no surprise that Sean also ended up playing for his church team as part of his upbringing in the Seventh-Day Adventist Church, and with Sean, they consistently won in their league. "He was such a well-rounded kid and, due to his faith in God, always kept himself humble with the Lord above," Pete Taylor said of Sean.

As a sophomore at Killian in 1998, Sean also tried out for Coach Kaufman and Coach Weissman, who ran the JV basketball program.

"Coach Weissman was very special in Sean's and my life," said Pete Taylor. "He was an administrator and made sure Sean had all his core classes right. After evaluating Sean's schedule and grades, he came to me and said, 'Mr. Taylor, your son needs to be in honors classes, especially when it comes to math and English.' We followed his direction, and it was a blessing, because Sean excelled even at the honors level."

Saul and Darren Weissman

Saul Weissman has been a guidance counselor and a coach at Miami Killian Senior High School for twenty years. Darren Weissman, Saul's son, was a friend and basketball teammate of Sean's. Pete interviewed both of them to get their perspective on Sean the superior basketball player. People are not aware that Sean Taylor could have been just as big a basketball star as he was a football star. Sean loved playing basketball almost as much as football, maybe even more. Here are two eyewitness accounts of Sean's talents from back in the day.

"I knew Sean when he entered Killian in ninth grade," Saul Weissman started. "At that time, I was the ninth-grade basketball coach. We had two JVs back then: we had a ninth-grade team and a regular JV team. Sean played basketball on the ninth-grade team. As a sophomore he played with the regular JV squad and was eventually moved up to varsity that same year.

"A lot of people don't realize how good a basketball player Sean was. In my opinion, Sean could have gotten a D-I scholarship in basketball had he pursued that sport over football. He was a great player, especially on defense. And who plays defense anymore?

"You never wanted to be guarded by Sean, because he was relentless. If you had the ball, you probably weren't gonna score, and if he fouled you, he hurt you. He was just that kind of player. He was never dirty; just a very hard, tough player."

Coach Kaufman, who was the varsity coach at the time, liked him so much he invited Sean to varsity practices. He started that when Sean was in ninth grade. So Sean was actually practicing with the varsity squad long before he joined that team.

"He was big for his age, and he could rebound," Saul Weissman said. "He could shoot and handle the ball. He was a quick learner, and any time he had to execute a defense, he was always in position. He had a great attitude. His teammates loved him. It was just a pleasure to work with him as a coach."

Then former teammate Darren Weissman spoke up. "I met Sean when he was in eighth grade, the summer before high school," said Darren. "That summer he would come to Killian for all of the open gyms to play basketball.

"He was very aggressive. Going up against Sean—well, he just wanted to make you look bad. He didn't let anything come easy. You were never comfortable with him guarding you. For that reason alone you wanted him on your team. But on the offensive end he brought his *A* game all the time because he was unselfish, and he always just wanted to win more than look good or score.

"I had the privilege of training with him. His father, Pete, would pick me up that summer, as well as in ninth and tenth grades. We would go from the field, to the gym. It was one of the first times I really worked hard off of the court, besides just playing the game.

"Sean was a great partner to work out with. You didn't want to get left in the dust, because that's where he'd leave you if you didn't keep up. He always pushed you to work harder, train harder. His energy was contagious. Then afterward we would always have a great time just as friends."

As Sean got older and left Killian for Gulliver Prep High School, he became a legendary football player. The boys lost touch for a while because they went to different schools. When Sean was at UM, they once again started training together.

"I began training basketball players for a living and still do," Darren Weissman said. "A lot of that is because of the workouts we had when we were younger. I would tell kids that I have a friend that plays football for the University of Miami, and they would ask who. When I told them it was Sean Taylor, they couldn't believe it. They were *huge* fans, and it was surreal to them. They would say, 'Sean Taylor! You know Sean Taylor?' They couldn't believe it, because he was a superstar!

"I never saw Sean as anything but a great friend, a great teammate, a great person to work out with," Darren said. "He was a guy that happened to be good at football. Further, he never carried himself like he was better than you or like a celebrity or big shot. He was very humble and down to earth. When he was playing with the Washington Redskins, he would come back home to Miami, and if he saw you at the mall, at the park, or on the beach, he would … if he saw you from far, far away, he would run up behind you and scare the heck out of you! You'd turn around and you'd see Sean with that big smile on his face. He was happy and joking and laughing, and sayin', 'I gotcha!'"

Saul picked up again from there: "I want the readers to know I was more a guidance counselor than a coach. Pete had asked me to keep an eye on Sean when he entered Killian and make sure he didn't get in any trouble—to make sure his grades were okay. That was a pretty easy job, because Sean never got into any trouble. He wasn't, you know, hangin' out with the wrong kids or any of that. We didn't have to worry about any of that stuff."

Academically Sean was a pretty good student. He took a mixture of honors and regular classes, and he did pretty well.

🏈

Darren is now known as Dr. Dribble, the world-record holder for running a marathon while dribbling two basketballs at the same time.

"We're very proud of Darren," Saul said.

"What's important is, Darren has an excellent work ethic. To tell you the truth, I don't know anybody who works out as hard as Darren.

"He started off in ninth grade. He didn't come in like Sean. Darren was a skinny little kid. But by the time he left Killian, he was really strong. Those four years in high school, he really worked hard, like with weights, thanks to Pete Taylor."

Saul added, "So now there's a little bit of Sean in all these kids that Darren is working with."

The Killian Incident

"In tenth grade at Miami Killian Senior High School, after receiving stellar grades, I rewarded Sean with three hundred dollars," recounted Pete Taylor. "This made him very happy. The thing was, I told him not to take the money to school with him. Did he listen? No. He put the money in his locker, and at the end of the day, when it was time to retrieve his wallet, it and the money went missing.

"I used to help out the football team in any way I could. I even helped break down film. I used to show Sean how to read defenses and offenses and show him what to look for. You know, like, show him the keys to the game. When we went to watch other teams play, we'd sit in a corner, and we'd be scouting opponents we'd be playing the following week. We were supposed to go to a football game the night of the missing wallet to check out the competition. I got off work around five o'clock, and I called home. I told Sean he needed to start getting dressed to go to the game. In a very mopey voice, Sean said, 'Dad, I don't want to go to the game.'

"It sounded like he was upset about something, so I asked him, 'Why don't you want to go?'

"Reluctantly, he answered, 'Remember that money you gave me? I took it to school, and it's gone, but I know who took it.'

"I decided to pick him up anyway, and when I did, I could see his jaws popping and his head hurting. He was just down.

Life Lesson

"I know this may sound odd, but I said, 'In most cases, the thief may need what he took more than you do. Just make a report with the school and move on.' I believe there's a scripture in the Bible that talks about not chasing after ill-gotten gains.

"Anyway, I pulled into a gas station to get a drink, and I asked Sean if he wanted anything. He declined. While inside, I went over to the ATM machine and I pulled out three hundred dollars, and when I got back to the car, I gave it to him.

"I said, 'Listen; let this be a lesson to you. Forget the money, but don't think I'm going to do this again for you if I find out you didn't listen to me.' This was a lesson I tried to teach him at fifteen years old so when he became an adult it wouldn't come back and bite him in the butt."

◗

"Around the age of fifteen, or even earlier, young men want to go out and experience the night life. I had two boys. Many years before, I used to see my father work with 'at risk' kids. He'd pick them up for weekends and take them out to events, or the beach, or picnics. He became a mentor to those young kids.

"Now, in Florida City, there's a program with our Florida City Police Department where we did something called a curfew check at night. Just like my dad, I also worked with 'at risk' kids and picked them up on the weekend and would take them to football games, movies, or the park. Although I was getting reimbursed to take the kids and their families out, just like my father, I became a mentor to the kids.

"I would begin my curfew checks around nine, and sometimes I would take my kids with me to show them that these kids needed to be home. I would knock on the door, and if the mom said they weren't home, I would have to write a report. If the kid was home, we'd chat, and for the most part the kids would tell me, 'Mr. T, when you come around, I will always be home, and I'll be listening to my mom.' And these were kids that had been in trouble before.

"I would take Sean and Joey, and I'd say to them, 'Let's see what's going on out there tonight.' Sometimes I would take them out around eleven p.m. or midnight to show them the streets. I'd say, 'Look who's out at this hour. You see those boys on the corner who may be trying to sell drugs? You see those guys over there drinking beer? There is nothing that's productive going on out here.'

"We went out countless numbers of times, 'cause you know when you start getting fifteen, sixteen, seventeen, kids change. They want to go hang out with friends and drink or worse. By showing my kids the traits of the street, I was trying to prevent them from doing the same thing and perhaps getting into trouble. We did this for almost two years, and you know what happened? Sean would say, 'Dad, you don't have to worry about me.' I said, 'I know. But now you know what's out here for you. Nothing but trouble.'

"Another thing I said was, 'Let's go by a park.' I did this to show them the other side of the coin. I wanted to instill the idea of determination and hard work, and this is where people trying to improve themselves would hang out. At the park there'd be those jogging or doing push-ups. Sean would say, 'I don't see anyone.'

"I said, 'Let me turn off the lights, and look again. Look. There's someone putting in hard work because he is competing against you or whoever or just for his or herself. While you're sleeping, they're working.' I said, 'That's what it's going to take for you to be the best. You're going to have to put in the work.'"

❦

T. J. Holten and Mike McFarlane

Coaches, roommates, and teammates were all very nice and very respectful, when it came to talking about their memories of Sean Taylor. It was beginning to feel to me as if nearly everyone was reading from the same script, as if they had all told the same Sean stories a million times. However, if you want the real skinny about someone, the truth, you need to seek out that person's friends.

Pete set up a meeting with Sean's homeboys T. J. and Mike at the Kendall Ale House in Kendall, Florida, on April 18, 2013. It was extra noisy that night; multiple ballgames were on the bar's many TV sets. Even the patrons had a little extra energy—which, by the way, made it difficult to understand the recorded interviews from that night when I played them back.

These two longtime friends of Sean gave me what they called "the real deal." And let me tell you, these guys were so much more than friends. They were truly brothers from another mother and had known each other for years, just hanging out or playing ball together.

To hear them tell it, no one knew the things they knew about Sean, and Sean had taken some stories about them to his grave.

For some of you, these stories may be completely out of character with what you think you know or what you may have heard or read about Sean. But as Sean's father, Pete, told me, he wants you, the readers, to get the whole and complete picture. He wants you to get a true sense of the good, the bad, and the ugly. What I didn't know was that I was about to spend two wild hours getting to hear stuff only these guys could know.

Make no mistake. I relearned something from these two. *Never* judge a book by its cover or a person by his dress, the color of his skin, or the way he wears his hair. *Never!* Big dreams and aspirations come in all shapes, sizes, and colors, and this story is a prime example.

"My name is T. J. Holten. That is spelled T-e-J-a-y H-o-l-t-e-n. [T. J. immediately starts laughing at his own joke.] Get that right, get that right." I could already tell this was going to be a challenge or, at the least, the funniest interview of the bunch.

"I met him for the first time … let's see, let's see …" T. J. was struggling.

"I think I was like fifteen. Yeah, about fifteen. We met at Colonial Park, and I know this because I played for South Dade, right across the street from the crib, and I hadn't really moved over there yet. I seen him training with Pete. I didn't have that help at home as far as that father figure. So I just kind of latched on every time I seen them training when we had a practice. Coincidentally, I ended up moving down the street. Then it just built from there. It all started from seeing him at the park.

"I was a year older. I turned thirty last year, in September. So once I moved over from my mom's house to my auntie's, we stayed right down the street from Pete and Sean. Then it was just like, all right, every day he was two steps away. We were always together from then on. From there, it's history," T. J. said. "We saw each other every day, but we didn't go to the same school.

"Then Mike [their friend Mike McFarlane] would come over. We played basketball fo' sho. That was like, we'd leave [football] practice, come home, sit on the porch, talk for fifteen to twenty minutes, and the next thing you know we'd see the black Altima come around the corner. That was Mike. Once we see Mike, we grab our sneakers and go on to Suniland Park to shoot some hoops. We had to get it in before it got late and get back to the crib. So that was pretty much our everyday routine. As long as we back on the block [before dark], we good. That's because we had other things to do in the morning. We had to go to school. We had responsibilities. We had homework, training ..."

After T. J. moved in with his aunt, he played wide receiver for Christopher Columbus High School, a local Catholic school. "I was supposed to go to Gulliver my senior year, but there was this day where I could have woken up and gone to Gulliver or woken up and gone to Columbus. I took the entrance test for Gulliver and everything. Pete hooked that up. But everything happens for a reason, and I passed on Gulliver. But I'm here, I'm happy, and I'm blessed," T. J. said.

As far as the football team goes, T. J. said, "Yeah, we had a great team. That was part of the reason I chose to stay there. I had friends on that team too. Plus Sean was my homie, and it was like, 'Come over and have dinner, then decide.' It was kinda like I didn't know what to do at that point, being that I had already been at Columbus for two years and I was doing good without them even featuring me. Anytime they put me in and I touched the ball, I felt content. I had a chance to go to another school, like Sean did, that could have featured me. [But I didn't go.] I played both sides of the ball, showing that I could do everything.

"Sean went to Gulliver Prep, a really small school, and their football team consisted of a mere twenty-seven varsity players, and he was afraid no one would see him play. No matter what, you got to show. With twenty-seven guys, that didn't mean you could play both sides."

But Sean played three sides: offense, defense, and specials. "So that's what I'm saying. It doesn't matter how many players you got. Can you stand to play all ways?

"Playing both ways was how I trained with Sean. I was built for that. Do you feel me? I guess I was just comfortable with the situation I was already in. The day I woke up and had to decide, I had some other peer pressure and didn't have a father to help me make a decision. I have five younger sisters, so I had to do it on my own. So I did what I had to do. If I could have done it over, I might have gone to Gulliver and probably would have been right there at UM with him [Sean]. I ended up getting a scholarship to FIU [Florida International University] the first year the school was open. I had all of the opportunities that any other kid that played football could get. I just didn't have it on that big a stage, just because of where I was."

Sean got hurt when he was at Gulliver. "From the point of that little injury in high school, he knew he was going to straighten that shit out. He always said it was more aggravating than hurt," T. J. said.

Sean's friend Mike McFarlane then spoke up for the first time. He said, "For two weeks me and Sean were sitting on the couch, and I actually asked him, 'Are you seriously going to play?' He said, 'This is the money game.' And they have a picture of him throwing up a hand sign … holding up his fingers: one, five, two. That stood for me, him, and T. J. That was our street. One Hundred Fifty-Second Street. He told us even before the game started, 'I'm goin' to take it to the house. I'm goin' to throw it up for y'all. One, five, two.'"

Pete Taylor sat and listened to our candid conversation. "And I'll tell you another thing," Pete said. "What happened was, he wasn't going to have surgery."

"He didn't want to mess with that game," Mike added.

Pete continued. "I told him if a horse is injured, they take them out and shoot them, so he went ahead and had the surgery.

"The coach said, 'He's got to rehab in two weeks.' I told him, 'I promise you he'll play. He'll be ready for that game and any game coming up.'

"Coach said, 'I don't believe you. It will never happen.' Pete said, 'Well, we'll see.' And Sean said this to me: 'I may have had surgery on my right arm, but that doesn't mean I can't knock them out with my left.'

"Here's something I bet you didn't know," Pete Taylor said.

"When Sean left Gulliver when school was over and we were on the way home, he wanted to work some more. So we stopped off at Palmetto High School. They had these big old two-hundred- and three-hundred-pound tackling dummies. So there he worked on jams; he worked on tackling and technique and everything.

"He said, 'Dad, why do you want me to hit three hundred pounds?' I said, 'Shit, if someone that big comes at you, you'll be able to knock his ass out too.' That's the way it was. I don't care how big they are. They got to fall. It's a mindset.

"Something that T. J. and Mike will always tell you is this: I must have been the toughest asshole as a parent," Pete said.

T. J. interrupted. "You had a program. You knew what it took."

"Sometimes Sean thought I was a little tougher than I should be," Papa Pete said.

T. J. didn't let Papa Pete finish. "It wasn't even that. Sean always respected everything you said. The way that he respected your words was the reason I wanted to be around. So it's not like he ever questioned you or second-guessed you. He was like, 'It's my dad.' And you built such a strong man. In fact, he may have been a little too strong, where he felt like he didn't need to come to you at all about certain things. He felt like he was built for this. 'I can handle this.' There may have been things he should have told somebody or asked for help. But he didn't because he thought he was ready for it all. So it's not like he thought you were a hard father at all."

Mike explained, "He wanted to prove he could be his own man like his father wanted him to be. He always accepted everything his father had to say. Now he had to execute everything that was instilled in him."

Pete then said, "He had to take the process and make it work for himself. It was like a boxing match. I taught him how to fight, get hit, and come back. But when it was time to get in the ring, he had to do that on his own."

"It was all about the punches," Mike said. "If you hit me, I'm going to hit you back. I know what it feels like, and I'm going to hit you right back." And that's how it was with Sean, too.

T. J. then took over: "After a hard night working out, we'd be sitting outside the house talking shit like, 'Man, Pete crazy.' But at the end of the day, we would look at each other and say, 'This shit is gonna work though.'

"You couldn't deny it. Even when you [thought] you were done, Pete would walk out there after we just got done talking shit and he'd tell ya, 'All right.' Right in front of the house, there was a little step, and he'd have us walk up, step down. Walk up, step down. Walk up, step down—just because we were sitting there. We had just finished. We were supposed to be done. I guess we looked too relaxed, so he made us walk the step. The one step."

"T. J., tell him about the tires," Pete said.

"Oh, the tires? Pete would make you pull the tires, push the tires, roll the tires. We'd have to take the tires to the hill. It was work. It was work. Right now I deserve a son just because I have so much to offer. I coached two years at Palmer Trinity, and [before I got there] the team couldn't win a game. After I went out there, all the players came to me, and I had them doing stuff they could never do before. It was just like, 'Wow, I could teach this stuff.' I quit coaching because maybe I was moving too fast. I needed to focus on what I really wanted. But it felt so good helping those kids. Maybe I'll be a coach one day. I felt like I shorted myself from going to the next level."

"Sean was a hell of a basketball player." T. J. continued. "When he came on that court, his mission was to dunk on your ass. And it was not just anybody. He wanted to dunk on the biggest man," Mike added.

Pete said, "He became a good basketball player at age eleven. But he couldn't control his speed."

"Yeah," Mike said. "He had only one speed—full speed."

"In basketball, you have to know how to switch speeds, but he didn't know how to do that," Pete added.

Everybody then said simultaneously, "*Full speed. Full speed. Full speed.*"

"On defense, you weren't getting by him," T. J. said.

"He started dunking in ninth grade, and when he did that, it was over," Pete added.

Sean could have played any sport he wanted. He was that good.

"In basketball, he would have been like a Blake Griffin [current NBA standout]," T. J. said. "He was a freak of nature. Sean was a freak. Griffin is a freak. He can't play basketball, but he's learning. Just give him the ball and get out of his way. That's the way Sean was. You either got out of his way or you were going to get dunked on."

"He would dunk on ya then knock you over," Mike added.

"He was something, man. He was our homie," T. J. said.

Connie Dingle

When Sean was sixteen, Sean's grandmother Connie Dingle gave Sean a Mazda RX7 sports car. Ms. Dingle said to her grandson, "Sean, we are so busy with everything right now; you're going to have to be your own man." So she gave him the RX7 to drive back and forth to school and practice. There was only one condition: he had to agree to be careful with it, as it was a very fast little car.

"Even when he finished practice, he got out of school, and that car was parked in the yard," Grandma said. "He was even a little different than his dad at that point because … I shouldn't say this, but … his dad was driving before he got a license. I hear sirens, and they [were] supposed to be home at a certain time, and that made me worry about him. Sean, he was a very obedient child. He was quiet, not arrogant."

Changing the subject, Ms. Dingle commented on Sean's "very large hands," which made him "very good in sports." She thought that with those hands he was going to be a basketball player.

But Sean and his father loved football, so that was his concentration. "He was great in track and stuff too," she said. "He was good at most things he did."

12

Gulliver Prep

HALFWAY THROUGH THE TENTH GRADE, PETE TAYLOR DECIDED IT WAS time to transfer Sean from Killian High School to Gulliver Prep after football season.

"Don't get me wrong. He liked Killian," Pete Taylor said. "However, there was just a little bit more Sean needed to get out of his education, and that could only come from a school like Gulliver Prep."

Pete wanted to make sure Sean had a better foundation for his education, and what better place to get that than from a top-notch college prep school. Oh, and it didn't hurt that they had a pretty good football program and Sean was a pretty good football player.

So in December Pete Taylor put in an application at Gulliver Prep, and Sean was readily accepted.

❡

Established in 1926 by Arthur Gulliver in the residential section of Coconut Grove, Gulliver Academy initially enrolled students from New England who were wintering in South Florida....

The most formative episode in Gulliver's history was the purchasing of the school by Marian Krutulis in late 1953.... Mrs. Krutulis envisioned Gulliver as a grand school home where everyone, both students and teachers, would feel they were part of a caring, inspiring family of learners....

Gulliver [Schools] serves students in grades pre-K ... through 12. With an enrollment of more than 2,200, Gulliver Schools offers the full spectrum of academic and extracurricular programs....

In the spring of 2008, Mrs. Krutulis transitioned into an "emeritus" status, and her son, John Krutulis, became Gulliver's head of school. [Mrs. Krutulis remained involved with Gulliver until her death in January 2013.]

Gulliver Prep is located off Kendall Drive in the Dadeland area of Miami. The minute you set foot on campus, the first thing you notice is that it looks like and feels like a little college campus with its various buildings and beautifully landscaped, sprawling grounds, as opposed to a single-building high school.

What the Taylors eventually came to find out was how nurturing Gulliver was with all of its students. Every day after school, they could get all the help they needed to succeed.

After practice, athletes are generally exhausted. When they come home, all they want to do is eat and then sleep. Gulliver was different. It was the type of school where the athletes couldn't even get on the field or the court until an hour after mandatory tutorials, which all of the teachers were required to attend. So if a child struggled in any class, he or she would have the opportunity to meet with teachers one-on-one after school. There, students could get help with homework or anything else not understood in class. This program continues to this day.

❡

On the field, Sean could do so much with the football. He could run. He could play QB, receiver, running back, every defensive position, and even center if he had to.

"So this was yet another reason I transferred Sean to Gulliver," Taylor said. "I knew if he went to a bigger school, he could get lost in the shuffle if he only played one position. But here he played many positions and he could really show off his talent, which made him stand out and help make a name for himself."

There are three phases to the game of football: offense, defense, and special teams. "If someone on one side of the ball makes it exciting, it could fire up the other parts of the team," Taylor said. "Sean wanted to have an impact on at least two sides—offense and defense. When all three phases kick in, you win games." Since Sean transferred to Gulliver in the middle of the tenth grade, he wasn't eligible to play football right away. He did get to play in the Jamboree Game, the summer game that takes place before the regular season starts. It didn't count for anything, so players could just go out and do their thing. Sean chose to shine.

Revelation

At Gulliver, besides football, Sean also ran track and played baseball. Yes, baseball. As a baseball player, Sean was occasionally used as an outfielder. However, he was predominantly used as a pinch runner because he was so fast and could steal bases. It did finally get a little overwhelming, so he stuck to his first love, football.

"You know who else played football, baseball, and ran track? One of my idols: Jackie Robinson. I love him for what he did for us. What an inspiration," said Taylor.

Mr. John Krutulis, Gulliver Head of Schools

It's been stated many times throughout this book that education was priority one for Pete Taylor and his family. So it was vitally important for him that we speak to the Gulliver Head of Schools and a few of the school's coaches, as it was here that Sean not only made his mark on the football field, but also in his classes.

Pete and I met with Mr. John Krutulis in his Gulliver Schools office. (Just like his mother, Mrs. Marian Krutulis, who was known as Mrs. K, Mr. Krutulis is referred to simply as Mr. K.) That was where we discussed his recollections and interactions with the Taylors. But before the interview began, something unexpected happened. Pete Taylor was overcome with emotion as he flashed back to those Gulliver years, so emotional in fact, that he asked if he could leave the office where we were chatting and come back when the interview was over. Mr. K and I looked at each other curiously, and then he said something like, "Of course. We should be done in about 30 minutes."

Our interview began when I asked Mr. K what his first meeting with Sean Taylor was like.

"I met Sean when his father brought him here and introduced him first to my mother, who was the director of the schools, and then me," said Mr. K. "Pete told us that he had a young man who he felt could benefit from a Gulliver Schools education.

"At first Sean was kind of quiet and reserved but very polite. He shook my hand and smiled an endless smile—one you'd never forget. Every time you saw him, he was in such a good mood and had such a nice disposition.

"We walked around with him [showing off the campus, and] Sean told us he played football and basketball … we said we have a very good athletic program. Pete knew that, and he said he wanted Sean to be a part of this school. After speaking with Sean for a little while, both my mother and I came to the same conclusion—that this was a very special young man and we'd like him to be a part of Gulliver Schools.

"One could see the apple didn't fall far from the tree. We saw where Sean got his manners and his personality, 'cause his father was the same way—very polite, just a nice person."

It didn't take long for Sean to make a lot of friends. According to Mr. K, "Sean had this attraction about him. People just immediately wanted to be a part of Sean's life.

"The teachers loved Sean. [Even today] when they hear Sean Taylor's name, they get a big smile on their faces and they talk about how pleasant it was to have him in class and what a great person he was."

Mr. K was endlessly impressed at how Sean never looked down on anybody despite his being a star on the field. On the football team he was a leader and a motivator.

Mr. K had some very fond memories of Sean's last year at Gulliver. "During our state championship year, when we were down and not winning any given game, just his aura would rub off on everybody else. He'd go down the line, boom, hitting them on the shoulder pad, boom—'Come on, guys; come on. We need to go out there and keep blocking, just keep going. We can beat these guys; we are better than them. This is our house, and we are not going to lose here.' You would see the players just light up," Krutulis said.

"'Just give me a hole. I'll run through it.' And the guys were like, 'Okay Sean, we'll do it, we'll do it.' The offense would run out there and, *bam*—Sean would run through that hole and score a touchdown, and everybody's mood would change. 'You see, guys, we can do this. We can do this. Let's just keep it going, keep it going.' We played some very good teams that year in some very close games.

"This was his senior year—the year we won the state championship with his good friend Buck Ortega, who was here as well. Buck was the quarterback, and Sean played all over the field. He was our running back, wide receiver, defensive back, and special-teams guy running back punts and kickoffs. He'd do whatever you needed him to do.

"I remember one game—it may have been against Chaminade[-Madonna College Preparatory School]—Sean just tore up the field, and one of our parents came up to me after the game and said, 'You know, Sean is like a man playing with boys out there.'

"We were battling for the regionals, and it could have gone either way. Sean just knew he had to do something. And when he ran back one of the punts, well, he was just twisting and turning, and he's bouncing off of guys, and he's jumping over them and high-hurdling people—just running down the field.

"After the game another father came up to me and said what most of us were thinking: 'That young man is going to be something, and I can tell you right now—he's going to go pro.'"

Mr. Krutulis and his mother took a great interest in Sean the player and the student. "We would sit down after games and we'd talk about how well he did. Of course, he was always like, 'Yeah, I know, but I can do better. I should've done this, I should have done that,' and I was like, 'Sean, you did more than ten people could have done.' He was such a humble individual with great talent. But he never bragged. In fact, he didn't like or want the limelight out there. He would look at himself as just another teammate, somebody who was just part of the football team."

The same held true during the school day. "Even though everyone in school walked around him like he was a superman, he didn't view himself that way."

Mr. K and Sean spoke about more than just football. They talked about family, his future, the University of Miami, and the Krutulises' support of the university. "We were getting bombarded with college coaches coming down wanting Sean. But Sean pretty much had it in his mind that the UM was where he wanted to play. I could name you top school after top school that would call and ask to speak with him. It got to a point where I would tell people they needed to show up by appointment only because Sean was spending more time out of the classroom talking to college coaches than he was inside the classroom."

Sean was also getting noticed for his accomplishments in print, such as in the *Miami Herald* and local sports magazines. "If I remember right, he broke the Miami-Dade County most touchdowns record." He had an amazing forty-five in one season!

"There are those who would say, because of the classification of our school—say if this were a 6A or 7A school—it would be a different story. I say no, because some of the teams we beat that year would have beaten most 6A teams. That's how good the competition was with the teams that we went through," Mr. K remembered proudly.

"Gulliver was probably three-quarters of the way down the totem pole with size of school, size of our football program, as compared to a school like Pace, which put sixty kids out on the field compared to the less than thirty athletes we had. It was the same with some of the other schools we played, where they too had sixty kids across the sidelines against us.

"In his senior year, everybody was after him," but he played on, Mr. K said. "He was like a pit bull out there. Sean was a huge factor in our state championship. We have a picture of Sean in that game versus Pace High School at the University of Miami field. It was a night game. [Gulliver played very few night games back then.] We were down, and Sean was running the ball. He just did a vertical leap at about the six-yard line, and one of the guys reached up to try and stop him. Sean did a helicopter around and just flew over and landed on his feet into the end zone. I have a picture of Sean completely vertical, spinning sideways, and he … it was just amazing. That was the talent that he had."

Mr. K eventually touched on how Sean was in class. "He was an above-average student, and he probably could have had all As, but he concentrated on areas he thought were important, and football was at the top of his list."

Once he moved on to college at nearby UM, Sean would sometimes come back to Gulliver to speak to the kids or just watch football games. He'd walk the sidelines and encourage the football players whenever he could slip away from UM practice. If UM had a week off and he was able to, he'd be at Gulliver before practice or during the school day.

"He'd come in on a game day to give a little pep talk, and you could see the players just light up when they saw him," Mr. K mused.

"Sean was loved here, and what happened to him—even students after Sean was here were very touched. It was just a very, very sad moment."

Sean made such a large impact on the Gulliver football program that in 2012 they named their football field after him.

"One more thing," said Mr. K. "Sean played basketball at Gulliver, though some [his future football coaches] were concerned about this. Both Sean and Buck Ortega had been accepted to the University of Miami, and we know there was probably a little whisper in their ear not to participate in too many other sports—you know, so as not to get injured. So they decided not to play basketball as seniors. They were our two leading scorers on that team. So we went pretty far, but not as far as I think we could have gotten if the two of them were there," Krutulis said almost begrudgingly.

While in high school Sean had typical teenage angst when it came to women. The one person Sean could always turn to for some solid advice and the woman's perspective was his stepmother, Josephine Taylor.

Josephine "Josie" Taylor

"Right around fifteen to sixteen years old, I remember him asking questions like, 'What should I do about this, that, or the other?'" Josie said. One day when Sean was already at Gulliver, "he came running in the house saying, 'Josie, I have to learn Spanish,'" recalled his stepmother. "I wondered why." It turned out he had met a Spanish-speaking girl and he wanted to impress her with some Spanish.

Josie said, "'Really, Sean?'

"He said, 'Yeah. Teach me a couple of words of Spanish.'

"I asked, 'Who is this person?'

"He said, 'Josie, her name is Jackie, and she's the most beautiful girl I ever met, and I have to have her.'

"I said, 'Okay, but do you really think you're going to impress her with Spanish?' I said, 'Sean, you just need to be yourself, because whatever you do in life, if it's not you, it's going to come to light anyway, and they're going to realize that's not the person they first met. You always want to be true to yourself.'

"'Yes,' he said, 'You're right. You're right. But you know, I still want to learn Spanish.' He probably picked up a couple of words, but that's it."

Buck Ortega

Buck Ortega became a friend and a football teammate of Sean Taylor in January 1999, halfway through their sophomore year, when they both transferred to Gulliver Prep High School. Buck came from Westminster Christian, and Sean from Killian High School. They were introduced by a mutual friend who played baseball at Gulliver named Travis Nesmith. Travis's father and Buck's father were good friends.

Once their mutual shyness dissipated, the two sportsmen, Buck and Sean, spent a lot of time together in school, on the practice field, at games, and at their favorite fishing spots in the Florida Keys. They became the best of friends. Buck talked about meeting Sean at school for the first time.

🏈

"Sean and I were both similar in size," Ortega began. "Travis was our exact size as well. So here are three kids with above-average size meeting in the hallway at Gulliver Prep, this little private school with two hundred kids in our graduating class. Travis was a year ahead of us, and when he introduced us, I just said, 'Hey, it's nice to meet you.'

"I'm very, very quiet, and if I don't know you, I'm not going out of my way to talk to you. Sean was definitely the same way. So it was 'Hey, how are you doin'?' And that was about it. So at first we were friendly, but I hadn't gotten to know him yet."

They both knew each other as football players—it was a small school—and Buck played basketball and baseball, and he ran track.

"Sean played basketball and ran track," Buck said. "I played baseball my sophomore year. It wasn't until spring practice that we started spending days and days together. We worked out together in the weight room, and that's kind of where we really got to know each other."

Sean and Buck were avid fishermen. So right after spring practice, heading into summer, they went fishing. A lot. "My grandfather has a little house in the Keys, so we were there nonstop," Buck said. "One of our linebackers, named Gonzalez, had a nice boat down in the Keys. So we all hung around and fished. That's when we became close friends. Sean was there when I caught my first sailfish."

On their fishing excursions, the boys talked about everything: sports, girls, who lost the most fish that day. "I mentioned that I'm quiet until I get to know you, just like Sean," explained Ortega. "When we did get to know you, we wouldn't shut up. He had that big smile. You know he was a jokester and a prankster.

"One of the interesting things I remember was when we went spear fishing. When we dove in water twenty to thirty feet deep, you have to hold your nose, and you actually blow air to equalize your inner ear. When you go down to the bottom, the pressure builds in your ears. I always do it so my ears don't hurt. When he dove down, he didn't equalize, and when he came back to the surface I asked him, 'What are you doing? Doesn't that hurt your ears?'

"He said, 'Not at all.' I kind of laughed because that's when I saw his superhuman attributes. Obviously he was superhuman on the football field. I was in awe of his diving abilities because it's just not normal for someone to dive down and not equalize. That was even before football season, where you'd see him hurdle over people coming to tackle him. So I think he was superhuman in a lot of ways."

The boys lived close to one another, so when Sean turned sixteen and got a car, they began to carpool to school. It worked out for Buck, since he didn't have a vehicle.

According to Buck (and many, many others), "Sean was one of the best high school players to ever come out of the state of Florida." He also remembered that because of an injury Sean sustained during his junior year, which Buck believed to be to his hip, colleges weren't going crazy over him. Sean missed the entire first half of his junior year because of that injury. "It was hard to believe, knowing what kind of kid he was and what kind of player he was, more teams weren't interested." That's why full-speed recruiting actually began in his senior year.

Revelation

Sometime during the eleventh grade, by the second or third game of the season, Pete went to Pinecrest High School, a prep school in Broward County, to see Sean play. During one play, Sean broke left, broke right, went up the sideline, and then he went down. Sean didn't get up. "What happened was, he ended up pulling a muscle off his hip bone as someone grabbed him to try and tackle him," Pete said.

An ambulance came and took him to the hospital. Initially Sean was going to be out six weeks, much to the dismay of his coaches. Sean did come back for the game before the playoffs; Pace beat them by 1 and knocked them out of the playoffs. Going for the two-point conversion, Buck Ortega kept the ball on a bootleg, and he got stopped.

🏈

"The summer going into our senior year, my dad drove me, Sean Taylor, one of his good friends T. J. Holten, and Roscoe Parrish, who went on to play for the University of Miami, to the Florida State football camp. While up there I remember they asked us to play some seven-on-seven, either with flags or two-hand touch, something like that. There was this player named Kevin Jones, a running back out of Chester, Pennsylvania, who ended up going to Virginia Tech. He was a huge recruit. Sean was a beast and wasn't recruited that highly, especially before his senior year. During the seven-on-seven games, this kid Kevin and Sean were getting into it. I remember the Florida

State coaches grabbing Sean, saying, 'You need to chill out because you are fighting with our prize recruit!' and 'Who do you think you are?'"

Buck just hung back and laughed, thinking, "*You suckers just made the biggest mistake, because Sean isn't going to back off.*" Buck then said, "Well, they didn't look twice at Sean, which was their second-biggest mistake. This might have given Sean some extra motivation in the games UM played versus Florida State.

"Watching his highlight reel, it's hard to believe teams actually punted to him," Buck said. "He ran back maybe fifty percent for touchdowns. On defense, if he got his hands on the ball, he'd intercept. On offense, he was a running back and I was a quarterback. But he could throw the ball too. He could do just about anything.

"There were times where I'd be in the single I-formation. I'd go in motion, and they'd snap it to him and he'd run it or he'd throw it to me. Or he'd go in motion and I'd run routes. I think in the state semi-final game he ran a touchdown in [and] threw a touchdown to me; I threw one to him, and I think he had a punt return for a touchdown. That was just the norm for him."

Revelation

"*UM Head Coach Butch Davis was recruiting Sean to play linebacker,*" Ortega said. "*Well, Sean didn't want to play linebacker at all. But the coaching staff kept saying Sean was going to play linebacker. Sean was not going to go to Miami if he was going to play linebacker.*

"Anyway, the minute Butch Davis left [he hightailed it to the NFL's Cleveland Browns] and Larry Coker got the head coaching job, my dad called him and said, 'Look.' And by the way, they hadn't offered Roscoe Parrish a scholarship yet, and—I don't know if I should be sharing this, but it really doesn't matter at this point—Frank Gore and Roscoe Parrish were very good friends, and if they weren't going to offer Roscoe a scholarship, then Frank Gore wasn't going to go to Miami. And since Davis wanted Sean to play linebacker, he wasn't going to go to Miami.

"So my dad [former NFL linebacker Ralph Ortega] called Coker and said, 'You need to call Sean and tell him he can play wherever he wants, and call Roscoe Parrish and offer him a scholarship.' I knew how good Roscoe was just by going to the camps with him, and obviously Larry Coker was humble enough to listen and made those calls, because everyone ended up going there.

"I wanted to go to Miami because I liked fishing so much and I loved the city. While I had committed, Sean didn't right away. He waited till the last minute."

Buck committed to UM early in November of his senior year. He didn't want to take any chances, knowing he wanted to go there. National Signing Day wasn't until February, and that's when Sean finally decided. "I wanted Sean to stay in Miami, since we had become the best of friends spending a lot of time together," said Buck.

What took so long for Sean to make a decision?

"It's because Butch Davis didn't leave until right before Signing Day, and Sean was *not* going to play linebacker. That's where Butch kept telling him he was going to play. So until the last minute, Georgia Tech was still in the mix. He was thinking very seriously about going there," Ortega said.

Pete Taylor

At the end of his junior-year season, Sean was already talking about leaving Gulliver and transferring again.

Pete asked, "You want to leave Gulliver? Why do you want to leave Gulliver?"

Sean said, "Well, I don't, Dad. But I don't think scouts are looking at me here. I don't think anybody wants me, and you know how much I want to go to and play in college. So I think it's best for me to leave."

He went on to question the attendance at Gulliver football games versus attendance at some of the other schools. He said, "Dad, only about two to three hundred people come to our games, but if you go to South Dade, Killian, or Homestead games, four thousand people show up."

"Something tells me someone had gotten to Sean—gotten into his head," Pete Taylor said. "So I decided to call his mom. I was pissed as hell now. So when Sean answered, I said, 'Let me talk to your mom.'

"I told Donna, 'I don't understand who's talking to Sean, but leaving Gulliver could be one of the biggest mistakes he'll ever make.'

"She said, 'What are you talking about?'"

"I responded, 'Sean is talking about moving in with you guys!' I wasn't going to fight or resist, because Sean was already seventeen going on eighteen yet still under court orders. However, if he wanted to go back to his mom's home, I wasn't going to argue.

"You know what? Donna actually took my side and supported me. She said, 'You know, Pete, it's not a good idea for him to come here, so he gotta stay with you. He's doing everything right, and look how far he's come, how he's excelling. And to tell you the truth, I don't know anything about what you're doing with him to make this all happen, so I'm not going to take that chance and see him take a step or two backwards.'

"She tells all this to Sean, and he decides to return to my house. He gets there on a Sunday and I'm at work. I get a call: 'Dad, I'm home, and I'm going inside the house.'

"I said, 'Oh, hell no, you're not. Don't you go in my house, and I'll see you when I get there.'"

Life Lesson

"If you listen to too many people, you could end up making a lot of wrong decisions. These people may not have your best interests at heart and may be looking at the short-term fix. You need to take the long view and look at all the important factors before making a potentially life-changing decision.

"Now, I have to give Sean credit. We had a nice, long conversation. Man to man. Father to son. And I told him these are the things he had to do before [he] could come back and live with me.

- You're going to have to work out.
- Read your books and do your homework.
- You're going to have to make good grades.
- You're going to have to bust your ass.
- Every day, you're going to have a workout task. Whether it's five hundred pushups a day, running for distance. It could be running up hills or six hundred sit-ups.

"So here's what I can tell you. Each day, he kept to the game plan. And the reason I know he kept to the game plan was because he would call me on my way home if I had to work the evening shift, to ensure he was doing what he was supposed to do and actually brief me on the day's events. So sometimes when he called he'd say, 'Dad, where you at?' because he wanted me to meet him so we could work out together. When I was available, we did. I took great pride and joy in the fact that he even still wanted to do this with me."

Gulliver's Championship Year

Gulliver Prep won the state football championship in 2001, and Sean set a new high school state record for touchdowns in a single season, which was officially forty-four. According to Coach Howey, who reviewed all of the season's videotape, Sean actually scored forty-five touchdowns.

By midseason, Frank Gore, who went to Coral Gables High School, was the leading rusher for Dade County. That distinction would not last out the season.

Right around the sixth game, everyone at Gulliver knew they had something special working. So they instituted the "Believe" program. The team believed in their coaches and themselves; they believed in the plan; they believed they could win. When they pulled it all together and began to believe in what they were doing as a team, they thrived.

That was also the year every Dade County football team got knocked out of the playoffs except one: Gulliver Prep.

"I'll never forget that conversation about the concern Sean had about fans not coming to his games," said Pete Taylor. "So when we all knew this team was going somewhere, I said to Sean, 'Let me tell you something. I hate to say it this way, but son, the other teams may be playing before crowds of four or five thousand, and a lot of those kids may even end up playing for twenty thousand people later on. On the other hand, when you graduate from Gulliver, you may end up playing for ninety thousand people or more.'

"Here's the thing. He didn't believe me. I told him, 'If you do a good job here, by the end of the season you're going to have eight to nine thousand people come watch Gulliver play.' He didn't believe that either. Guess what. Halfway through the season, he did have seven to eight thousand come watch. By the end of the year, he [got] off the bus at one of his playoff games and I said, 'Hey, remember I told you you're going to make it to the playoffs and the championships one day?'

"He said, 'Yeah.'

"I said, 'Check the stands out. There are fifteen thousand people about to watch you play tonight.'

"Sean said, 'Dad, why are you always right?'

"I said, 'I'm not always right, but everything I told you you're going to see happen, happened.'"

Gulliver ended up winning that night. They beat Chaminade-Madonna College Preparatory School. Gulliver's next opponent was Immokalee High School, which is located near Naples, Florida.

Gulliver Prep Head Football Coach Steve Howey

Pete Taylor puts the success of the Gulliver football program squarely on the back of former Head Coach Steve Howey, and Steve Howey puts the success of his Gulliver football program on the back of Sean Taylor.

Currently Steve Howey is the athletic director and head football coach at St. John Neumann Catholic High School in Naples. That's where Pete and I met him to hear what he had to say about his high school superstar Sean Taylor.

"The first time I met Pete, he came to an open house in the middle of Sean's sophomore year. He introduced himself to me in the gym, and all he said was, 'My son is a sophomore over at Killian. He's a pretty good football player, and you might want to, you know, take a look at him.'

"For me, that was a typical story. It kinda tells you how modest Pete and Sean were," Steve Howey said. "As it turned out, Sean was the best football player I've ever coached and probably ever will. So to say he's a pretty good player was definitely an understatement."

The first time Steve Howey saw Sean play football was the summer between Sean's sophomore and junior years on the Gulliver seven-on-seven league team. Steve Howey said, "Right then I could tell Sean was going to be a monster on defense."

Sean was the most aggressive player he'd ever seen in seven-on-seven. "I know it's supposed to be two-hand touch, but he was knocking kids around." At the time Sean was already 6'1" and about 205 pounds and was playing free safety. He hit 220 by the time he was a senior.

Opposing coaches and parents alike complained he was too aggressive, so he had to be calmed down. "I shouldn't say calmed down, because that's just how he played," Coach Howey said. "We had him stay in check, where he wouldn't lower his shoulder or kind of run through kids. We had to remind him every week when we went over there that it's seven-on-seven."

However, nobody stood up to him or questioned him. Those kids just went back to their huddle and complained or even took themselves out.

"There weren't many times he played for us when we were down, but it didn't matter if we were up or down," Howey said. He was one hundred percent full speed on every play, and he hardly ever came off the field. He played offense, defense, and special teams. "He was our kick returner and punt returner. He probably had four or five kick returns for touchdowns his senior year.

"Half the time we'd be up by thirty points and by halftime he was out. I couldn't put him in the game the second half. He would always be the first one to say, 'Coach, give the ball to someone else.'

"When we were up by thirty points, we weren't looking at a state record or anything like that, but we knew the game was in hand. It was my decision to take out a lot of the starters that year—not just Sean, but a lot of the guys— so we could get the younger guys in and give them some field experience.

"The record-setting forty-five touchdowns Sean had were for all touchdowns, including interceptions. Even in the championship game as a split receiver, he had two catches for touchdowns. He could do it all!" Howey said.

Sean didn't speak much. He was a quiet leader. Most of the time, he set the example, both on the field and off. Whether it was in practice, in the weight room, or in a game, he would set the example.

"I do remember our one-on-one talks, when he would come down at lunchtime to my office, watch game film with me, and go over stuff. He always wanted to learn and to pay attention to what our opposing team had on offense and defense. Ralph Ortega was our defensive coordinator, and I know Ralph spent time with him looking over game film. Sean would kind of relay that to the players on the field at practice. He was like a coach out on the field, whether it was on the offensive side or the defensive side of the ball.

"The one time I remember Sean speaking up was in the first game in the playoffs in his senior year. We were playing American Heritage [School] up at Dade Christian [School], and we were down 21 to nothing at halftime. We felt we had a good enough team to win the state championship or at least get to the state championship that year. So when we were down 21 to nothing, we went into the locker rooms, and there wasn't a word said. Coaches went in, spoke about offense and defense, and made adjustments we had to make. And then Sean and Buck Ortega came up to me and asked if they could have five minutes with the team without the coaches in the room. You know, when you are down 21 to nothing, you'll try anything.

"The coaches walked out, and they closed the door. You could just hear Sean and Buck and some of our other captains just going off on the team. And I remember them coming out, and Sean kinda leaned in and said, 'Coach, I don't know if we're gonna win or lose this, but we're not goin' home without givin' it one hundred percent.'

"I remember the first play in the second half when they got the ball. Our defensive end, Alfredo Pascal, came in on the blind side and just crushed their QB, and kinda set the tone for the second half. Then our kids just took over. We ended up winning 24 to 21 and movin' into the second round. It was their talk to the players that made the difference."

Coach Howey gave a lot of credit to Pete Taylor for pushing Sean hard. He also gave him credit for part of their state championship because he had the kids motivated too. "He spent a lot of time on the sidelines getting them fired up," Howey said. "I remember his dog calls to the players. Every time the kids did something well, he and Mr. Jones, Marcus Jones, would cheer the kids on and be so excited.

"I know we had a full-house power backfield, and whenever I put that in, you could hear these guys yellin'. I know they loved it, because we'd go right down the field on most of the teams we played. I look back, and you know, we were down to our fourth-string center and we had a center snap-off going into the state championship game. And that kid—all three of those kids—had a part in that. I know Sean and Buck and Alfredo and Mike and Alex were the top players. We only had twenty-seven players on the team. Each one of them contributed somehow.

"You know how sometimes it's better to be lucky than good? Well, we had an opposition field goal go off the goalpost in one of our final-four games. So you know there was a lot of luck involved. The ball hit the goalpost and bounced out. It was Immokalee. We were tied going into the last minute of the game, and they went, I think, for the extra point. And the kicker hit the upright. We were playing at FIU, so they had the college goalposts, which are two feet shorter and narrower. We went into two overtimes, and in the second we decided to go for two after a touchdown. It was Sean who ran it in for the two-point conversion. He dove in, and I still have the picture at home. Every time I look at that, I get a good feeling, because that was such a great play.

"After beating Immokalee, we felt like that was the hardest game of the playoffs, so we felt very confident going into the championship. After all, it was Immokalee who had one of their best teams ever."

🏈

In the two years Howey coached Sean, he saw a lot of growth "as a young man and as a player." He got a lot of recognition going into his senior year. He was ranked on the top of www.rivals.com and some of the other recruiting sites. Georgia Tech, Clemson, and Miami were all over him.

"He became more confident when he was going into his senior year," Coach Howey said. "We had a good group of seniors during Sean's junior year that took the lead, and Sean—again, being very respectful of his teammates—took on that backseat role and did what he had to do to help the team. Then, his senior year, he knew it was his team. He worked it and showed the other players how to work hard to win, to be at practice every day on time and get the work done. You could just see his confidence really build the first couple games into his senior year, and from there he just took over games.

"Sean knew all along that he wanted to go to the University of Miami. Assistant Coach Larry Coker would always check and see how he was doing. He was very good at recruiting Sean. When Sean and Buck went over to the UM camp, it was pretty much a done deal. Buck and Sean wanted UM, and UM wanted them. So I didn't get involved with a lot of recruiting.

"In the curious case of Miami football, Coach Butch Davis looked at him first. He was going to be his coach. I think a day or two before or after Sean said he was committing to Miami, Butch went to the Cleveland Browns. For Sean, that wasn't a problem. He wanted to go to Miami, and it didn't matter who was coaching. It just so happens I think Larry Coker and the entire defensive staff were great coaches for Sean. It was a good move to stay in town. I loved it because I could go to every game, and I'm sure Pete felt the same way.

"Most coaches were looking for defense. A couple of coaches talked about him returning the ball. I remember he returned one for a touchdown in his freshman or sophomore year at UM, on a kickoff return. It kinda showed that yeah, he can return kicks and punts. I think most of them wanted him for defense, because how often do you have a kid that's 6'2" and 225 playing free safety that could run and hit like Sean could?"

Coach Howey even knew about Sean the ladies' man in high school. "There were many ladies after Sean. There were older ladies that thought the world of Sean, too. Lots of girls wanted to date him. And I'm sure it got more interesting for him in college. But Jackie Garcia is such a sweetheart. She was a great choice. She met him at Gulliver. I still have tapes from the championship game with Jackie and her white T-shirt on that says 'TAYLOR #1' and she's in the front row cheering him on. She was supporting him."

Gulliver Prep Assistant Coach Ralph Ortega

Ralph Ortega played football in high school, college, and the pros. He was an All-American at the University of Florida (UF) and was chosen twenty-ninth by the Atlanta Falcons in the 1975 NFL draft. He was a middle linebacker for four years with the Falcons and was on the team that set the all-time record in 1977 for the fewest points allowed. That line later became known as the "Gritz Blitz." They had only 129 points scored against them, which is still the record for a modern-day defense playing fourteen games or more.

Ralph was traded in the off-season of 1979 to the Miami Dolphins and spent his last two years there. That's where he injured his knee, and he never played again. So all together, Ralph spent six years in the National Football League.

As a Gulliver Prep coach, Ralph brought the 3–4 defense. This gave Sean an edge in knowing how NFL teams ran their defenses. Several pro teams ran the 4–3 defense, which gave Sean a second option if he were to make it to the NFL.

After football, Ralph went into the financial planning and mortgage business, where he became, and still is, very successful.

●

"I didn't know Sean or Pete Taylor until both of our sons transferred into Gulliver Prep in 1999," Coach Ortega began. Ralph's son Buck entered Gulliver Prep at the same time as Sean.

"Shortly thereafter I agreed to become Gulliver's defensive coordinator. From there the fantastic journey of knowing Sean Taylor and his family began."

Ortega began coaching at Gulliver in the spring of 1999. At first none of his players made him think they were anything spectacular. He just had some "good-looking players." It wasn't until the spring game that he thought he had a few diamonds in the rough.

"Honestly, it was like an epiphany, like watching something in a movie. When I saw Sean play in his first competitive game against another team, it was literally incredible, so much so that I told Sean I wanted to talk to him after the game."

The two met after, and Ralph told him about his college and pro background. He told Sean he thought he had a pretty good eye for talent, and he made it clear that Sean had the potential not just to go on to the next level, but also to be one of the greatest players in the National Football League. Ortega said to Sean, "'There's just something about you. If I had to tell you exactly what it is, I can't, but there's something about the way you move and the way you play; your instincts are amazing. All I'm telling you is, do not sell yourself short. If that's something you want, think about it and then pursue it. You and I are gonna continue to talk about it.' That was the first time I realized that Sean was beyond something special.

"Sean had what I called the 'pit bull look.' He could literally look expressionless. He hit you with this look and you didn't know if he was happy, mad, glad, or sad. He'd look at you with that dead stare and it was unreadable."

This is the perfect look to have if you're a poker player—which, by the way, Sean later became.

"He was a pleaser in that he loved to be told he did something well. At the spring game, again, I'm dealing with this kid who is basically expressionless unless he was goofing around, etc. When I told him at the spring game what I thought he could be, he lit up like a Christmas tree. He had this big, huge smile. In a way, I think we tend to understand people who are like us. I'm very much like that."

After four weeks, Sean was playing on offense and defense. According to Ortega, there was a kid named Jeremy Hannah on that team who was going to be a good player. Ortega thought his son Buck had a chance to be a good player too, but there's a big difference between good players and what he saw in Sean.

In his junior year Sean incurred a season-ending injury. He hurt his hip, and team Gulliver lost their best weapon.

"Let's talk about Sean the person for a second. He was never a bully, even on the football field. Some of the lesser teams had no business playing against teams like ours, and that's when Sean would turn it down a bunch of notches. Where he could have destroyed guys, he wouldn't do it.

"By the same token, I started to learn about what I thought were some of the key ways to motivate Sean. He had a lot of pride. I think he had a great fatherly instinct in him, a protective instinct. He would protect guys he needed to protect, be it family, friends, or players. So I could tell you, you didn't want to tick him off.

"I remember one game against a particularly good football team. I believe it was Florida Christian. It was supposed to be a close game. At one time their defensive coordinator had been one of the coaches at Gulliver. It was a crosstown rival. There was a lot of talking going on off the field the week before the game.

"On one of the plays where Buck reversed field, Sean came back and hit a kid. I'm not joking. It looked like something from *The Exorcist*. The kid's helmet not only came off his head but literally went about ten yards parallel to the ground. It looked like something on a bungee cord. The crowd started whooping. However, I knew this kid was hurt. It wasn't something you wanted to be yelling about. They did bring an ambulance, and thank goodness, the kid's neck wasn't broken. But I'm sure he had a few bad dreams for a while about that lick.

"In that one play, you saw the intensity and the viciousness Sean could bring to the field. It was an absolutely clean hit, but no one was worried about CTE [chronic traumatic encephalopathy] or head concussions back then. It wasn't a penalized hit. I'm sure he didn't intend to knock the kid's helmet off or even to knock the kid out. It was just a part of football back then. In my era, there was no shame in knocking a guy out. Quite the opposite, if we had an opportunity to knock a guy out, we were gonna do it. It's how the game was played.

"I'm reminded of something. I invited one of my big investors in my mortgage business to come see a Gulliver game. To this day he tells people what I call 'Sean Taylor stories.' That's how it seemed to him ... he tries to describe how Sean would run and the things he'd do on the football field. Some of what Sean did was just indescribable. Some of the other things that come to mind ... when I met with the owner of Gulliver Prep, whose husband had been one of my high school coaches, we talked about expectations. 'Mrs. Krutulis,' I said, 'you realize a small school has never won the championship out of Dade County.' There's a reason for that. When you go to Immokalee, or you go to, say, Sebring, any of these other schools, there is no other school in the county. We are in Dade County, and what inevitably happens is, these small schools develop a kid, and when he gets to his senior year, they tell him he needs to go to a 6A school if he wants to get a scholarship. So you end up losing your players. Sean wanted to leave, and we had to convince him to stay.

"In Sean's junior year we lost in the second round of the playoffs. We lost to Pace High School. However, they go on to lose 7-0 against the team that eventually wins the state championship. That's the first time I realize we are physically strong enough to win it all.

"So now we fast-forward to Sean's senior year, where he and Buck became very close. He spent many nights at the house in Miami and at our house in the Keys. Sean caught his first sailfish with Buck. Eventually they roomed together in the dorms their freshman year at UM, and in their sophomore year, they shared a condominium out here in the Kendall area.

Life Lesson

"I responded well to my dad because he was always telling me what I could be. He was never negative. He never pushed me with, 'You're never going to be anything in life.' He was the opposite: 'You know, you could be this or that,' and just always giving me a bar to try to achieve my goal. I sensed that with Sean. If you told him, 'This is the challenge and you are the man for it,' he would put on the Superman cape and achieve it.

"I want to go back to the game before the state championship for a moment. It was the semifinal game, where we played Immokalee HS. They were beating teams by about thirty points. And that was the proverbial small high school. There's no other school besides Immokalee High in their area.

"Immokalee [the town] is a community with many kids growing up on farms. Some were migrant kids, who are traditionally tougher than kids out of a rich prep school in Miami. But I had had a lot of contact with Immokalee High because I had been involved in a fundraising program where we'd go to Immokalee every year. I knew the athletic director from the school and the big boosters. They brought four Greyhound busloads of boosters to our game. They had more people in the stands than we did, even though the game was here in Miami.

"The state final was in Gainesville, Florida, where my alma mater, the University of Florida, is. We were going to play Mariana High School [located northwest of Tallahassee] for the state championship. From having watched the film, I thought we were a better team than Mariana, but the day before the game, the dairy association gave a trophy to the 5A-6A player of the year and the 1A-4A player of the year. They had given it to the tailback and an outside linebacker from Mariana who had signed with the University of Georgia as the best player from the 1A-4A.

"I'm doing some interviews up there, because again, in Gainesville the sportswriters knew my background. The subject of best players of the year came up. Actually I think I brought it up on purpose. I said what a mistake the dairy association had made in picking this other kid. They thought I was nominating Buck, my son, who was the quarterback, as the best player. I said, 'No, we have another kid who is the best player.' I said, 'Look, I'm not telling you this kid is the best 1A-4A player; I'm telling you he's the best player in high school football. And I'm not saying he's the best player in the state of Florida; I'm saying he's the best player, period!'

"Now they are joking around with me, not knowing much about Sean Taylor, and I said, 'You'll get to decide tomorrow.' After that interview, I had a little talk with Sean about how everybody thinks this other kid is supposed to be a better player. Well, the end of the story is that we ran over Mariana. Sean had—oh, I forget how many touchdowns—but he was extremely dominant. But the interesting thing is, to a man, all the sportswriters who were there the day before came up to me and said, there was no doubt, 'That's the best kid we've ever seen play ball!' The moral is, he responded when he was challenged.

"Anyway, we get up there for the state finals, and I forget what the stats are. If you look at the *Miami Herald*, I believe, the headline was either 'Gulliver Prep' or 'Sean Taylor Dominates Game.'

"Off the field, we talked about football. We also discussed life in general. Sean had a fatherly instinct that was not common in kids his age. It's interesting. I don't know if that's why Buck and he hit it off so well. Buck was also a very fatherly type. He had a younger brother, as did Sean. I don't know if it's something they build up early in age, because they are used to holding the baby of the family and taking care of him. For all I know, some neighborhood kid picked on Caleb [Buck Ortega's brother]. Did Buck take care of the situation? Of course he did.

"One of the things I later told the Redskins coaches was, I used to go watch the boys play seven-on-sevens. Roscoe Parrish played too. So he ran a takeoff route. The ball was overthrown, and Roscoe gets tangled up a little bit and ends up going down. Sean got tangled up on the same play. But Sean did something with his feet and was able to hurtle Roscoe as he was tumbling, stay on his feet, and never fall over. It's one of those things, if you are an ex-athlete and can recognize or just respect what you just saw, where you end up with your mouth agape. How in the heck did that guy just do that? It's not something you can train for. It just comes with natural abilities. You just can't duplicate it."

❦

Pete Taylor was a big fan of Ralph Ortega. "Ralph brought me over to his house so we could just talk," Taylor said. "While we were at his house, he'd explain the 3–4 defense to Sean. He would explain green ninety-five or mention what other colors or animals meant. He taught Sean how to think through the calls, and that eased Sean's transition into the NFL.

"In the middle of the season, they were running eight 200s, eight times around the field, walk back, and then go again, to build their lungs. He told the kids, 'You guys think I'm making you run for your health?' Coach Ortega asked. 'You gotta be in shape. They hit very hard in the NFL. They'll knock your teeth out! The game coming up—we don't want to play with them. We want to knock them out!' Then he turned away from the kids, flipped out his dentures—the kids didn't know he had no teeth—and turned around bare-gummed. The kids were shocked! He added, 'Make sure you wear your mouthpiece and your hardhat, and play ball!' He slapped his teeth back in. 'Do you understand me?' Ralph yelled. The team went on to win!"

Pete Taylor continued

Sean's dad remembers a time during Sean's senior year at Gulliver when the team was getting ready to play Berlin. Coach Howey put in his front line and put Sean in the backfield. There were Pascal, Coviglia, Burns, and Dunn. At practice, Sean got the ball and kept scoring touchdowns.

"Ralph started calling blitzes, one after another. Sean came through the hole, and he was like fifteen to twenty yards down the field. Pascal came from an angle, heading at Sean. He hit Sean and got in a good lick. Ralph wanted at least a tackle. So the coach called the same play again. Sean ran the same play and came out thirty yards downfield this time. He made a U-turn. Then he ran full speed back into Pascal. When the coach asked him what the heck he was doing, he responded, 'Coach, he hit me, and I'm hitting him back!' He was setting an example—if you are going to bring it, bring it all the time!"

Gulliver Prep Assistant Football Coach John McCloskey

John McCloskey spent fifteen years at Gulliver High School as both an assistant principal and a football coach. Currently McCloskey is coaching football at the Gulliver Academy (the middle school). His office prominently displays his trophies, plaques, and pictures from those glorious years—the football years with Sean Taylor. McCloskey had many Sean Taylor stories to share; following are but a few.

Not pulling any punches and right off the bat, McCloskey said, "His death was very upsetting to me, obviously, and to everybody I know. Especially the part after, what the media had reported incorrectly about him. You just wanted to say to them, 'You don't know Sean, and you don't know his father like I do! None of the stuff you're saying is true.' I was very upset about that."

McCloskey wants people to know the truth about Sean Taylor. "He was just a fabulous young man. He brought his *A* game every day and he loved to play football. He was not a very vocal person but did his talking on the field. Every day, day in and day out, at practice, just doing what he's supposed to do—following the guidelines of his coaches. His goal was to be better every day.

Coach McCloskey said, "To be able to coach Sean was one of the thrills of my life. I don't think I've ever seen a more talented athlete. He could do anything and play anywhere on the field: offense, defense, special teams. I don't know if you remember [he cast a look at Pete Taylor], if the kickoff team wasn't going down and making coverage, he wanted to get in there and make it happen. I was so very blessed to be able to know him and to coach him.

"I could remember only a couple of times where he was having a bad day. We aren't portraying him as being perfect. But that's the definition of being human; you are not perfect.

"If his effort would not be the same, we'd take him aside and ask what was happening. Again, he wasn't real verbal so he wasn't going to tell you [everything]. Maybe something happened at school earlier in the day, or maybe it was something else. And you'd just say, 'Come on, we're here, we need to pick it up.' Inevitably he responded to that. Don't get me wrong; those bad days were very few. But it was really how he responded to things like that. When he wasn't feeling himself, you knew."

Remembering that very first off-season scrimmage, the spring game, Taylor reminded McCloskey of his rah-rah speech.

"I made my rah-rah speech?" John asked.

"I think it was just before the Booker T. [Washington High School] at Gulliver game," Pete Taylor said. "The teams met up on the field, and the Booker T. players tried to intimidate our players. They race over and holler, 'Get back. Get back!' Neither team moves back. Sean is a latecomer, but he comes over to the front of the group and starts hollering, 'We aren't moving back. Don't mess with my teammates. If you don't back up, y'all are gonna have some problems!' The coaches started pushing Booker T. players and Sean into the locker room.

"The kids thought they'd get in trouble, but you came running, screaming, into the locker room saying, 'Boo-ahh-ahh-ahh!'" Pete Taylor said, doing his best McCloskey imitation. 'That's what I'm talking about, gentlemen, football! And I love it! Let's do football.' The kids get all fired up and go out and win!"

"I swear to God, I don't even remember that," the perplexed McCloskey said.

"You did," Pete replied, amused by the recollection.

"If he says I did it, then I guess did it. But I don't remember," McCloskey said.

"I almost died," Pete said, laughing. "You said, 'We're in trouble, we're in trouble … ahhhhhh!'"

"You know what? We were having fun. We were having fun, so I'm sure I did something like that." McCloskey said.

Pete said, "The kids were scared—'What did *we* do?' they thought."

"I was just trying to get the kids fired up," said McCloskey.

"So anyway … the first year, as I recall, didn't he get injured, Pete? Yeah, he was injured that first year, and I think he only played maybe half the year or something. We knew he was a very good talent, but we never got to see him play a full season. So we weren't quite sure what he'd end up doing."

In year two of the Sean Taylor era, "We played a preseason game against Westminster Academy. He played very well there. And then, once the regular season games started, that senior year of 2000 and 2001, he was just incredible.

"You know, the key to his success was that he was consistent. There's no doubt in his second year that Sean was the leader of the team. There were some other guys there: Buck Ortega, a few others, Casey Dunn, and them; they were leaders, too. He never shunned that. He stepped up to it.

"He would be verbal with them at times, but it wasn't a big long rah-rah speech bringing them together. He mainly did it by his performance on the field, his leadership, doing it the right way.

"I remember Sean came here, not only to the high school, but he came to the middle school and met with our kids. We have a picture of him with a couple of our staff members from that day. And so selfishly I was like, 'Man, you know, he's such a good ambassador to come back for the kids, to see and talk to them.' And so whereas in high school he was kind of reticent and didn't talk that much, he opened up big time through college and especially when he started playing professionally. The kids didn't really want anything from him. When you're a pro player, everybody wants something," McCloskey said.

Pete Taylor

Pete Taylor also vividly recalled the Gulliver-Immokalee High School game, the one before the state championship. "We got scouts everywhere. We played them before but never beat them, but we could tell when they got off the bus by the looks on their faces they came to beat us again. But that's not what happened.

"That day, University of Miami's offensive coordinator Larry Coker and running back coach Don Soldinger were on the sideline. I see them and I say to no one in particular, 'We got some Miami scouts in the house.' There were other scouts at the game as well.

"So having a pretty good relationship with our coaches, I'm always roaming the sideline with the team. I never interfered with their practices, but I had a keen eye for what was going on. I was just there to help the team in any way I could.

"The game starts. We have the ball, and the Gulliver coach, Steve Howey, called a dive play. Sean hit it, and they gang-tackled him. Coach calls a sweep. They don't even look at Sean, just all pursue to the corner. Sean's not making any yardage. What they were doing was over-pursuing. So the coach tells Sean to, 'Run the play, just run the play.' He does, but Immokalee was over-pursuing so fast, they get him again. Sean wasn't seeing the belly back, but from the sidelines, I could. So Sean was kinda upset—very frustrated. He comes to the sideline, and I say, 'Hey what's going on?' Before he could answer, I continued with, "What do you see out there? I'm obviously seeing something different than what you're seeing.'

"I saw Coker looking at me, but he didn't know what I was saying to Sean. But some time later he asked me, 'What did you tell him the day Don and I were out there?'

"So I told him the belly was wide open, so just belly back. 'Sean, if they all flood left, and you're running to the right, then belly back and go the opposite way. Stop getting upset.'

"We could see our team wasn't moving the ball and it was going to be a tough game. I told Sean, 'Champions fight and they scratch and they claw, and in the end, they win.'

"Coach calls Sean's number to get back in the game. As he's running on the field, he looked back at me and he said, 'The belly was wide open?'

"I said, 'Yeah, wide open. They're over-pursing.'

"I'll never forget it. The coach calls a P-sweep. So he goes in and he does a fake-down like he's gonna run a sweep but instead runs the play, and as he turns to go outside, he looks up and sees the defense pursuing but also sees he was wide open on the belly.

"He bellies back and runs the other way and picks up ninety-seven yards. Next play, *bam!* Touchdown! All of a sudden, there's a momentum shift. It was a good, hard game. I'm not sure how much Gulliver won by, but that win got them into the state championship—which, by the way, they also won."

🏈

Sean went on to play in the championship game against Mariana High School out of northern Florida. At that game, nine thousand people were sitting in the stands. It was standing room only, much to the chagrin of both Sean and his father, Pete Taylor.

The game began and Mariana jumped out in front, but Gulliver responded. Mariana had planned for Sean again, so Gulliver ended up putting Sean at wide receiver. That's something Mariana had not planned for. Quarterback Buck Ortega just started throwing the ball to his favorite target, who in this game lined up as the wide out.

Gulliver also had a kid by the name of Pascal running the ball, and they just couldn't stop him either. And that was that. Gulliver ended up winning the state championship.

Pete said to his son, "'I told you you'd win it. I told you you'd win it.' Finally Sean looked at me with those 'now I believe you' eyes."

"'We did it,' Sean replied."

Side Story

At the time Gulliver won the state championship, Steve Spurrier was the head football coach of the University of Florida Gators. "So when I got to the stadium for the championship game, I [went] down to the field and I started walking around," recalls Taylor. I said, 'Man, it's gonna be a beautiful day.' Both teams started their warm-ups, and when they were done, they [went] back inside to their locker rooms.'"

A University of Florida assistant coach approached Pete Taylor on the sidelines and informed him Coach Spurrier would like to see him. "So now I am back in the stands when this same guy comes to get me to go see Coach Spurrier. I wanted to go the quick way, so I headed down the stands and headed for the field so I could cut across. He was sitting in a booth on the opposite end of the field. A police officer stopped me and said, 'Don't you go down there.'

"But Coach Spurrier wants to see me, and that's where I was going."

"'I'm telling you, don't you cross that field or I'll poke you,' the officer said."

A friend of Pete's piped up, and two other coaches came over to apologize and have words with the officer. "'Can't he come with us? We will escort him across the field. It will be okay.'"

Pete spoke with some irritation to the coaches. "You heard what the officer is going to do. He wants to poke me. So the only place you're gonna catch me is back on I-75 heading south. You don't have to worry about poking me anywhere, because I'm not going across no field to see anybody."

Gulliver won the game, and when it was over, they tried to get Pete to meet with Coach Spurrier. "Hey, I'm telling you I'm not coming," Taylor reiterated.

They pleaded with Taylor for a third time, but for them it was not to be a charm. They asked again.

"I said, 'No, I'm not coming with you. I'm headed south on 75 just like I told you before! I have to respect the police, and he said no, so it's no.'" So Taylor didn't take the meeting with Spurrier. Perhaps he looked at it as a sign to say no to the Gators.

After the win, the Taylors attended many UM practices and had the opportunity to speak with former coaches Larry Coker, Don Soldinger, and C. J. (Curtis Johnson), as well as Coach Stoops (now at Kentucky) a few times. Johnson was the wide receiver coach for the Hurricanes, and today he is the head coach at Tulane University.

With the Gulliver win and the state championship under his belt, Sean was invited to the Dade and Broward All-Star Game. Sean went to one of the workouts, but the next day he told teammate Andre Maddox he didn't want to go anymore. He instead let Maddox use his car so he could get back and forth to the practices.

At about the same time, Sean was invited to the Florida–California All-Star Football Game. It was what one would call a showcase game, but they called it a special Florida–California football bowl game.

Half Brother Joseph Taylor

Younger half brother Joseph Taylor also remembers Sean's high school years. "He was a good kid. I mean, if he did get in trouble, it was because of his school grades—academic trouble. That would be it," Joseph "Joey" Taylor said.

A few short years after Sean, Joseph also attended Gulliver Prep. Joseph commented on getting the extra help needed to get students' grades up, the nurturing atmosphere, the teachers that were there to make sure they succeeded. "They were a truly dedicated group of professionals," Joseph said.

Joseph also said he never got in trouble, having learned from his brother.

Besides succeeding in the classroom, Joseph competed in sports as well. "So in high school I competed in cross-country events and played basketball," Joseph Taylor said. "I went to Gulliver for four years. After Sean left after his senior year, I came in. He is three years older. He was born in 1983; I was born in 1986."

Another Taylor athlete—no surprise there! But when Joseph got to Gulliver, were they expecting another Sean Taylor?

"As you can imagine, I was known as Sean Taylor's little brother in ninth grade until I got my own name. Then they knew me as Joey. I played basketball there all four years. That helped in establishing me as my own person. We had a good team," Joey said. "I also ran track my sophomore, junior, and senior years. And cross-country."

As far as his father Pete's pay for As program, Joey said with a smile, "When I was young, I made a lot of money. But then we started taking all Dad's cash because we were always getting good grades. I guess the program ended for us, I'm sorry to say. I used to love that program!"

Since many of Gulliver's students came from the area's elite families, the parking lot was filled with high-end vehicles, such as Mercedes, BMWs, Range Rovers, and the like. It wasn't like that for the Taylors.

"Sean used to come in with that old Corolla, and he walked out of that car as if it was one of those Mercedes," Joseph said. "He didn't really care. When he got out of that thing, he knew he was something special, but he never flaunted it. It never really bothered him. He was that big guy coming out of that little Corolla. It was kinda funny!"

It turns out that car became a hand-me-down.

"I got my brother's car. That Corolla got passed down to me. Personally, I loved it. It used to have that dark tint, and I had my [sound] system in there. I felt big-time in that little Corolla. I used to call it the Green Machine."

When it came to music, Joseph said Sean was into Tupac, Bob Marley, and Snoop Dogg. "He had a Marley shirt. He had a lot of Bob Marley shirts, actually. I have a couple of them too."

Joey said he was into R&B and a little bit of rap. He liked 112, Jay-Z, and other artists like that.

When it came to one-on-one time, the brothers would talk about a lot of things, especially girls.

"He was my teacher," Joseph said with a laugh. "Another thing, he was a protective brother. If anybody would mess with me, he'd be at their door asking, 'Why are you messing with my brother?'"

Joseph then offered this: "In seventh grade, somebody punched me in my face when I was walking home from school for no apparent reason. Next thing you know, I heard Sean was knocking at the guy's door, looking for him, protecting me. He knew how to take care of business. He made sure nothing happened to any of us.

"He was loved everywhere, especially at Gulliver—except, of course, by those that messed with his family."

Joseph loved watching Sean play football. "Yeah. We used to go to all his games. I was going to Southwood Middle School at the time. Whenever Sean had a high school game, my dad would 'fly' over to Southwood and pick me up, and we'd all ride over to Gulliver to go to the game."

13

Recruiting Sean

THERE ARE MANY RULES RECRUITS MUST FOLLOW TO BECOME ELIGIBLE to play college sports. One of those rules has to do with the number of college visits you can take. Recruiters can come to you at home or high school and discuss playing for this college or that. But you only get up to five college visits away from home. So the Taylors' thought process was to take a visit far from home as a vacation and take a few closer by, so Sean could compare different campuses and facilities and check out the surrounding areas.

Over 150 coaches tried to talk to Sean. The high school has a written record of who came to see him. At each game, there could be ten to fifteen coaches who wanted an audience. This helped Pete build his portfolio of coaches.

Schools called all the time. They called the house; recruiters came to the school; they even tried to pull him out of class. In the end, the Taylors ended up with a bag of about three hundred letters.

"Then there's a part of the season that is quiet. That's called the dead zone," Taylor said.

Originally Sean and his family scheduled five trips: University of Southern California (USC), Georgia Tech (GT), University of Miami, and then Clemson. He had already been to the Florida State University (FSU) campus in Tallahassee at a summer training camp.

"George O'Leary was the coach at Georgia Tech," Pete said. "He came twice to see Sean. The first time, he came and spoke to both of us. Trying to get on Sean's good side, he stated, 'Sean, you could play anywhere on the field [meaning offense or defense],' as he wanted to see Sean play for Georgia Tech.

"So I sent Sean up to GT to visit the campus and spend time with my brother-in-law. I think he liked it, and it made his 'possible list.'

"Coaches Don Soldinger and Larry Coker of the University of Miami would come to his games at Gulliver and observe. It never dawned on me that they were interested in Sean. Miami is the kind of school that waits till the last minute then makes its rush," offered Taylor.

Once Sean decided on UM, he wouldn't go on any other trips. He liked the idea of being in his own backyard.

"Butch Davis was the University of Miami's head football coach. Davis pulls up to the house in his nice car, comes in, and starts talking to Sean. Davis is one of the coaches I spoke to about giving Sean an opportunity to play safety or running back, but not linebacker. But Davis had been a linebacker coach and liked linebackers.

"I know Butch Davis. He was with Jimmy Johnson and the Dallas Cowboys. So I'm sitting there listening as he talks to Sean about all the reasons to attend UM.

"Just before National Signing Day, GT's George O'Leary comes back to the house. He appeals to Sean: 'Dare to be different, Sean. I would like to see you come here [to Georgia Tech]. We know what you can do and where you can play. Dare to make a path of your own,' he said."

Sean had also briefly thought about going to Florida State University. But while there on a visit, Sean noticed that Bobby Bowden didn't seem to be interested in him. So when he played against FSU and the University of Florida, he had a bone to pick with both schools—the ones that didn't want Sean Taylor.

"Anyway, Sean had already signed with Miami, and a few days later we see a story on the TV news about Butch Davis and Pete Hernandez leaving UM and heading to the Cleveland Browns to start a new era. Gee. I hope it wasn't something Sean said," kidded Pete Taylor. But "It's a good thing Coach Coker still wanted Sean, because Butch's departure had no impact on Sean's choice. We always believed that UM was a good fit for my son."

Gulliver's Got the Juice

Orenthal James "O. J." Simpson, the famous (or infamous—whichever you prefer) former professional football player, sat next to Pete Taylor for most of the Gulliver Prep football games. What brought O. J. to the games? When the Simpsons moved to Florida, away from the turmoil of Southern California, O. J.'s son Justin attended Gulliver Prep. Justin tried out for but did not make the football team; instead, he played basketball for Gulliver. So O. J. often attended both football (for obvious reasons) and basketball games.

"So Justin ended up playing basketball with my son Joseph," Pete Taylor said. "Justin Simpson came in and played hard." He was Joseph's age. Sydney, O. J.'s daughter, also went to Gulliver. She was two years younger than Sean.

Gulliver Prep is a very prestigious private school that is highly respected and often the school of choice for the five- to eighteen-year-old children of the well-to-do. It's not unusual to find a myriad of celebrity children from Miami's elite at the school.

"O. J. admired Sean's ability," Pete said. "He once said to me, 'Listen, your boy is very good. Have you ever thought about sending him to California? To USC?' And before I knew it, he's making a phone call to the USC coach to let him know there's a kid he might want to look at and offer a scholarship to. O. J. said, 'This kid has great qualities—very explosive—and I think he'll fit into the Trojan program. I'd like to bring this kid out.'"

However, USC was no longer on the Taylors' radar. On the other hand the fact O. J. even made the effort to try to entice them to go out there and look around, and to encourage Sean to go there, was quite impressive.

"During games, O. J. picked out things for Sean to work on," said Taylor. Besides football, the range of conversation spanned from family, to golf, to Sean's performance on the field. Taylor said they never discussed his trial and all that ensued.

"Golf was his morning cup of coffee and his midnight cup of tea," Taylor said of O. J. "He talked about the nine holes or eighteen holes he was going to play that day.

"Sometimes he would speak about his surgery. Did you know he has a titanium knee? I used to ask him how it felt, because I had a knee injury myself and I was thinking of having some more work done to it. He told me if I was going to get something done, make sure it's titanium. He hadn't had any problems with his titanium knee since. He was obviously experienced with injuries and bad knees; he was a great running back. So for me, he was somebody good to talk to about that."

Think of him what you will, but Pete Taylor said, "When we were all together, the kids and family, we just sat around with my friend Coach Marcus Jones, and we all just laughed and joked. At home he was more of a parent than a celebrity."

Was Sean excited to meet a former pro player? "Sean was always humble," his father said. "He met many former pro athletes, and he always welcomed any and all information about how to transition from high school to college to the pros. He would get insight as to how to carry oneself, or how the NFL worked. O. J. imparted information of that nature. He especially cautioned Sean about how to protect his finances so he'd have money at the end of his career.

"O. J. said, 'You have to be on the job, doing what you're supposed to do, to last in the NFL.' O. J. also preached 'knowledge of expectations.' That would include what to expect from coaches, teammates, and fans. Sean was *very* appreciative of the information and stored it away for future use."

When Sean made it to the pros, he always remembered the things taught to him by O. J. and an assortment of former players.

National Collegiate Signing Day

It was the evening of February 18, 2001, the night before National Signing Day, the day high school student athletes across the country would get to announce to the world which college they were choosing to play for. As the evening went on, Sean told his father he had made up his mind. He wanted to wear the orange and green colors of the University of Miami and play for the Hurricanes. The Taylors were thrilled.

🏈

On February 19, Gulliver Prep scheduled a 9:00 a.m. National Signing Day ceremony for Sean and Buck Ortega, who both played football for their Gulliver Raiders.

"Buck's father, Ralph Ortega, and I met up in the morning and we went inside and saw the tables all lined up, complete with pens and the papers they would have to sign and fax over to the school of their choice. There were small hors d'oeuvres being served, but I wasn't hungry. I was too anxious to be hungry," Taylor said.

"We moved to the gym that was so elegantly decorated with information about all of the seniors. There was even a retrospective video.

"When the boys sat down to sign, they looked at each other, and at that point I knew they had decided to sign for the same school, but still not one hundred percent sure.

"Sean picked up his pen, and then Buck did the same. Then Sean began to ink the NSD [National Signing Day] paperwork of the University of Miami, and just as I had suspected, Buck did too. It was a proud day to be a Miami Hurricane. A proud day to know they'd have a chance to go to the school of their choice. I was thrilled he chose Miami, because I wanted to see him play in his backyard, in the community he grew up in, not to mention close enough for me and my family to attend most, if not all, home games. I still have the picture of Sean making the announcement in my office," said Taylor.

It was a very proud moment for Sean. The signing was shown before the entire student body over the internal cable network. The rest of his classmates responded by throwing up the sign of "the U."

For Gulliver Schools owner Mrs. K, it was also a very proud moment because not only was she the head of Gulliver, but she was also a proud graduate of and major contributor to the University of Miami. So when Sean declared he would be going there, Mrs. K was very excited.

Pete continued, "Another reason I was so proud of Sean, was that he was to be the first child in my family to get a scholarship to a D-I [Division 1] college and play on that high a level. Generally universities are ranked by size and scope of their athletic offerings. There are D-I, D-2, and D-3 schools. Only D-I schools could offer 'scholarships.' So that was an exciting time, my friends."

Shortly after the ceremony, Sean returned to class. It was business as usual, though he now knew what his future held. But first he had to prepare himself to graduate from Gulliver.

A few months went by, and Sean was doing well until one day Pete got a call from Mrs. K. Taylor remembers the conversation going something like this:

"Mr. Taylor, we have a problem." Mrs. K said. "Sean is required to give a speech on graduation day. But he's refusing."

"What do you mean he's not going to do a speech?" Pete Taylor asked.

"It's part of his public speaking curriculum, and he doesn't want to do one."

"Let me handle it," Sean's father said.

"When Sean came home that day," said Pete, "I asked him about the speech. All Sean could say was, 'But Dad, how did you know?'"

"So I told him about the phone call and said to him, 'I have to tell ya, come graduation night, you *are* going to do that speech.'"

Everyone who knows Sean knows how painfully shy he could be. Public speaking under that much pressure just wasn't his forte.

Despite his misgivings, Sean's graduation day at Gulliver was great. Pete remembered it clearly. "It was a proud day seeing my son walk across the stage to get his diploma. He walked into the room, standing tall with his braids, in his cap and gown. It's the day he gave his speech in front of eighteen hundred to two thousand people—thanking everyone, thanking his parents.

"So just to see Sean standing in front of that crowd at the graduation ceremony and delivering that speech was a very proud moment. Just knowing Sean and how he was, I knew that took a lot out of him. This whole thing did remind me of Sean as a child, when we asked him to read his books to us out loud. Well, I guess in the long run it paid off."

The lady of the hour, Mrs. K, was there. When Sean had first come to Gulliver, she told him he had to work on his academics and always strive to be better than the day before. "At Gulliver," Mrs. K said, "they'll do everything to help you, but you need to work."

"I knew the message had gotten through and Sean was working hard," Taylor said. "I remember we had a neighbor across the street whose kid was struggling with math. The kid came over, and Sean tutored him. That's how I knew he 'got it.' Guess what—the kid got an A on the test! Imagine—Sean the tutor!"

On the night of the graduation ceremony, in front of his mother, father, Buck Ortega, and all of Gulliver Prep, Sean delivered a great speech. Many in the news media used to say that Sean didn't like to talk, and that made their job that much harder. When push came to shove, he could do it; but we all know Sean liked to do his talking on the field of battle, and believe me, if a picture speaks a thousand words, his hits spoke a million.

Today there's a requirement that NFL players speak to the media, so I guess he would have gotten used to that, too, and perhaps all of those nasty things that were written about him could have been avoided.

❧

Even before official enrollment, the UM football organization encouraged their new recruits to start working out with the team. So the summer before officially entering the U, Buck and Sean began their workouts.

Two days out of the week they'd run seven-on-seven drills. This was done with just players and no coaches. Because Sean had volunteered to play safety, he worked out with a player named Ed Reed, who was a very good, very aggressive player and great role model. Sean believed he'd have no trouble playing behind Reed.

"The defensive guys like Ed Reed already knew the plays," Pete said. "So when they got through, they'd run twenty-one 100s or do whatever drills they needed to do. I'll never forget Ed Reed being one of the smartest players on the team. He would get on Sean to make sure he was keeping up. They'd start running, doing their conditioning. Some thought Sean was going to start off fast and finish slow. Instead he kept up with the veterans.

"Sean's objective was to come in and immediately contribute to the team. Freshmen Kellen Winslow, Jr., Frank Gore, Antrel Rolle, D.J. Williams, and most of the other players had goals to start fast and contribute as well," said Taylor.

❧

Getting back to the conversation we had with Sean's friends T. J. and Mike, Pete Taylor reminisced about the times Sean was seen working out late at night at UM before he was a student there.

T. J. said, "Yeah! We jumped the gate. We did it a million times. Like we did the sand pit at UM. I loved it. I'd do it because it helps you get better. It would give you an edge. So yeah. We'd do it all the time. Three, four o'clock in the morning. We'd run the 40. We'd do 110s. We'd be out there. All these people that used to play with him, they can't tell you what he did in his off time, which was probably the same thing—working hard. They can't tell you, because they didn't know. He didn't share it. This is the stuff he'd do early in the morning."

Pete added, "My thing is, you do what's required during the day, and you come back at night to do what was needed to get better. So he was working while—"

"His competition was sleeping," T. J. said, finishing Pete's sentence.

Pete said, "Yeah. That was our motto. I just left Naples, where I spoke to a group of high schools kids. I said, 'Look, what made Sean different?' I told them I used to take Sean out at night and we'd be working out or jogging. He was putting the extra work in. Hard work. That's what it was."

PART III

14

The Boys Land at the U

In August 2001, Sean Taylor and Buck Ortega entered the University of Miami together.

According to players and coaches alike, in the 2000–2002 seasons, Miami Hurricane football players were even more popular than Miami Dolphins football players. They called it the UM swag. So what was it like being part of that superstar team?

Buck Ortega

"We were all-stars, and going out to South Beach, for example, meant we were VIP," Buck Ortega said. "Obviously Sean was a lot bigger star than I was."

Revelation

"You know Sean and I grew up in Miami, and at Gulliver Prep there are plenty of kids who had plenty of resources, so in high school we could get into any club. That's just how those kids lived. So we had already experienced South Beach life. Truth is, we were partying right alongside a lot of the UM guys even before we were at Miami.

"I remember our official recruit weekend at UM. Normally the players would take you out. I remember talking to my host player, Joaquin Gonzalez, and I'm not sure who was Sean's host, and he asked 'Do you want us to take you out?' And we were like, 'No, not really.' Not to be snobs or anything but we'd already been there, done that. So it's kind of a unique situation when you come from a little prep school [where lots of students have cash in pocket]. For us, it was just a continuation [of the good times], going from high school into college and hanging out with those guys. However, now we were hanging more with the UM guys and not high schoolers, because we were now part of the team.

"Sean and I were roommates our first year on campus. As sophomores, and part of our junior years, we lived in an apartment, off-campus. In my fourth year I actually moved back home. Now that I think about it, Sean was done and out of UM before his junior year was over, because he was drafted by the Redskins. If you come out [declare your intent to take part in the NFL draft before graduating] when you are a junior, you're done after your third season mentally and physically. That's because you know you are going to the pros."

After Sean left, the boys slowly drifted apart. "I was juggling school, football, and everything else. So we didn't speak daily by any means," Buck said. In fact, Sean was busy trying to learn the playbook and get settled into his new surroundings, so it was unusual for them to speak even a couple times a month.

Sean adjusted well after he became a Redskin. He always appeared happy, according to Ortega. "Normal things would get him down, like family problems, girl problems, just the normal life headaches. But if you'd crack one joke, that smile of his would come right back out."

❧

"Sean met 'Mommy Jackie' [the mother of Sean's daughter, 'Baby Jackie'] at Gulliver," Ortega said. On the other hand, "it was just a little fling. I don't think they were serious boyfriend/girlfriend then. You know, we were all really good friends. She'd come down to the Keys and hang out with us. At UM she played soccer. The baseball players, kids from other teams, we all hung out.

"Sean and Pete were a big part of my life. Pete really worked us hard. He used to have the parachutes out behind us when we ran. He would do anything in order to help Sean make it to the next level—college—then on to the next phase: the pros. That instilled something in Sean. I remember jumping over the fence to run the steps and the track at nine o'clock at night at UM. It's not normal, but I think we both had strong fathers, and they both instilled 'the craziness' in us."

Sean already knew a lot of the guys who were in the Miami Hurricanes freshman class. There was Antrel Rolle, whom he had played with at six years old at Dick Conley, and again in eighth grade with the Florida City Razorbacks. Besides Antrel, there were Frank Gore, Kellen Winslow, Jr., his high school buddy Buck Ortega, Rocky McIntosh, and Eric Winston, all out of South Florida.

Pete Taylor

Speaking of Frank Gore, Pete Taylor said this: "I love Frank to death. He is a competitor. He would work out at night just like Sean. He would do whatever it took to succeed. He wanted to play in his first year in college just like Sean. One day at practice I saw them talking. I asked Sean what it was that he and Frank just talked about. Turns out Frank had asked him to ease up. The key was to impress the coaches. In practice, every time Frank cut left, cut right, or run, every time he broke, Sean was right there, wrapping him up.

"I told him he had to understand that they may all be friends, but they were all competing for a job. If you do what someone else asks, it could cost you something. Sean told me he just wanted to listen to what people have to say. I told him he was going to make Frank better and Frank was going to make him better, so he had better make sure he went hard. That was the main thing—Frank had wanted him to stop breaking touchdowns. Sean told him he was on defense and he couldn't let that happen. He and Frank ended up with a pretty good bond."

During Sean's sophomore year of high school, he met Andre Johnson, who eventually became the tight end for the Houston Texans. Sean and Andre met at camp the summer before school started, and they competed. They met as opponents in the playoffs at Miami Killian Sr. High in Miami. They met up again at UM and together they played successfully for two and a half years.

Roscoe Parrish was a special kid, too. He came to UM from Miami High as a quarterback and receiver the same year Sean came in. He worked on his track speed like Sean did, and they became good friends.

Locker room leaders included Jonathan Vilma, Clinton Portis and quarterback Ken Dorsey. That team was very well built.

When it came to the campus, Sean thought he knew the U because of all the working out he did there. He discovered that wasn't the case when some older students rounded up the freshmen for a little hazing. They took them somewhere blindfolded, and when the blindfolds were removed, they didn't know where they were. They eventually figured out they were on campus and made it back to the dorms.

The kids would play around and wrestle with each other in the locker room, so when Sean went to his dad's house he would ask about specific wrestling moves. He wanted to know how to get out of a hold, how to put someone in a submission hold, etc. Pete explained, "I asked him what was going on at school. Sean said everything was fine. Then he came by the next day and gave me a thumbs-up. He told me that move worked and he was on top. Then he asked about another move. After about three weeks of this, he stopped asking about wrestling moves. I don't know if being on top meant he had bested these guys or if they just stopped wrestling with him.

"As a parent, you try to make sure your kids have everything they need," Taylor said. "On the other hand, there are things they don't need, like tattoos or earrings. I always told Sean he couldn't have a tattoo until he went to college. So when he was moving into the dorm, sure enough, he took off his shirt, and his name, 'Taylor,' was tattooed on his back. That was the first tattoo I had seen on him.

"All in all I could see he was doing well. The guys and girls in the dorm seemed to be having a good time running around. I knew I didn't have to worry about him. The next week I called and told him I was coming up.

"Many times I told him he couldn't wear earrings. So I show up and he's wearing a skully cap that covered his ears. A little later he took off his cap and I noticed two earrings!" Kids!

What Pete really liked about UM was the camaraderie among the parents. "When you talk about family atmosphere and fanfare, we would all meet up at games and tailgates; we would all fly to games together and cheer together, etc. It was awesome. We knew all of the players by name and they knew the parents by name. I loved it," Pete said.

Ralph Ortega

"At one of the UM practices, Sean Taylor and Kellen Winslow, Jr., went at it. Sean literally threw Kellen around, and he was maybe 230 pounds, 6'4"—he was a man. But it looked like Sean was dealing with a little kid or something. It was physical; it was part of the play. When Sean grabbed him by the shoulder pads and flipped him over, it was a 'that was something' moment."

Ortega spoke on. "It was NFL Day at the University of Miami, and I didn't know anything about it. They wouldn't let me on the field, and the security guy—who I didn't recognize, who I guess was part of the NFL or something—tells me I'm not allowed on the field. I tell him, 'You don't understand. I come here every Saturday to watch the seven-on-sevens.'

"I see Donnie Soldinger and I ask him how I can get down there to watch. Soldinger asks me if I know a guy named Don Brough, who was one of my college coaches. I said, 'Sure.' He said, 'Well, he's here with the Washington Redskins.'

"So I get in to see Coach Brough, but I didn't know Coach Joe Gibbs was back [there] with the Washington Redskins. Here's the thing. Don Brough tells me that they are trying to work a trade out for Clinton Portis. He goes, 'And how much do you know about the players here at UM?' I said, 'Well, how much do you want to know?' I told him I went to a lot of their practices and workouts for about three years since my son was a Hurricanes player. He told me they had the fifth pick in the NFL draft that year and were thinking about taking Kellen Winslow, Jr., and asked what I thought about that. I said, 'What about Sean Taylor?'

"He asked, 'What about Sean Taylor?'

"So I started telling him Sean Taylor stories. I literally raised my hand about as high above my head as I could. From the players that you are talking about, I had Sean Taylor up here, and then had Vilma as the next choice above Kellen Winslow, Jr., and then I said, 'I think D.J. Williams is going to be a great pro.'

"By the time I'm finished telling the Sean Taylor stories, he asked me if I would repeat them to Joe Gibbs, which I did. It turned out I not only told them to Joe Gibbs but to his entire staff: Joe Bugel, Gregg Williams, a few others that I didn't recognize. There were at least six coaches there."

UM Head Coach Larry Coker

Larry Coker spent twelve years with the University of Miami—six years as assistant coach under Butch Davis and six years as head football coach. As the assistant coach, Coker recruited Sean Taylor out of Gulliver Prep. He is currently head football coach at the University of Texas–San Antonio and was formerly with ESPN as an analyst.

Few could have imagined the player Sean Taylor would turn out to be, let alone UM Head Football Coach Larry Coker.

Despite Sean Taylor's being a record-holding, touchdown-scoring running back machine in high school, UM played him on the defensive side of the ball. How did that come about?

"Well, let's start with the need factor," said Coach Coker. "We needed him on defense, and we felt like he was going to have a great future there. Most people thought Sean was going to make a great linebacker when he was recruited. We were just experimenting with him at safety. He never did play linebacker with us. When I saw him at running back [at Gulliver Prep], I knew he had great hands, and I've always said he could do it all."

When Coker had his private time with Sean, they talked about keeping up with study hall, doing what he had to do to remain academically eligible, and making sure he got his degree. "Like most kids he dealt with a variety of issues, like adjusting to being away from home for the first time, time management, and the pressures of being a college athlete and all that entailed," said Coker.

What was it like coaching that fantastic Hurricanes team back in 2001?

"It was a great experience. It was also a great pressure from the standpoint of I had high expectations for the players and the players had high expectations for themselves. Anything less than getting that national championship would have been considered having a bad year! There were some great players on that team, but the game I will remember most is the one against Florida State. It was in the rain up there in Tallahassee."

In a very matter-of-fact voice, Coach Coker continued: "The reason I remember that one is because Sean had a particularly bad practice on Thursday and we almost didn't take him. But on Saturday he picked it up, and in fact he blocked a punt and scored two touchdowns, and I don't think we could have won without him."

The players competed against each other as well as the other team. Who could lift the most? Who could run the fastest? Who could hit the hardest? So what was it like dealing with those egos with each one of them believing he was better than the other guy?

Coker's answer was simple: "When you are with guys just as talented as you, your ego is held in check. Sean had his ego, for example, but he was there playing next to Kellen Winslow, Jr., and Jeremy Shockey, so that sets your ego in check right there, because those guys are great too. They kept each other in check. Hard practice during the week would test them for the things they saw on Saturday."

In the end, Coach Coker saw Sean as "a very quiet person. He was certainly one of the best football players I had ever been around. As far as his private life, he got his life in order just before the tragedy happened. It was such a shame—but certainly the way things were going for him made it even more tragic."

UM Coach Don Soldinger

Pete and I met with Miami Hurricanes Sports Hall of Fame inductee (April 2013) Coach Don Soldinger at the Kendall Ale House in Miami, Florida, for a little dinner, soft drinks, and a few great stories. It didn't take long to realize how great a coach Don must have been to play for and what a huge supporter of Sean he was.

"The year Sean went to the Pro Bowl [Sean's UM teammate], Frank Gore, who I coached at the University of Miami, flew my wife Phyllis and me out to Hawaii," Coach Don Soldinger said, beginning his first of many stories. "We were at picture day, and I was very excited when Sean walked over with a mini helmet and a football for me. We talked for a bit, and I told him how great he looked and how happy I was that he was doing so well.

"How are you doing?" Coach Soldinger asked Sean.

"He said, 'I got a great girl and a new baby, Coach. Everything is falling into place.' He followed with, 'This is the best time of my life.'

"That's what he told me when we were at the Pro Bowl, and I was thrilled to hear that.

"That guy was just getting it together, and that's why this is so sad. When this thing happened to Sean, I was devastated. I knew him since he was a little kid. My point is, when Sean played the game of football, he was all business. Off the field, he was a totally different guy. He actually became a great friend. He really cared about people. On the field he was always fired up, getting ready to hit you. Not that guy off the field.

"You know, I was pretty tight with Sean. I liked him, and he liked me."

Coach Soldinger talked about Sean and his buddies. He said Sean had a lot of friends at the U. "He hung around with all the top guys. There was Portis, Rolle, Moss, Quadtrine Hill, and Buck Ortega, who played with Sean in high school. Ed Reed and Sean were good friends too. They would play basketball together. Even Edgerrin James joined in when he came back to work out. That team was like the who's who of college football. All those guys were unbelievable, and while you'd think the competition was between them and their opponent, they actually competed against one another.

"Even before the U, Sean was known for his workouts. I used to go to the weight room a lot myself. I was very big on weights in high school. You want to get bigger and stronger? Lift weights. You should have seen it. These guys were squatting—putting as much weight on as they could—and they were competing against each other. That's what made them so good. No matter what one guy lifted, the next guy had to put on more weight. Sean was that way. Some of these guys were off-the-charts strong. McGahee was like that; D.J. Williams too. Whether it was lifting or running, they used to challenge each other. It was fierce competition all the time."

As far as Sean's learning skills, "he got the plays and understood the playbook right away," Soldinger said. "Now some said Frank Gore would have a little bit of trouble in college because he had dyslexia and didn't read like the others. Sean was a little better prepared for college than Frankie. But no one can deny what a brilliant career he is having in the NFL. Frankie is super sharp, and his football intelligence is off the charts, as was Sean's."

Frank Gore was offense smart. "Sean had a natural ability on defense to know where the ball was going to be. If Sean had come over to play offense, he would have been the same way. He was given a gift, and he could play ball. He was just special.

"When you got him off the field and sat down one-on-one with Sean, he was a special cat. We would not have won as many games as we did without those guys being of high character. They were all good kids trying to be real successful.

"We talked about everything. Like if he ever got in trouble, he would come to my office and we'd talk. We'd talk about going out. We talked about grades.

"We talked about this incident at FIU where Sean and a couple of his friends were playing basketball. Don't quote me, but there was a little scuffle—over what, I don't know. But because he was from Miami and assumed to be a bad kid, he got the finger pointed at him. He caught some bad vibes off of that, and he was just in the wrong place at the wrong time."

T. J. and Mike

According to Sean's buddies, this is how that FIU incident went down:

T. J. began: "I went to FIU, so Sean was either at my campus or I was at UM [working out or just shooting hoops]. So that day I was on the basketball court while he had practice, If I'm not mistaken, there was this big dude—6'9", 7'2"—called the Crushin' Russian."

Mike added, "He was there with Carlos Arroyo." Carlos went on to become a very successful NBA player.

T. J. explained, "Now, this big guy was fouling us, playing all rough. So the big Russian guy and Mike got into it. He thought we were going to back down. But instead, we were getting ready to fight the big Russian."

Mike added, "So I drove double baseline one time and he pushed me out of the air."

T. J. repeated, "He pushed him."

Then Mike said to the Russian, "'If you push me out of the air again, I'm going to fight you.' So he pushes me out of the air again. He did it again! So I walked to the bathroom and grabbed a fire extinguisher and I head back out to the court. Everybody started coming up at me, so …"

T. J. interrupted and said, "'Chill out. Chill out.' So Mike is gonna whoop him. Then you see the Russian get all Hercules."

Mike continued, "And he seen we serious and we not scared of him. So I'm a little guy—I couldn't even punch him in the midsection, and I would practically have to jump to do that … literally … not even exaggerating. I'm being dead serious here."

"So while all this going on, Sean calls and says, 'Whatcha all up to?'" said T. J. "'Well, we just playin' ball.' He said, 'Well, I'm coming too.' So this going on and I say, 'Bro, we about to leave,' and Sean says, 'I'll be there in two minutes.'

"So Sean gets there, and the Russian is still going off. When Sean gets there and sees this, he says to us, 'This guy going off on y'all?'"

T. J. said, "This was like how we got down. It didn't take nuttin' for us to pop off, ya feel me? If you bother him and I saw it, I'm gonna get you for bothering him. I'm gonna get you. Me. So once Sean sees this 6'7", 6'8" dude going crazy, he told him straight up, 'Don't disrespect my homeboys.'

"So the Russian got in his face, and the next thing you know, we all up on the Russian. We broke him down!"

T. J. and Mike spoke in unison: "So now the big Russian goes from big bad guy to haulin' ass out da gym."

"He's trying to retreat," T. J. said. "So that's all an incident of us having each other's back." So they ran. "They got all big and bad, but when it was just us and the fire extinguisher, he was ready to fight. But when Sean pulled up it was like, uh, now they the victims, and they ran. That's what it was. They took off full speed through the gym."

Don Soldinger continued

"So that's what we'd talk about [grades, going out, dealing with trouble]. No matter. All these guys are millionaires now. A lot of guys got a place in Key Biscayne. Portis got a place there. E. J. [Edgerrin James] got one. Reed got one. The bottom line is, you have to know who's with ya and who's going to help ya or hurt ya. He was a big-time player, and they tried to mess with him, and he wasn't going to take crap from anybody. So once they started messing with him, he wasn't the type to say, 'Okay guys, you won.' Whatever he did, he was going to win, and a guy could get in trouble that way.

"We started to get a lot of publicity back then. In fact, from the mid eighties until very recently, I could say the Hurricanes were more popular than the Dolphins or any professional sports team in Miami.

"So when guys would go out to clubs and there's trouble, it's the players that get pointed at. When guys got in trouble, they'd come in and say, 'What do you think, coach?'

"Most of the coaches in the school were pretty good guys, and we all had an open-door policy. Myself and other coaches like Art Kehoe did anyway.

"Some of them came from out of town. I was born in Miami. I became a fan before I became a coach. So I've seen these kids grow up, which is why they all felt comfortable coming into my office.

"I'll tell you what they didn't come to talk about. They'd never say stuff like, 'Hey Coach, I got laid last night.' They wouldn't talk about that. They felt they could talk freely about anything for any length of time, but not about that."

●

"It was Pro Day at the U, and the Washington Redskins had brought their entire staff down for a look at our guys," Soldinger began this story. "They had Coach Joe Gibbs, Don Brough, Earnest Byner, and Joe Bugel, and they're all sitting in my office. So they ask me to tell them about Kellen Winslow, Jr.

"I loved Kellen. He was one hell of a ball player. I said, 'Kellen is good.' Then they asked about Sean Taylor. So I said, 'He's been coming to our camps since he was six years old. I watched him in high school, college—that guy is real special.' Then they started asking me about Clinton Portis, who was at Denver at the time and his contract was up. I said, "If you go after him, you've got yourself one heck of a football player. He was one of the fiercest competitors I've ever had," And the rest is history.

"Things have changed quite a bit from even a few short years ago. I think that's why they're going through some growing pains at the University of Miami right now. Al Golden is super organized, but everybody there is treating football like a business. I don't know if that's a good idea. I think you have to make it personal.

"In six years we were sixty-four wins and ten losses under Butch and Larry, and Coker fired four or five guys. Just like that. Let me say that again. Hurricanes football was 64–10! Fired. For what reason? I don't know and I may never find out. Then they had a season when they went 7–6. Right now the team is under five hundred since they let us all go. That's the nature of this business. They didn't like 9–3, but they haven't seen 9–3 since they let us go in 2005.

"There was this incident in the Peach Bowl where Dwayne Bowe out of Miami Norland Senior High School, a receiver from New Orleans that played on LSU [Louisiana State University]… we got whipped up pretty good … one of the worst losses I've ever taken at Miami, and they swiped a ball out of the ball boy's hands as he was running it back to the locker room. Jon Beason went and chased him to get the ball back, and a huge fight broke out. After the fight, instead of firing Larry [Coker], they fired a bunch of the coaches and then brought a bunch of new guys in. They said to us, 'We're going in a different direction.' *What direction is that?* I wondered. *Maybe 74–0?*

"If I asked right now if they'd take 64–10 again, I bet they'd give up a right arm to get there. It was tough, because we were close to the kids and they were close to us.

"When I got hired on at Miami, it was like hitting the lottery. Some people hit the lottery and get a lot of money; I hit the football lottery. Kinda like Coach Spoelstra hit the lottery when he got hired to coach the Miami Heat. I mean, think about it. Start naming the guys [on the 2013/14 team: LeBron, Wade, Bosch, Allen]. Then there were all the guys I coached: Hester, Taylor, James, Reed, and Lewis. I loved it.

"Even our special teams players scored points. We had four more defensive touchdowns than Virginia Tech had offensive ones in the five years I was there. No one even acknowledged that. We were good. We were really good.

"As far as Sean goes, I am convinced he'll be in the Miami Sports Hall of Fame. Furthermore, he may even make it to the NFL Pro Football Hall of Fame. He's eligible. He played and has been out of the league long enough. I think he only needed to play three and a half years to get in, you know."

(Sean Taylor, along with Jonathan Vilma and others, will be inducted into the 2015 UM Sports Hall of Fame in April 2015.)

"I always said he was a special cat. He was with a group of guys that were all special. That's what made us great. They all wanted the same things, and Sean was their ringleader. He was respected by all those guys. Talk to Santana or Clinton; they loved and respected Sean. That's the way it was.

"Sean was one of the greats at the U. The way he ran, the way he hit, whatever he did was unbelievable. To tell you the truth, I wish I had him as a running back. He was an unbelievable running back in high school. I'm not talking average; I'm talking record-breaking unbelievable. He was just as good as the guys I coached when I was at Miami. He just leaned toward defense because he was so aggressive. As a matter of fact, when I go around to high schools, I show this PowerPoint presentation called 'Attitude of a Champion.'

"First there's desire. I use Devin Hester for that model because he didn't pass his SATs coming out of high school. So when the next year came around, he kept taking the test and finally passed. He knew once he passed he could have gone to any university he wanted but he always wanted to be a Hurricane so he stuck with it … with Miami.

"Hester entered the University of Miami as a sophomore and was the first player in the university's recent history to play in all three units of the game [offense, defense, and special teams]. He was drafted in the second round in 2006 by the Chicago Bears.

"Frank Gore wasn't ever going to play again because he blew out both of his knees. He had two flat tires; it was me who told him, 'Frank, you gotta play! God made you and built you to be a football player, and that's what you are.' So I use courage with him because he came back after rehab. He never got himself into the shape he was in when he first got there, because he had a little bit too much weight. He still had a great career at Miami, but not the way it could have been. He comes out early and ends up being drafted by the San Francisco 49ers. What a career he's having in San Francisco.

"I use Sean for aggressiveness. The three things you need to succeed: desire, courage, and aggressiveness. Sean certainly had all three. As a matter of fact, I remember when we were at the Pro Bowl and the punter had a bobbled snap or something and he takes off … Sean killed him. From everybody in the stands you could hear 'Whoooooo' … like that, you know? Some people said he shouldn't have done that to the punter. At the point, he was a runner, and that's the way Sean Taylor plays football.

"I was just telling Pete, Gulliver Prep had a couple of good players like Sean and Buck Ortega [Soldinger was good friends with Buck's dad, Ralph]. Anyway, they had a couple of guys that were pretty good. They were playing Immokalee High School, Edgerrin James's old team. James had already graduated, and they're playing over at FIU. So UM asked me to go out and watch the game. Because I was recruiting in Orlando, Tallahassee, Gainesville, all upstate, I didn't really get to see Sean play. The thing is I've known him since he's been in our camp, and I knew he was coming here. So they sent me. I was on the field that game, and he must have had two hundred forty or two hundred fifty yards rushing, something like that. I just said, 'Wow.' I wanted him as a back. I always wanted him as a back, but the defense kind of snatched him away from me.

"The thing I want everyone to remember about Sean is his passion for what he did," stated Soldinger. "A lot of people called him crazy. I called it passion. He was passionate about everything he ever did. Whatever Sean set out to do was done one hundred percent, and I credit his father Pete for that. Sean came to the U like that. It's nothing we taught him. He was a fabulous kid."

Don't Mess with Sean T.

Warning: This section contains the *N* word.

"There's a story about a South Beach club that's since been closed," Sean Taylor's friend T. J. remembers. "I think it was on Eighth Street. You wanna hear about a brawl? I mean it was all the UM players. This may be a story no one ever told. I'm talking about Vilma, D.J. [Williams], all of them. All of them came to the rescue this night. And it all started with me, Sean, Jackie, and one of Jackie's homegirls.

"Me and Sean walk in the bathroom, it's like three thirty in the morning, and there's a dude in there popping off at the mouth. He's talking to another dude while me and Sean were standing at the urinals. This is the truth. This one guys says, 'I'll knock any nigga out for twenty-five hundra dollars.' Nobody say nuttin'. We still pissing. So I look at Sean. We hear the conversation. He says, 'I'll knock *any* nigga out for twenty-five hundred.' So I say to Sean, 'Hey, you gotta say something.' So Sean says, 'Twenty-five hundred? Let me see the money.' Wait. It gets better. Well the fool pulls out his money. But he only got four or five hundred dollars. So Sean says, 'My nigga right here will knock you out fo' dat; I'm not gonna even fight you fo' dat.'

"So I say, 'Chill out. Chill out. The girls are out there. Let's get back out to the table.' So they looking at us, and I'm telling the dudes, 'No, we good.' ... Just then this *big* 6'6" chico come walking out of the bathroom stall ... bald head ... straight off steroids. He says, 'What's up? These guys want to get in on it? What, they got a problem?'

"Now I'm looking at Sean like, look what you got us in. So I'm saying to myself, 'Oh God.' So I'm telling the big guy, 'Nah, nah, we just joking. We heard these two guys talking, and there's no problem.'

126

"The big dude says, 'Nah, it sounds like you guys got some pressure.'

"I say, 'No problem, we good.' So we go back to our table and we sit down in the VIP area. So you know, during his last year at UM, the UM players got more love in the clubs than the Dolphin players. You hear what I'm saying?"

T. J. continues. "They [the UM football players] were the celebrities. All the groupies flocked to them. They would walk up to the front of any club and walk right in. So we in the VIP chillin', and we see this commotion kinda building up. So I say, 'Oh look, man. Those guys from the bathroom are trying to get to us.' So the bouncers are letting them in the VIP. And there's five or six of them. And it's just me and Sean. And I'm like, 'These niggas are trying to get to us.'

"We see one dude jump the railing. Now the dude that started the actual conversation that said he would knock anybody out, he's standing directly in my face. Sean is standing there, and we got the girls standing behind us. Nobody could get behind us, because our backs were against a wall. We can see everybody in our line of sight. So now the big chico is standing in front of Sean, and the dude that was talking is standing in front of me. And he's like, 'What's up? What's up?' This is a big black guy with four of his front teeth missing! And he's talkin' he'll knock anybody out? That's why Sean said anything in the restroom. It's because of all those missing teeth.

"So Sean was like, 'Let me get this quick twenty-five hundred dollars. You ain't got no teeth. I know I can knock you out.' So he's standing in my face, sayin', 'What's up? What's up? What's up?' So me and Sean give that last look at each other like something is about to happen. So we look at each other and kinda nod. By the time I turn back around, the guy is swinging. As he is swinging, I move out of the punch's way, and before I could hit him, Sean done cleaned him out. Like, night-night.

"When Sean hit toothless, chico jumped on Sean. So I take a bottle, just like in the movies, and hit chico in the head. *Boom!* He falls off Sean. Another member of the UM football team, D.J. Williams, is literally 2 feet away from us. He sees this whole thing going down. Now five, six guys are coming. Me and Sean are fighting the chico. Next thing you know, D.J.'s foot comes out of nowhere and we're all fighting the chico. So then D.J. is fighting somebody, I'm fighting somebody, Sean fighting somebody. Next thing you know, they throw us out the club.

"Wait. I get thrown out first. Then I'm at the front door trying to get back in. They won't let me in. They throwin' Sean out. They throwin' the other dudes out, and now we all on Washington Ave. in South Beach. So as we gettin' thrown out, Sean calls another club, and before you know it, here comes five, six more UM players. They on their way full speed, drunk, shirts off. I mean full speed down the beach. You see five, six big niggas just running. They get down there, and now it's on. We meet them halfway. We tell them what happened, and we say those niggas are standing right outside the club waiting on us right now. So now it's, 'Let's go.'

"So we're walkin', walkin', walkin' ... we get right in the front of the club, and this random dude is just leaning on a car ... we didn't even know this guy. Sean was leading us, in front, so when he gets to the dude leaning on the car, *pow*, he sneaks a punch at Sean. It was the worst idea this kid ever had in his life. Actually all that guy did was push Sean, but when he hit him back, *bam*, all you saw was this dude slither down the car door. Sean almost put him through the car. And it started from there. That's what started the brawl in the street. That guy hit Sean first. It was on. We were right in the middle of the street, in the middle of traffic. No police for fifteen, twenty minutes. It was a full-out brawl.

"But Sean didn't want this dude. He wanted the big chico. And that was who he was gonna get. By the end of the fight I had to stop Sean because he had him on a palm tree. I heard Sean say as he was poundin' him, 'I done told your ass ... *whop* ... I told you I was gonna get you ... *whop* ... I told you ... *whop* ... I told you.' He kept saying, 'I told you. I told you I was gonna get yo' ass.'

"So I'm like, 'Fool, we gotta go. We gotta go.' He said, 'Aw right, let's go.' He literally made sure he got his message across to this guy. 'I told you I was gonna get you. I told you I was gonna get you.' That's what he kept saying every time he hit him."

T. J. didn't know exactly how many were involved, so he guessed. "We had about eight, nine. I don't know how many they had. They were just coming out of nowhere. If you wasn't wit' us, I felt like you were against us. So I don't know who they had. But if you were standing around and you acted like you in it, and we didn't know you, you were gonna get it. We weren't worried about how many they were; it seemed like a lot though.

"So we all got in our cars. Left. There was no incident report. No police reports. No press; just the talk of the players. But yeah … what a night on South Beach!" T. J. said.

"Don't get me wrong now," Pete said. "At the end of the day he still had a good time. He still worked out, and he still was a good kid. It wasn't like you did a fight on top of a fight."

"No. The best thing was, people didn't try us," T. J. said. "We never got into fights [other than the ones described herein]. We never got in trouble. We were still around all the people that got in fights, that got in trouble, that did the wrong thing. But we didn't have time for that, because we were playing football or we were running track. We were always occupied. So the incidents that we got into we did because we were inexperienced. We shouldn't have done it, but we did it anyway. But hopefully you learn from your mistakes."

Pete Taylor

"When it came to practice and games, it was all business at the U," Pete Taylor said. "That UM team was focused. It was a determined team. The year 2001 was the last time UM won the national championship and won it in the Rose Bowl.

"I was very familiar with how to play the safety, corner, free safety, and strong safety positions. The U let us watch the guys practice, and I took advantage of those opportunities. I got to see how much fun Sean was having. So what I'd do is show Sean how to break on the ball—basically what to look for. I was trying to help him with the transition. Sean knew I was good at evaluating talent. For example I knew how hard and how fast he could go. What kind of talent was in front of him. When I saw some of the other players, I told Sean, 'Oh, you gonna give this guy a push. You're going to give him a run for his money.' And he looked at me with that 'Okay, Dad' look.

"He was working hard because he wanted to play. He had to earn his keep as a freshman. He was on the kickoff team and special teams. His main thing was to stay focused. He was just glad to be roommates with the guys. I got him a little car, and he had a girlfriend. He was interested in his books, having a good time, and playing.

"We had many talks about fans in the stands attending Gulliver Prep games," Taylor said. "I told him on a number of occasions not to worry about those sparse crowds because one day [he'd] be playing in front of thousands of people."

On the day of Sean's first UM game, there were more than 100,000 people in the stands at Beaver Stadium in what is affectionately known as "Happy Valley," home to Penn State. It was nearly impossible for Pete Taylor to find a hotel, what with the invasion of the 106,572 rabid Penn State fans descending on Happy Valley that day. By the way, that is the official number of seats, but according to Pete, a lot more than that can fit in that stadium.

"I called Sean on the phone to report in," Pete said. "'Sean, I'm here in Happy Valley, and there are one hundred six thousand people going to be at this game. Do you remember what Dad said? When you put the work in you're going to be playing in front of huge crowds and you're going to be enjoying life.'

"Well, that was the true start of his illustrious career, albeit a humble start. He played on special teams that day, and by the end of the game he was a little pissed off because he didn't get a lot of playing time and he wanted to make more of an impact. All the freshmen do."

Sean's father said to him, "You're a freshman, man. They didn't have to put you on the plane and bring you up nor put you in at all."

Then came one of those father-son chats. Pete said, "Let me explain something to you, Sean. When you're on the field and you see a guy wearing a different color than you and he has the ball, go after him and make the tackle. If you can't make a tackle, make sure you crack somebody. Put someone on their butt so they'll see you making your impact.

"From that day forth, every time he came down that field and if he wasn't in on the play, he'd level somebody. And that was it. Sean got to have his fun, and coaches noticed.

"So here I am at the game where I run into a bunch of Miami fans. We're walking around all over the place carrying on, making noise, screaming, and flashing the sign of the U. They're wearing their orange and green, and they're just as proud as can be. We had a great time."

Miami Hurricanes Coach Curtis Johnson

Coach Curtis Johnson has had a long and illustrious career coaching football. He spent a decade at the University of Miami and was with the winning 2001 national championship team. At UM, where Johnson was the kickoff/returns coach, he coached Andre Johnson and Santana Moss, and he also recruited standout safety Ed Reed.

After leaving UM, Johnson went on to coach under Head Coach Sean Payton at the New Orleans Saints (2006–2011) and was part of the 2009 Super Bowl XLIV winning team. As of this writing, he is the head coach at Tulane University.

Then Head Coach Butch Davis, Larry Coker, and Don Soldinger, along with Curtis Johnson, recruited Sean Taylor from Gulliver High School.

The interview Pete and I had with Coach Curtis Johnson was both entertaining and enlightening, and here's some of what he said.

🏈

"I've known Sean's father, Pete Taylor, for a long time," Coach Curtis Johnson began. "He used to come by with his son [Sean] and do some workouts at our UM facility; so most of the coaches were familiar with the Taylors. Sometimes Pete and Sean would come up to the office just to talk. But when Sean used to work out, you could see how athletic he was."

Coach Johnson first saw Sean play in a Gulliver Prep High School game at the University of Miami. According to Johnson, "Sean was one of the best athletes I'd ever seen."

Originally they were looking at Sean's Gulliver teammate quarterback Buck Ortega, but after seeing the dazzling Taylor, they thought it would be a good idea to start recruiting Sean as well.

Johnson said, "Sean, while not a kick return specialist, always told us that he could return kicks. In fact, he returned quite a few at Gulliver."

In one 2003 University of Florida game, the UM kickoff returner was Hurricane Devin Hester. That day he ripped one for a ninety-eight yard return. So naturally UF had no intention of kicking to Devin again. So UM put Sean in as a kick returner, and when UF kicked it to him, he ran it back for a touchdown. UF was out of options.

🏈

"Upon Sean's arrival at the University of Miami, we were all in the gym playing basketball. I wanted to test Sean's competitiveness and see how verbal he was, because he didn't talk very much. So some of the other

131

coaches were standing next to the basketball court, and I said, 'You know, we should play Sean in the best possible position for us. And I say he's a linebacker.'

"Sean said, 'Oh—I'm a defensive back.'

"I said, 'No, you're a linebacker.' Remember, I'm doing this just to pull his chain a little. I said, 'We'll give you a chance to play, but at linebacker.'

"Sean was so adamant; he kept saying, 'I'm going to show you, Coach. I'm going to show you.' I always teased him about the conversation after that.

"Sean was a very physical basketball player too. He was physical as hell. So we would have this ongoing rivalry, and we began to compete. It was strength coach Swayze, me, and a bunch of the other coaches and players who would get together and play basketball. Pete used to bring Sean around while he was still in high school, and we got into it hot and heavy. That's when I said in the staff meetings that I really liked this kid's attitude. Since he didn't say very much, Larry [Coker] asked, 'How do you know?'

"Here's another tidbit. Sean was very, very observant. I told Sean if he's going to play linebacker, [he needed] to watch Chris Campbell. So he would say, 'If I'm going to play safety, I'm going to watch Ed Reed.' Then he'd say to me, 'I'm going to be better than Ed Reed.'"

Johnson found that amusing but at the same time saw Sean's drive.

"I used to tell Ed Reed, 'You have to teach Sean,'" C. J. said.

"Sean didn't miss many classes, and he didn't miss many practices either. But a couple of times when he didn't call in, I really had to lay it on him. I had to remind him about the players that came through before him, and Sean was very receptive to that. I'll bet sometimes he didn't like me because I was always straight up with him.

"When it came time to practice, I would always put Sean against Andre Johnson because I felt Sean was the best corner. We had Antrel Rolle, Phillip Buchanon, but I always thought Sean had corner skills, so I would always put those two together. Sean would come to my office, and we'd watch film on corners."

With all that talent, deciding whom to put in and whom to keep on the sidelines was a challenge, to say the least.

"With our secondary, we won a national championship in 2001, and here's why: In our meeting room we had Ed Reed, Antrel Rolle, Sean Taylor, Phillip Buchanon, Michael Rumph, all good, all young.

Revelation

"Basically, in their first year, we relegated Sean and Antrel to special teams. They would have been starters anywhere else in the country. I will also tell you that as a safety, Sean had more of an impact on the game than Ed Reed did. Ed needed to push Sean a little bit, but I'm telling you, Sean was a better overall player."

Coach C. J. said that whereas Ed would motivate the team with his speech, Sean motivated with his actions. The whole secondary changed when Sean took over the leadership role.

"Incidentally, Ed had the most tackles, but Sean had the most knockouts," said Johnson. "I had to remind Ed when he went to the Super Bowl that he became a good DB [defensive back] because of Sean Taylor.

"I wouldn't exactly call this a weakness, but initially Sean was very cautious about everything and everybody. So in the beginning he didn't trust the guys in the field. He didn't trust what was going on as much as he should have, being a true freshman in a program like ours.

"I think his strength was his high confidence in his own athletic ability. I could tell he had a great background, because of Pete.

"I remember before the Florida State game he said he was going to take out one of their receivers because he was running one of his routes. And he did it. On one play he hit P. K. Sam so hard he turned him around three times in the air. But that's the kind of player Sean was. He had great speed for a guy that size.

"Tennessee beat us one time with their best player, but when we had Sean, he stopped this kid—caught him in midair and took him out just before he crossed the goal line. Sean basically took away the middle, and he did not let them beat us with this guy. There was no way he was going to allow him to score that touchdown."

Revelation

"Here's what people don't know. Sean spent a tremendous amount of time in the summer learning the game. He also spent a lot of time in the film room. He was putting in the work. So here are these guys in the film room watching then discussing the opponent's skills and plays. That's the kind of guy Sean was off the field," added Coach C. J.

"I got another story for you. I was one of the coaches in the 2006 Pro Bowl. Sean was a late edition. Now, the Miami guys had a reputation. Take [Jeremy] Shockey for example. Everybody thought he was this big shot, a big talker, but he wasn't. Maybe on the field he was, so when he got to New York, he didn't talk a lot, so he really didn't change much [after college]. Sean Taylor was a good kid; a great kid. But people around the league thought that he was a bad kid.

"So the Saints lost to the Bears in the NFC Championship Game, which was why we were coaching the NFC in the Pro Bowl that year."

At the Pro Bowl, "No one was showin' Sean Taylor any love, so he and Head Coach Sean Payton rode from the stadium back to the hotel together. After that, Payton told me that Taylor was the nicest guy in the world. He couldn't believe how sure he was, how he had it going on, how intelligent he was, and how great of a conversation they had. He told me, 'No one knows that kid is like that.' [Coach C. J. knew because he had coached him at UM.] Payton was very impressed and said he wanted to get Taylor on our team [the Saints]. But that wasn't going to happen. Payton wanted him because he was our kind of player. He was a Miami Hurricanes kind of player."

Changing it up, C. J. said, "I think Pete and Sean had one of the best father-son relationships I'd ever seen. They were almost like brothers."

Back when Sean played, the competition was fierce and everybody wanted to be great. C. J.'s thought on that competitive environment was this: "That was the difference between Miami then and … Miami now. I told you how we stacked the players up against one another. We had Vilma going against Sean Taylor, everyone against Clinton Portis, Sean against Andre Johnson—those were epic battles. Antrel and Roscoe [Parrish] and I don't think you'll see competitiveness like that again."

UM Roommate/Teammate Jonathan Vilma

Pete Taylor and I met one glorious Miami Monday afternoon at a restaurant called Brother Jimmy's, which is one of three owned by Sean's former UM teammate and freshman roommate Jonathan Vilma. This location is just a stone's throw from the American Airlines Arena (known as the Triple A), where the Miami Heat play their home basketball games. Brother Jimmy's is a Carolina-style barbecue restaurant and bar, and Vilma bought it and two other franchises with his partners, who are also former Miami Hurricanes and New Orleans Saints players.

Because of Vilma's connection with the Bountygate fiasco, the restaurant is rumored to have signs up banning NFL Commissioner Roger Goodell. The signs read, "DO NOT SERVE THIS MAN" and bear Goodell's picture, circled with a diagonal line through it. After a one-year ban, Jonathan Vilma was reinstated by the NFL.

After finishing a brief meeting in his office, Jon Vilma joined us at our corner table and was ready to talk—but only about Sean.

Sean came to the U the year after Vilma did. In Sean's freshman year, they were roommates. They also both played on the defensive side of the ball with the Miami Hurricanes.

🏈

"I remember my cousin came to visit from Germany and he kept telling me about this guy he went to Gulliver with—this guy named Sean—and he heard he was going to play for the U!" Jon Vilma said. "I kept telling him there's no way a guy from Gulliver Prep can go to UM and play top-notch football.

"He said, 'I'm telling you, there's this guy—Sean something ...'

"I remembered this guy Sean who I played against at Killian when I was at Coral Gables. But he kept telling me about this guy Sean from Gulliver.

"'He's really good; he's really good,' Vilma's cousin kept repeating.

"And I'm saying, 'Ah, I don't want to hear it.'

"My cousin continued. 'I'm telling you, he's going to Miami.'

"So I said, 'Yeah, I can't wait to see a Gulliver guy going to Miami.' Well, this Sean did go to Gulliver and had a tremendous career there, and after high school he did go to Miami." It was, of course, Sean Taylor.

Jon said, "I played against him one time when he was at Killian, but no times versus Gulliver, which is why I completely forgot about him. All I knew was he was good at Killian even back then. He was really good."

At the U, Vilma's first interaction with Sean wasn't much of an interaction at all. Sean was a safety, so they didn't see much of each other on the field.

"We had different coaches, so the only time I would see him was when we'd go eat, like in training camp," Vilma said. "So my first interaction wasn't much of one, besides saying, 'Hey freshman, go get me something to eat.' [Pete, Jon, and I all laughed at this.] Outside of that, there was really no interaction. I'd see him at practice, but that's it." It was soon after that the two became roommates.

At first, this Gulliver kid made a limited impact on the team. "The class under me was so talented that everyone was good," Vilma said. That was an understatement. That class included Frank Gore, Antrel Rolle, Sean Taylor, and Kellen Winslow, Jr. And they were all freshman.

"At first he [Sean] was on special teams and did a great job, and we knew if he had to step in for us, he could. We didn't know just how good he could be."

Sean came to UM as a safety, and his demeanor, his size, his attitude— everything—said he was a defensive guy. "It wasn't until a year or two later when I saw his high school highlights that I saw how good a running back he was." But according to Vilma, "He was made to play safety."

A particularly memorable play came in a game against FSU. Jon easily remembered. "It was my senior year, his junior year, and he was phenomenal in that game. He had two interceptions, returned one for a touchdown; he was lighting people up … I remember FSU had Greg Jones, who was a running back … a really big boy about 250 pounds. I remember on the goal line I hit him low; Sean Taylor cleaned him up high. We stopped them on fourth and goal. We ended up winning the game fourteen to ten or twelve, I can't remember now. It was one of those real 'knock 'em, bruise 'em' games. He was lights out. He was fabulous."

Jon Vilma went on to describe another Florida State game that took place during his junior year (Sean's sophomore year). They were significantly behind Florida State when all of a sudden they began rallying back. "Sean Taylor lit up their receiver, P. K. Sam." Vilma and others have described the hit with P. K. doing a complete 360 in the air before finally falling back to earth. "Right there we knew how talented Sean was. When you make plays like that in the biggest game of the season, you know you have something special."

"That was the momentum changer," Vilma said. "It didn't cause a fumble or anything like that, but when we talk about one of those hits that instantly energize a team—that was it. After that, we were ready to play. Ready to play."

Was Sean a trash talker on the field?

"When did he not trash talk on the field?" said Jonathan.

What did he say?

"I can't repeat any of that," joked Vilma.

"Yes, you can," I said, laughing. "This is an R-rated book."

"Nah, I can't. That's okay. That's okay. Just know he liked to talk. And he'd back it up.

"People knew he trash talked on the field and didn't say much off the field. So they didn't know what to make of him. He was really a good guy, a nice kid. On the field, he was aggressive, you know? Nothing wrong with that, especially playing football.

"I knew Sean on a more personal level because of the time I spent with him the night before games home or away," said Vilma. "Also, when I was a sophomore and he was a freshman, we were roommates, and the first thing we'd do at night was we'd wrestle. Our ritual was to wrestle before we went to bed. Don't ask me why. I think that's just how he used to get ready for games. That told me a lot about his competitive drive. He loved to compete and, more importantly, win. And that means win at anything all the time.

"You know, Sean Taylor was really misunderstood by a lot of people. When they saw him on TV, they saw the Sean Taylor who talked trash, and then they didn't hear much else after that," related Vilma. "So students would see him walking around campus, and he was one of those guys who didn't want to say hi. So what. To each his own. So what if he didn't feel like saying hi to you. He just liked to keep to himself. That's just how he was. It didn't make him a bad guy or anything. That's what people tried to make him out to be, but he wasn't at all."

Moving on to specific conversations, the roommates/teammates discussed anything and everything. "You just get to hear a man's thoughts, like thoughts about the season, thoughts about him coming here [UM], his family—things like that. At the time, he liked Jackie. He hadn't started dating her yet, so that's what we'd talk about."

Pete Taylor, who had been sitting quietly, listening to the interview, suddenly chimed in. "I'm surprised you said that before," he stated, remembering a conversation from a few minutes prior. "So he used to win at wrestling?"

"I think it was more like fifty-fifty," Vilma replied.

Pete said, "They reason I asked is, I used to wrestle, and uh, Sean would come home and he would say, 'Dad, show me a move.' So I'd show him a move. 'So if a person does a certain thing, show me that move; you know, how to get out of it.' So I would show him, but I didn't know why I was showing him these moves."

A curious Vilma asked, "So he would ask you that back then?"

"Yes," Pete said.

"Well, that's why," Jon said.

"'Well, show me how to do this or show me how to get out of that,' Sean would say. Why was he asking these questions about wrestling every weekend?"

"Pete, every night. It never failed. We'd go get our dinner, go upstairs, whoever got in there first would try to hide, surprise the next one, and bop! [Pete laughed at this.] We're wrestling. We're wrestling. We're wrestling," Jon explained.

"I did not know if they were doing freshman pranks on him or something," Pete said.

"No. No. No. And to this day I don't even know why we started wrestling."

Training Tip

"That was part of our regimen," Pete explained. "We would wrestle all the time while we worked out. We would do pushups. We'd do pyramid pushups; we'd do all kinds of stuff. With wrestling, you have to move all of your body. He'd stretch for forty-five minutes, and then we'd wrestle. That makes you stretch your body out. It makes you twist and turn. So he told me about the wrestling, but I thought y'all wrestled in the locker room."

"We'd do that," Jon said. "Those were the freshmen against all the upperclassmen."

"Oh?" Pete said, sounding a bit surprised.

"But that was in training camp. That was normal. Then, when we'd start playing the games every night, I was dog tired and he's jumping around."

"I couldn't figure this out. He never told me why. He never told me who, I just put ... well, he just wanted to know moves, and more moves and more technique," Taylor said.

"Cause we had two beds, and we'd go at it. We'd tear the beds down...."

"An eight-year mystery solved," I blurted out. Everyone laughed.

"That's good detective work there, young man. Another mystery solved by Chief of Police Taylor. And here's your key witness right here," I said, pointing to Jon Vilma.

"Never failed. Never failed. Yeah. So that's what I remember about Sean. I don't care what they put out there. That was the Sean I knew. A real good dude."

Jon Vilma spoke a little about "Mommy Jackie." Jon said, "I think he started dating her in the spring after we won the championship." Jon turned to Pete and asked, "Am I right on that?"

"Yeah," Pete agreed. (Actually Jackie and Sean dated a bit at Gulliver.)

"I met Jackie through Zulu [a girlfriend of Vilma's] first, so he didn't have to introduce me to her. I already knew her. So that's when he started dating her." The rest is history.

(See Appendix A for a recap of the 2001 season.)

15

UM Years Two and Three

Many of Sean's "greatest hits" didn't occur during games, but rather at UM practice, when he put some colossal hits on his own teammates, like Kellen Winslow, Jr., and Jeremy Shockey. Sean had only one speed—full—and that was the case even in practice.

Coach Curtis Johnson always stayed on his wide receivers—Kellen Winslow, Jr., and the others. Johnson noted Kellen always talked trash, saying things like "I'm the best receiver; no one can touch me." (This is how players would get into other players' heads.)

Once, after a hard practice, Kellen said something to Sean. So C.J. yelled out, "Kellen, we saw that last play, but you know Sean would have gotten you, right?"

Kellen responded, "No, Sean wouldn't have touched me." So on the next play, Sean leveled him. Coach Larry Coker sprinted thirty yards down the field and grabbed Sean's facemask. Screaming at Sean, he said, "What the hell are you doing? You are going to kill all my damn players and I won't have anyone else left!"

Remember, they were still kids, so Sean said that Kellen started it. No matter. Kellen continued to talk trash, but by the end of the season, he had become a good friend of Sean's.

◗

Pete Taylor

"Before his third year, I decided to go to New Orleans," Pete Taylor said. "I took both of my sons and my little nephew. We were going to the Tom Shaw speed camp in 'Nawlins.' [Shaw trained Hall of Fame cornerback Deion Sanders.]

"At camp we were having fun. Just as I was planning to go to Bourbon Street, I twisted my ankle, so I headed back to the hotel to put ice on it. I told the big guys they could go out, and they both came back with tattoos."

Kids!

"The next day, we drove over to the facility and worked on drills. That's where I met Darren Sharper. He was the defensive back for the Minnesota Vikings at the time, and he was there working out."

On the second day, Sean was supposed to be back at school. C. J. called because UM defensive coordinator Randy Shannon was angry. The team was mad that Sean wasn't there. They wanted him back in Miami on the next plane. So Pete flew Sean back.

That night Sean called his father and said something to the effect of, "Dad, guess what? I'm on the seventh string. They were pissed at me. It will be a while before I get back to first."

"At practice, C. J. told me about Shannon," Taylor said. "Sean was now playing seventh string against the third and fourth stringers. So he's making hits back there. *Pow. Bam.*"

The other players couldn't run through him; Sean was laying people out. He was once again proving his worth. Sean used tight end Jeremy Shockey as a tackling dummy at practice. He worked his way back up to first string in a matter of three weeks. Before the first game, "I sent Sean a message: make sure you have your ass in place," Pete said.

"Florida State games were some of my favorites, and mostly because Sean was pissed off at Bobby Bowden, their head coach, for not recruiting him," Taylor said. "They had this running back, a bruiser named Greg Jones. If you've ever seen him, you'd know he is about 6'3" and weighs 250. If you've ever seen Greg Jones run, you know he was definitely 'the man.' He comes up the sideline, and Sean levels him and practically throws him out of bounds. He comes up the middle and Sean hits him and levels him again. UM won that game 49–27, ending their [FSU's] unbeaten home winning streak of fifty-four games.

"When we played Ohio State in the championship game, once again our team played awesome. Sean was all over the field, making hits against some of the great members of that team. That was 2002, when Miami was up for the national championship.

"The game was very intense, and Ohio State won when Miami was flagged for pass interference at the end of the game. Damn. We should have won that game," said Taylor.

Back in those days, the U was awesome. Ed Reed played for the University of Miami and was drafted by the Baltimore Ravens in 2002. After he left school, Reed returned to the U with seven other players.

"I'll never forget this," Pete said. "These eight guys were all going to be drafted, and Sean had an opportunity to see these guys as they all drove up in their new Cadillac Escalades. At the time, that was the hot truck of the day. So they all drive up and park in front of the university.

"It was great how past players would even come back to the university just to work out. That place was always about hard work, coming back and giving back to the young guys. That was very inspiring for me and Sean. Especially when you go to games against Ohio State or Florida State, you'll see these guys fly back in to show their support.

"In 2003, we played Florida State again in Tallahassee. That's the game where Sean flattened P. K. Sam in a helicopter spin in one of the most classic plays I had ever seen. But he wasn't done. He leveled their receivers and their running backs. He had a hell of a game."

That game was played in the rain, and Bobby Bowden was left scratching his head. At the end of the game, Bobby said, "We played against the team, but that Sean Taylor *was* the damn team today. We couldn't block his ass. We couldn't stop his ass. We couldn't do nothing. He just disrupted our whole offense."

It was one of those careers. Sean just got better every year. He listened to the coaches. He gave the fans what they looked for. He played hard. "He just did what Sean do!" his father said.

"While in his third year, I went into the UM locker room," Pete said. "There's a big U on the floor. All the players are walking by, but they are walking around or across the U but not on it. So stupid me, I step on it. Sean hollered at me, 'Hey, Dad, you don't step on the U!' That was the first time I understood what pride and sacrifice was and what it meant to be a part of the core. Every team has something they use to motivate the players. That was what the U used. There was something special about that team; they believed in and cared about each other. They had 'the swag.'"

In the back of his mind, Sean thought that if he did a good job, there was a possibility that he could come out after his junior year.

"Pete Hernandez [former UM assistant compliance director] called Lloyd's of London, and they told him I could insure Sean," Pete said, "So we took out a policy against injury which assured him if he got hurt, he would be taken care of for a long time. Well, at least he'd have money in his pocket anyway. Since he was insured while playing for UM, we really didn't worry about him getting hurt. Sure, it would hurt his draft status, but like I said, he would be covered."

So there you go. Sean was insured for about a million while he was still in school. And he continued to play.

"I'll never forget it. In his fourth or fifth game of his junior year, he makes a tackle and messes up his labrum. He had a little tear. He thought it wouldn't hurt, but in his sixth game it hurt to play. This kind of injury takes about eight weeks to heal. The trainer came over and said they didn't want him to have surgery during the season. The team was doing well. They were on a roll. And I said I just wanted another opinion.

"We went to Dr. Uribe for that second opinion. He suggested surgery, but it was up to us—we could do it now or after the season.

"As a father, once again I thought about what happens after a horse race when the horse can't run anymore. They take him to the pasture and shoot him. Horrible thought. I know. But this was the second time Sean was facing major surgery.

"I told Sean he could be ready for the second game after surgery. There was a game midweek that wasn't that important, then they had a bye. I tried convincing Sean and his coaches he'd be ready for the second game. But no one believed me.

"When we told the UM head coach he was going to have surgery, Coker was concerned. In a phone call from the coach I explained that he needed to have surgery, but I [could] guarantee Sean [would] be back [in three weeks]. At that time, they went along with me and agreed with me. I said, 'He's maybe out for one game.' Then they had a bye coming right after it. They accepted my decision."

So Sean had surgery on his right shoulder in the middle of his junior year. That's why his strength in that arm was weak that season—he couldn't bench press with that arm. He came out of his quickie rehab, and in the next two games before the season ended, he gave spectacular performances.

"We take him home, and a week later he goes back to school. Everything did come out normal. It didn't matter to the team, though, because they still thought Sean wouldn't be able to play the next few games.

Pete knew he could play, so they simply put extra padding over his shoulder. Pete told him "to use his left shoulder more to make tackles." He didn't have to change sides. It didn't make any difference. Sean was Sean.

"He came out swingin' the next few games, and he whacked people as if nothing had happened to him. It was like he hadn't missed a game. They ended up making it into the bowl game. That was the game where we really thought he'd be coming out. It was UM versus their longtime rival Florida State in the 2004 Orange Bowl. This was the first time these state rivals actually met in a Bowl game! Miami won it but it was very close, 16–14, and Sean had a great game that night.

"I supported Sean's decision to come out and go pro after that game. I left the game to go fax the declaration papers for him, and at the same time, Sean was being interviewed, declaring that he was going into the draft."

Shortly afterward, the NFL announced that Sean Taylor was entering the 2004 draft.

Three and out

Athletes in their junior year can go to the compliance office to petition the NFL to see what their draft status is. Many do so. At the time of Sean's declaration to enter the draft, the prediction was that Sean was going to go in the first round as a junior. So the Taylors did their homework and saw that Sean was rated as one of the top safeties coming into the draft. Not only that, but he was also being considered for the 2003 Jim Thorpe Award. (See Appendix B.)

"The night of the award, I felt Sean was the best safety, but it wasn't up to me. So we went to Orlando to see if Sean was going to win it. He didn't. Unfortunately for Sean, he came up a little short. A kid from Oklahoma by the name of Derrick Strait won it. We accepted that. But it still pissed Sean off, because he knew he was better than all of them and even thought he was the best college player that year, period."

Sean's neighborhood friend Mike added, "As a junior at UM he was the defensive player of the year, but all you heard about was Vilma and everything about offensive player Winslow. At the end of the day, he always had a plan, and that was to be the hardest hitter. In his sophomore year he'd still let you know he was going to hit you hard. His junior year, he'd let you know he could get that ball out of the air. He accomplished everything he set out to accomplish; there was nothing left to prove. So it was time to move on to the next level—the professional level.

"Three short years later, he was just unstoppable. If he could have played in the NFL maybe another four more years ... he would have been a Hall of Famer."

Scouts, Agents, and Access

Pete Taylor was given the opportunity to watch on-field UM practices and talk with Sean on the sidelines. He got to meet with Sean's professors and his tutors. "It was and always will be education first in my family," said Pete Taylor. "Any of my kids will tell you that. I was there so I would know what my child was doing. Now, you can't direct them all the time. But you can see who's hanging around, who's who—who knows who and what they wanted.

"I found out there is something called runners. Runners are the people who are paid to get on the inside [and are often seen on the sidelines]. They want to meet you; they want to take you out to a dinner. 'Everything will be taken care of,' they'd say.

"One thing you're always cautious of is, if someone buys you something, before you know it, someone finds out and you're suspended for team or NCAA violations and you can't play until your name is cleared. I talked to Sean about that. I told him he had to make sure not to get into any alleged jams, because you'll have to fight like hell to get out of it. So he was always aware of things of this nature. The good news was, his name really didn't come up in any of those discussions, and he was never suspended. The guy you want to ask about this [Sean] isn't here, so I can only tell you what I know.

"During the school year, affiliate scouts from NFL teams might reach out to the kids and coaches, but the teams don't contact you directly. They're not supposed to talk to you until after you have an agent. Having an agent also means you are no longer a student/amateur athlete, and you could lose your scholarship. That's why timing is so important, especially if you decide to finish school and get your degree.

"Scouts always hang around practices and the like, but they can only go so far. So they have runners who find out where you're going out to dinner that night, what movie you're going to see, etc.

"It was kind of interesting to learn how it all worked. If they couldn't talk to Sean, they'd call me. Or they'd call someone in the family close to Sean to see if they can get to him. But we made a commitment not to agree to anything without talking about it together first. We both kept our word. After he declared, it's just like high school recruiting, where college coaches put the hard press on to get your kid to play for their college. The NFL and the agent business are just the same. Agents and wannabe agents will call you and try to get your kid to sign with them; sometimes they'd call until twelve midnight. There could have been fifteen to twenty agents contacting us."

The agents usually contact the players, but it was the teams that had direct contact with Sean. They would call his cell phone to ask if he had an agent yet. The protocol is to work through the agent, as the agent knows the business. If players say they don't have an agent, the teams will request to meet directly.

Good agents serve many purposes, and most earn their commission. All of them negotiate contracts, but there are those who will go the extra mile and do everything for their clients. You might say they serve as in-house concierges, and in no particular order they'll make dinner reservations, answer the mail, secure endorsement deals, and basically handle most or all of their personal affairs.

Remember, the agent is only as good as the player. There are a lot of agents in the business, but many of them don't have any business or connections. They don't have the players either.

Then there are those agents who are in it for personal gain. Nevin Shapiro, for example, an agent and ardent UM football booster, got in trouble for running an elaborate $930 million Ponzi scheme. During the investigation, Nevin told authorities about the thousands of items given to seventy-two players over the course of eight years. The issue is, no NCAA player is allowed to accept anything from agents.

"The bottom line? So many people hung around the parks, the field, and the campus, and before long they just started to look familiar; like they belonged," Taylor said. "In the end, you never knew who was up to no good, because after a while they just blended in.

"Now here's something I want kids to understand. Once you're part of the U, or any college, you can't be talking to agents. But once you declare for the NFL draft and the school thinks you have an agent, you can no longer participate in college activities. Therefore, anything Sean did, like continue going to school, he'd have to pay for out of his own pocket. This is because when the school knows you're leaving, they also know agents are starting to put things in motion, like take the kids to workout centers to get them ready for Pro Day in March, the combine, and the draft in May. There's no time to play around. So immediately after declaring for the draft in January 2004, at the end of his junior-year football season, Sean stopped working out at the University of Miami."

When Sean first came out, Edgerrin James, who was then with the Indianapolis Colts, had an agent Sean liked. That agent wanted a meeting so he could talk to Sean. Sean started discussions with this agent without his father's knowledge.

"I had spoken to Drew [Rosenhaus] and thought he was a better fit for Sean," said Pete. Sean decided on Edgerrin James's agent, with whom he felt comfortable. "What could I do? I had to support his decision."

Kids Will Be Kids

In Pete Taylor's opinion, "kids are supposed to be at the university for an education, but what tempts them are the parties, the girls, and having fun. When you're a football player coming from a prime-time school like UM, everybody wants to be around you. The kids are going here and there, and you start feeling left out if you don't go. If you have good people around and family members who care enough to keep you grounded, you'd be okay. Kids are still going to do what kids want to do. That's just the nature of a kid.

"Let me give you an example. [After Sean had already declared for the draft], I'm sitting home one day and Sean calls me. He said, 'Dad, I'm catching a flight to Las Vegas in thirty minutes.'

"Number one, Vegas is not called Sin City for nothing, and number two he's going to go out there and maybe someone is going to try and strike a deal with him and have him sign papers, and before you know it, it's going to be crazy.

"So Sean said, 'Yeah. I'm going to fly out there for a day or so, and I'm coming right back.'" Being that Sean was no longer a UM student, he could come and go as he pleased. So he went out there with a couple of friends.

"In any event, a red light went off. 'What are you going to Las Vegas for?' I asked. 'Are you sure you're not going to meet with anybody? You're not going to meet with an agent and you're not going to get caught up in some stuff are you?'"

"No. I'm just going to go out there just to have a good time," Sean told me.

I said, "If you do meet with anyone, would you at least please tell me before you do something crazy?

"He said, 'Yes, Dad.'

"He jumps on the plane and he flies out there. He calls me to tell me he landed and where he was. Nevertheless, the whole time he was there I thought someone was going to set him up with a deal. A deal I may or may not approve of and he may regret.

"Sean gets back from Las Vegas with no deal and no agent. Needless to say, I was relieved."

Sean Taylor
Photo Album

Early Sean

Baby Sean (Photo courtesy of Pedro Taylor)

Baby Sean and his grandmother Connie Dingle
(Photo courtesy of Connie Dingle)

Youth basketball
card (Photo courtesy
of Pedro Taylor)

Sean and half brother Joseph
Taylor in tuxedos (Photo
courtesy of Pedro Taylor)

Sean on the Florida
Razorbacks (Photo
courtesy of Pedro Taylor)

Sean looking sharp in a
tuxedo (Photo courtesy
of Pedro Taylor)

The High School Years

Killian High School Basketball Team photo
(Photo Courtesy of Killian High School)

Gulliver Prep Football Team photo (Photo courtesy of Gulliver Schools)

Sean on the move for Gulliver Prep (Photo courtesy of Gulliver Schools)

Buck Ortega and Sean Taylor—friends on and off
the field (Photo courtesy of Gulliver Schools)

Sean going full speed for Gulliver Prep (Photo courtesy of Gulliver Schools)

It takes more than two opposing players to catch Sean T.
(Used with permission of Alex Mena and the Miami Herald)

Sean eludes a tackle (Photo courtesy of Gulliver Schools)

Sean wins one for Gulliver Prep (Photo courtesy of Gulliver Schools)

Gulliver Prep
Assistant Coach
John McCloskey
(Photo courtesy of
Gulliver Schools)

Gulliver Prep's Memorial Scoreboard (Photo by Steven Rosenberg)

Gulliver Preparatory
Football

National Signing Day
February 7th, 2001

Sean Taylor

Will sign his letter of intent to play football at The University of Miami on Wednesday at 8:00 am in the Gulliver Library.

2000 2A State Champions
1997, 1998, 1999 District Champions

Football Office ✦6575 N. Kendall Drive ✦ Miami, FL 33156
Phone (305) 666-7937 ✦ Fax (305) 665-3791 ✦ Beeper (305) 290-9947

National Signing Day Flyer (Flyer courtesy of Pedro Taylor)

Proud dads and sons on National Signing Day—Ralph & Buck
Ortega and Sean & Pete Taylor (Photo courtesy of Gulliver Schools)

The University of Miami Years

Sean Taylor on the Miami Hurricanes (Photo courtesy of The University of Miami and JC Ridley)

UM players posing in the weight room (Photo courtesy of The University of Miami and JC Ridley)

UM players working out on stationary bikes (Used with permission of Alex Mena and the Miami Herald)

Sean leading the gang tackle for The U (Used with
permission of Alex Mena and the Miami Herald)

The Sean T.
Miami Swagger
(Photo courtesy
of The University
of Miami and
JC Ridley)

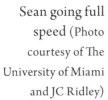
Sean going full
speed (Photo
courtesy of The
University of Miami
and JC Ridley)

Sean breaking away (Photo courtesy of The University of Miami and JC Ridley)

Sean on the move (Photo courtesy of The University of Miami and JC Ridley)

Super Taylor's
flying acrobatic
catch (Photo
courtesy of
The University
of Miami and
JC Ridley)

Sean laying out his opponent (Photo courtesy of
The University of Miami and JC Ridley)

Sean scores ... again ... for The U (Photo courtesy
of The University of Miami and JC Ridley)

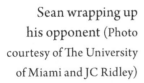

Sean wrapping up
his opponent (Photo
courtesy of The University
of Miami and JC Ridley)

Sean doing a little high stepping (Photo courtesy
of The University of Miami and JC Ridley)

Sean holding half sister
Jazmin Taylor (Photo
courtesy of Pedro Taylor)

Sean immortalized on UM practice field wall (Photo by Samuel Jazzo)

Life after the University of Miami

Sean Taylor (Photo courtesy of Pedro Taylor)

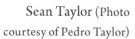

Sean Taylor (Photo courtesy of Pedro Taylor)

NATIONAL FOOTBALL LEAGUE

January 21, 2004

Sean Taylor
University of Miami
15542 SW 107 Place
Miami, FL 33157

Dear Mr. Taylor:

Congratulations on being invited to the National Football League's annual scouting camp at Indianapolis (National Invitational Camp) for draft-eligible players. Selection to participate in the combine means you are one of the best prospects coming out of college football this year.

In recent years, a few players have failed to take advantage of the opportunity to display their skills. There is no downside to participating fully at Indianapolis. The Combine provides you with the unique opportunity to work out in the presence of representatives of all 32 teams, including head coaches, general managers, personnel directors, and owners. A favorable first impression in any job evaluation is a positive step.

Moreover, the turf at the RCA Dome is one of the fastest surfaces in the National Football League, as demonstrated by the performance of past and present Indianapolis players such as Marshall Faulk, Marvin Harrison, and Edgerrin James. In addition, the schedule of events has been arranged so that you will not run your 40-yard dash until approximately three days after the administration of the Cybex test, permitting sufficient recovery time.

If you do not perform as well as you expected, you have ample opportunity to schedule other timing and testing sessions at your campus or residence in the weeks that follow. Since NFL teams will base their evaluations on your best workout, you should take advantage of any opportunity to display your skills in Indianapolis.

Best wishes for a successful workout and a long career in the National Football League.

Sincerely,

JOHN BEAKE
Vice President for Football
Development and Operations

Sean's invite letter to the NFL Scouting Combine (Courtesy of Pedro Taylor)

Sean Taylor
15542 SW 107 Place
Miami, Florida 33157

February 09, 2004

Mr. John Beake
NFL Football League
280 Park Avenue
New York, New York 10017

Dear Mr. Beake:

Thank you for your recent letter and gracious invitation to participate in the scouting camp at Indianapolis. I look forward to the opportunity to demonstrate my abilities as an athlete.

I am exciting in participating in this unique event that will hopefully open many doors in my NFL career.

Thanks again for the invitation.

Best regards,

Sean Taylor
ST/pt

Sean's thank you letter to the NFL (Courtesy of Pedro Taylor)

The Washington Redskins Years

Washington Redskins' Super Bowl trophies (Photo by Steven Rosenberg)

Sean Taylor and Coach Joe Gibbs (Photo courtesy of the Washington Redskins)

Sean Taylor addressing the media (Photo courtesy of the Washington Redskins)

Sean pregame on the field in Tampa Bay (Photo by Steven Rosenberg)

Sean Taylor rockin' rookie jersey #36 (Photo
courtesy of the Washington Redskins)

The Cowboys can't catch Sean T. (Photo courtesy of the Washington Redskins)

Sean going full speed (Photo courtesy of the Washington Redskins)

Sean Taylor putting a wallop on Philadelphia Eagle Mike
Bartrum (Photo courtesy of the Washington Redskins)

Sean's pick and run (Photo courtesy of the Washington Redskins)

Teammates Carlos Rogers and Lemar Marshall congratulate
Sean after he scores (Photo courtesy of the Washington Redskins)

Sean and half brother Joseph Taylor (Photo courtesy of Pedro Taylor)

Extreme Sean Taylor Fans

Extreme Redskins fan Michelle Harding and Sean (Photo by Casey Ward)

Angel Sean digital art (Digital art courtesy of Rachel Gresham)

Gone, but not forgotten...

Sean Taylor
1983-2007

Sean Taylor digital art (Digital art courtesy of
Rachel Gresham, Photo by Josh Miller)

Charlie White's Sean Taylor 21 arm tattoo (Photo by Charlie White)

Steve Tosi's back tattoo (Photo by Millie Sarmiento)

Sean Taylor SUV tribute (Photo by Charlie White)

Sean Taylor SUV tribute (Photo by Charlie White)

Painted football by Paul Nichols (Painted by Paul Nichols, used with permission of Paul Nichols Art)

Fan standing next to Sean's locker located on the Club Level, FEDEX Field (Photo by Steven Rosenberg)

Wes Johnson holding his framed Sean Taylor jersey (Photo by Kimberly Barrett Johnson)

With Special Thanks

Pete Taylor & Dan Snyder (Photo courtesy of the Washington Redskin)

Sean Taylor & Former Gulliver Schools owner
Mrs. K (Krutulis) (Photo courtesy of Gulliver Schools)

Gabriel Taylor: The Next Generation

Sean's younger brother Gabriel making a tackle for his Florida
Razorbacks (© Kelsey Toomer/Royal Photography, Inc.)

PART IV

16

The 2004 NFL Draft

Warning: this chapter contains the *N* word.

AFTER THE REDSKINS TRADED DEFENSIVE CORNERBACK CHAMP Bailey to the Denver Broncos for Clinton Portis, Portis knew the defense needed some help. At the time, Portis thought Sean Taylor was the man for the job.

Every time Clinton Portis walked by Daniel Snyder or Coach Joe Gibbs, he'd whisper, "Sean Taylor … Sean Taylor." Former players always come back to UM, so they always know who the really good players are. "Sean Taylor … Sean Taylor," Portis said relentlessly.

Multiple sources have confirmed that Portis also said to Gibbs, "Coach, I've never seen anyone hit a guy the way Sean hits guys."

🏈

"About a week before the draft, my shy son came to me and said, 'Dad, I'm thinking I'm not going to Radio City [Music Hall in New York where the NFL Draft takes place]. I just want to have a party with friends and family in the Keys where we can all get together and celebrate.' Sean's friend had a place in the Keys, and that's why he decided to have the party there.

"Well, the NFL knew where we were going to be," Pete Taylor explained. "So the morning of the draft, the local media, ESPN, and the NFL TV cameras and uplink trucks were out in force, all set up and ready to get the partygoers' reactions when the announcement was made.

"By the time the last guest arrived, there must have been a hundred fifty people inside that house," Pete Taylor said. "We're sitting around eating and talking, just having a good time. The draft started around twelve o'clock in the afternoon, and history tells us the draft can take some funny twists and turns. I went over to Sean to first congratulate him, then to ask if he was ready."

The first team to pick was the San Diego Chargers. They picked Eli Manning. "Before the draft, Eli, Sean, and a few other guys signed Reebok deals, so we were all in New York for the signing and the shoot," Pete Taylor said.

The Taylors speculated Sean was going to be a top-ten pick, but they didn't know exactly which team would take him or when he would be selected. "So I told Sean, 'You wait and see. You're not going to be on the board that long,'" his father said.

"Things were getting a little tense, because sometimes teams are on the clock for a long time, especially if they want to trade up or down. Some teams wait until the last minute to get a deal done. Then we get a call welcoming Sean to the Redskins ... Boom. It was over. We got to enjoy the moment. Then we took some pictures, shook hands, and before you knew it, everyone left the party," Taylor said.

Sean's friends T. J. and Mike were also at that party. T. J. related to me that before the draft, newly hired agent Drew Rosenhaus (Sean's third agent) begged T. J. to make Sean cut his hair. "Tell him if he cuts his hair, he'll go top ten," Rosenhaus said.

T. J. said, "So one day we were sitting around and I said to Sean, 'Hey, cut your hair.' He said, 'Nah, my nigga, it ain't happening.' We both had afros, so I went in the bathroom and took the clippers and handed it to Sean, and I said, 'Here, give me a haircut.' So he cut my hair off. I guess that bothered him. Not even fifteen minutes later, I hear him in the bathroom ... buzzzzzzzzzzzzzz ... So I go in there, and I'm like, 'Yeah, he's getting a haircut.' Next thing you know, he's the fifth pick in the draft. I think it was a surprise to us. It was just crazy. So when we left the party, we turned it up for like two days."

Of the top 32 players chosen in the star-studded 2004 NFL Draft, there were six UM Hurricanes: Sean Taylor, picked fifth by the Washington Redskins; Kellen Winslow, Jr., picked sixth by the Cleveland Browns; Jonathan Vilma, picked twelfth by the New York Jets; D.J. Williams, picked seventeenth by the Denver Broncos; Vernon Carey, picked nineteenth by the Miami Dolphins; and Vince Wilfork, picked twenty-first by the New England Patriots,

Other '04 draft notables included: the aforementioned Eli Manning, chosen first overall by the San Diego Chargers; Larry Fitzgerald, chosen third by the Arizona Cardinals; Philip Rivers, picked fourth by the New York Giants; Roy Williams, picked seventh by the Detroit Lions; DeAngelo Hall, picked eighth by the Atlanta Falcons; and Reggie Williams, chosen ninth by the Jacksonville Jaguars.

For the complete first round draft list, check out:

http://insider.espn.go.com/nfl/draft/rounds/_/year/2004

17

Conversations and More Life Lessons

LIKE MOST FOOTBALL PLAYERS WHO GET DRAFTED, SEAN WAS PULLED IN a million different directions. "So many people call you. They try to be around you. They want to fly you here and there, and we're talking to everybody from friends, family members, agents, to sponsors, to charities, you name it," Pete Taylor said. "The bottom line is, you have to be very careful, because you don't sign a contract until maybe July or August. There's nothing guaranteed until you sign. The other thing is, you don't have anything in your pocket yet. Therefore, you're still just a draft pick. Of course your name has value to some people, but once again, you have to be very careful not to overextend yourself, etc.

"One would think a person wouldn't need to prepare himself to have a lot of money. Players do, though, because so many of them don't know what to do when they get it, how to save it, and what to do so they don't go wanting when their playing days are numbered. So I spoke to my friend Kellen Winslow, Sr., all about the subject. Being a former player in the NFL, he had some insight to share with me and Sean.

"Kellen Winslow, Sr., was like a mentor to me. We talked about how important it was to give the draftee some money in his pocket so when he gets it for real, he wouldn't lose his mind. Remember, his son was about to enter the draft as well. Turned out Kellen Winslow, Jr., got picked sixth— right after Sean, who went fifth.

"We would always talk about the business of agents, marketing, dealing with financial planners, etc. He was very well-versed on a lot of things, and that's how we were able to set up Sean's finances when he came out. He was going to be financially set.

"When Sean knew he was about to come out, me and Kellen Winslow, Sr., talked. Kellen said, 'You know what, man? I know my boy is good with money, but I don't know how good he is with a lot of money. So here's what I think I'm going to do. I'm going to call Wells Fargo, and I'm going to take out a loan. I'm going to put a lot of money in his hand and let him fuck it up. I want to see how long it takes him to spend it. He can do whatever he wants to do.'"

After their talk, Taylor and Winslow, Sr., agreed it was a good plan. They each took out a $250,000 loan for their boys so that when they got the big money they wouldn't "go crazy."

"If you give someone a lot of money and they're already used to dealing with it, they won't do crazy stuff afterward," said Taylor.

The dads wanted their sons to hold, feel, touch, and smell big money. They told them to do whatever they wanted with it so they could see how easy it could be to blow through $250,000. It was a test of sorts.

Pete continued. "Another advisor I sought out was my friend Jim Ferraro, who was also a former agent and very knowledgeable about the NFL. His son played for Gulliver, too. He also had financial connections, and he advised me about obtaining money for Sean as well.

"When Sean signed his contract, all he had to do was repay the loan to the bank," said the forward-thinking Taylor. A surprise came when Sean put a good deal of the $250,000 aside in a bank account and didn't blow through it like he could have.

Taylor added, "It worked out great, because when Sean finally started receiving his NFL money, he didn't go crazy."

During our conversation with Sean's friends T. J. and Mike, Pete asked, "Did you guys know about this?"

Mike said, "Well, yeah. Who do you think he's going to spend the money with?"

Pete said, "Yeah, but you may not know the back story ... the things that I know and did."

T. J. countered, saying, "Yeah. And you didn't have to know everything we know."

Pete chuckled and then continued, "What I tried to do as a parent was expose Sean to different things, knowing that he would do some good and some bad stuff. It's like getting a new car. What are you going to do when you get it? You're gonna get in that bitch and driiive ... but after about a week, you know what you may say? 'I should've gotten the other damn car I was looking at.'"

T. J. said, "Sean was good with his money."

Mike added, "Sean always had at least a hundred dollars in his pocket since eleventh grade."

Pete said, "And where do you think he got the money from?"

"Of course we know," Mike said.

"I always made sure he had a couple of dollars in his pocket so he wouldn't be a burden on no one else," Pete said.

"Straight up. And when he got into that other class, it wasn't even a hundred no more; it was like, keep a stack on you. It was like, have it someplace where you can go touch it. You never know what's going to happen and when you're going to need it. If you can't put your hands on the stack, you ain't out here livin', bro," said T. J.

"You gotta have a hundred. That was our line," Mike added.

T. J. then said, "As far as the money and being that flashy guy, wanting you to know 'I'm Sean Taylor,' nah, that wasn't him. Sure he was that superstar on the field, but when he came off the field, he threw on some Chucks [Chuck Taylor sneakers] and some shorts and a T-shirt and he'd be ready to go. It was all about better living. Ya feel me? It was like if he had it, we had it. Yeah. And it wasn't you gettin' it because I got it. You gettin' it because you earned it. He wasn't that type of person. It was never like, a handout. He'd walk up to people and make people do certain things to get certain things from him because he didn't want you to feel like it was a handout. People respected him for that, because he looked out for everybody. See what I'm saying?

"There's lots of stuff we can't even speak about when it comes to what he did for his family. That's for another day. Just take it as this. There isn't anything he wouldn't do for his mom or his brothers and sisters. And when I say anything, I mean literally anything. He'd walk around barefoot ..."

Then there was just silence.

After a short pause, Pete continued, "When these guys get a big payday, they're really not sure what to do with it. Sometimes they're just scared to make a move because they had to work so hard to get it and they don't want to lose it. You can't make someone do what he or she doesn't want to do. Advisors can only advise."

Wisely, Pete had conversations with his son about his future (although Sean would never be able to benefit from that wisdom). Pete explained, "There was a point where we were sitting and talking and I said, 'Listen, Sean. How much would it take for you to retire? And how much would you like to live off of? How much money would you like to have as a monthly income? And when he answered the question, I said, now multiply that by twelve months, then multiply again by fifty years if you think you're going to live that long. Only you can decide on what lifestyle you'll want to have and for how long, but you have to prepare for that.'"

Sean and his dad had a frank discussion on a subject most families do not have with their kids. They talked about the possibility (not the eventuality) that maybe someday Sean would become addicted to drugs, alcohol, or even pain pills. Perhaps there'd be a career-ending disability. Who knows?

"It's not as far-fetched as you might think," Sean's father said. "How many times have you seen or read about this or that celebrity checking into a rehab center for some kind of addiction? Plenty."

So Pete Taylor asked his son, "How much do you think it would cost to set you straight? Three hundred thousand? Four hundred thousand? Well, whatever it is, put that money aside just in case."

The two spoke about the off chance Sean would become permanently injured and the kind of lifestyle he wanted if he couldn't play another day in his life.

"When Sean first went into the league, he was going to have several million dollars in the bank. I tried to make Sean understand that's only going to last for so long. 'Sean, I want you to keep in mind you haven't met the league minimum of three years yet to get any kind of pension from the NFL.' So over a ten-year period, the number he came up with was six hundred thousand before he could touch his retirement money.

"So I said, 'Based on the contract you signed and what you're going to get, you have to put your money in certain places so it will get interest. You don't even need to get high interest. You just want to keep it somewhere it will be safe. This is the no-risk money for later, and don't touch it. What I was trying to convey to Sean was, you can't let yourself go broke. You have to put money away. If you make it past the league minimum, you'll have your retirement income. Basically, you have all your bases covered.'"

So Sean knew about saving. He also felt he still had obligations to family members and friends.

Life Lesson

"I know for some of you this is going to be hard to fathom," Pete Taylor explained. "After all, we're talking about big numbers. What I do want everyone reading this to understand is, even though you may not be at this place in your life, I'm telling you, don't spend everything you got. Watch what you put on credit cards, and don't let yourself go into debt. And please put money away for later. If you don't, you may be very sorry."

There's another thing Sean and Pete spoke about—the community programs and schools that helped him get to where he was. Pete advised him to always give back—to Gulliver, the University of Miami, and even to local programs that give a little extra help to kids who need it. "He did that, and I loved him for it," Pete said.

"I taught Sean early, as I did with all of my kids, to write down goals," Pete said. "Every day that you don't make one of those goals means you probably failed at something. Where do you want to be now, and where do you want to end up? So it's not like Sean wasn't guided in the right direction. He had goals, and if he stumbled, there was nothing wrong with that, just as long as he gave it his best.

"In life, everyone is going to see obstacles on the left, the right, and even right in front of and behind them. So if you fall down, you just have to look up. Now, the thing about Sean was, once he set a goal, he not only reached it, he conquered it."

18

The Redskins Got Their Man

WITH THE DRAFT OVER, IT WAS TIME TO HAMMER OUT A DEAL WITH THE
Washington Redskins. Pete Taylor continued talking to people, gaining
knowledge and understanding of the process. He made it his business to
learn about finances and the "business" of the NFL.

Pete said, "Sean and I meet up, and he is going to sign with this agent
[one not of dad's choosing]. 'That's okay,' I said. 'If that's what you'd like.'"

Sean was working out a deal, but something came up. "Wait a minute!
Now I'm thinking Sean was going to change his mind and go with Drew
[Rosenhaus], but in the middle of the process he decides to go with yet a
different agent," said Taylor. "So I jump on a plane with this new agent and
fly to Long Beach, California, from Miami, where the meeting with then
Redskins general manager Vinny Cerrato was to take place.

"I get there about three to four p.m. Miami time, noonish their time. By
nine p.m. I'm dead-ass tired. So I take a nap. I wake up two a.m. Miami time,
eleven p.m. West Coast time. Despite the hour, the agent, Vinny Cerrato,
and I decide to go out to eat. Little did I know they roll up the sidewalks at
eleven o'clock at night in Long Beach—no beer-drinking, no nothing! So
I'm like, damn, there's nothing to do. Then I remembered what Shaq said.
'After eleven o'clock, you can't party outside of L.A.' So now I'm experiencing
this for myself, and I realized he was telling the truth. No wonder so many
Californians come to South Beach to party!"

After just a couple hours of sleep, it's meeting time.

"Vinny comes in the meeting room after his morning jog and workout. He's all refreshed and looking casual but sharp. The agent arrives. So now it's Vinny, me, the agent. We get Sean on the phone because he didn't want to make the trip to L.A. Now we're going back and forth, and at the time, the Redskins needed him in camp, but we needed to get a deal done first.

"After day one, Vinny and the agent can't get a deal hammered out because Sean rejects it. We know how much Sean is going to make, but as everybody knows, it's all about the incentives. There's also the part on *how* you want to get paid. Do you want it all up front? Do you want it back ended, or do you want to put it in a trust of some sort, etc. So here I am in Long Beach, and I have to spend another night. I'm thinking, *Now what I am going to do tonight?* I didn't do much of anything.

"So the next morning, things start up again. We go back at it, and by four p.m. we finish up and have a deal. Sean approves. It's also agreed upon that Sean is going to report for the beginning of camp. So now I get to fly home to Miami."

So it was a done deal, right? Well, that's what Sean's father thought. With a signed deal, Sean was expected to report to camp. Pete took the red-eye home, and by the time he landed the next morning, Sean felt there was something not quite right—and all of this, after he approved the deal.

"So now Sean is thinking he should have signed with Drew Rosenhaus, the agent I originally recommended. Sean voids the contract, fires his agent, but still pays the man his commission, and Drew Rosenhaus is hired to revise the deal."

Agent Drew Rosenhaus

Agents have to do a lot of things to keep their clients happy, and sometimes they find themselves dealing with some very unorthodox situations. Agents make it their business to know everything about their clients: their likes, dislikes, wants, needs, and deepest desires. From Drew's perspective, he and Sean had some ups and downs, and the client and person who first came to Drew was not the same person who lost his life far too early.

In 2003, sports agent Drew Rosenhaus recruited Sean Taylor out of the University of Miami once he declared he was foregoing his senior year and entering the 2004 NFL draft. Over the years, Drew had represented many of UM's superstar athletes, and he had a direct line to Sean from both teammates and UM alumni. In the case of Sean Taylor, Drew was hired as Sean's agent of record, but was later released by Sean. After some contentious negotiations with the Washington Redskins and other agents, as stated, Sean decided to nix his deals. Working through clients Santana Moss and Clinton Portis, Sean contacted Drew and rehired him after a separation of just a couple of months. After Rosenhaus was rehired, he represented Sean for the remainder of his NFL career up until the time of his death.

🏈

"The thing that jumped out at me about Sean most was his progression—not so much as a player, but as a person," Agent Drew Rosenhaus said. "Sean had a chance to become one of the better safeties to play in the NFL. I really thought he had a shot at a Hall of Fame career. What I was really impressed with, though, was his maturation off the field.

"My relationship with Sean had its ups and downs, and at the beginning there were some maturity issues. However, the young man developed into a really outstanding person. In the beginning he was a high-maintenance client and a little hard to work with. In the end he became a wonderful client and a terrific human being. He had a great personality, but at times he could be a bit moody, especially early on."

There were times when Drew would go days without hearing from Sean. "Toward the end of his career, toward the end of his life, he was very professional, very accountable, and a great communicator," commented Drew.

Speaking about the Redskins, Rosenhaus said, "He developed a great relationship with his head coach, Joe Gibbs. He also developed a very special relationship with Defensive Coordinator Gregg Williams, as well as the team's general manager, Vinny Cerrato." But his best relationship was with Redskins team owner Daniel Snyder. "I had a lot of conversations with all of those gentlemen about Sean throughout his career."

Drew spoke of the "Sean highlights" he experienced while representing him and beyond. They were as follows:

- NFL draft day, when Sean became one of the highest-picked safeties of all time;
- watching Sean play in the Pro Bowl in Honolulu;

- Sean's being inducted into the Redskins Ring of Fame; and,
- Sean's being voted one of the top eighty greatest players in eighty years by the Redskins fans in 2012.

"I remember doing a lot of off-the-field things with Sean. These things were very important to him and his dad, who was very active in the community. Pete Taylor did a lot of really positive things including giveaways and charitable endeavors. His father was very committed to giving back, and Sean followed that lead. I always thought that Sean and his dad had a very good relationship."

After a brief pause, Drew continued: "We were on very positive terms when he passed away. I was one of the speakers at Sean's funeral."

♦

Pete Taylor

"So now my son Sean is part of the Washington Redskins, and just like when you're drafted, you go visit the team. Mr. Snyder sends his private jet, *Redskin One*, to pick Sean up in Miami.

"Sean, Drew Rosenhaus and I fly up to Washington, DC's Dulles Airport. I didn't even know there was a Washington Dulles Airport until we flew into it. I guess we flew in there because it's close to Ashburn, Virginia, near the Redskins training facility. When we get to Redskins Park, we meet with Daniel Snyder and Coach Joe Gibbs.

"The thing about Mr. Snyder is, he always treated us like we were part of the family. When we met, you could tell he was honestly happy to see Sean, and he says to me, 'Have a seat, Pete.' So we sit down inside his office and have a little chat. You always imagine what this day is going to be like, but when you get there, you realize just how special the occasion really is. Snyder then tells us the Clinton Portis story—about how every time he saw him [Snyder] or Coach Gibbs, he would whisper, 'Sean Taylor ... Sean Taylor.' Portis repeats, 'Who you gonna draft? Sean Taylor ... Sean Taylor.' So we're sitting around just laughing and having a good time."

Pete remembered the initial meeting with Snyder and the Redskins fondly. Along with Mr. Snyder's and Joe Gibbs's offices, Sean was shown the

Redskins facility, including the football practice field, the weight room, the locker room, and then the pressroom.

"Everybody was genuine and welcoming, from the secretaries to the trainers, as well as the other players. They all shook Sean's hand and gave him a great big welcome.

"Now remember, he had just been drafted, so basically it was just a meet and greet. We didn't get to do anything," said Pete. "After all that, there was a press conference introducing Sean to the media, and that's when Sean gets his Taylor number 1 jersey, which is held up for the cameras."

Washington Redskins Team Owner Daniel Snyder

A meeting was set up at Redskins Park, in Ashburn, Virginia, at noon on June 6, 2013. Pete Taylor and his (current) wife Simone Taylor met me outside the main entrance of the park fifteen minutes early. We said our good-mornings, chatted for a moment, and entered the official reception area, where we were asked to wait until an earlier scheduled meeting was over. We did. Just beyond the receptionist we could see the Redskins' three Super Bowl trophies serving as a reminder of the Super Bowl glory years.

Within a few minutes we were ushered into Washington Redskins owner Daniel Snyder's conference room, which is located just outside his office. We were there to meet him for a rare interview. Once inside the conference room, we were greeted by Tony Wyllie, Redskins Senior Vice President, Communications, and Mr. Daniel Snyder.

"Please come in and sit down," Mr. Snyder said. After the Taylors received their hearty handshakes and hugs, we did.

"I'm normally not dressed this way," Snyder added. That day he sported a crisp button-down shirt, slacks, and tie. "I usually come to the park in sweats, but I am flying to New York for some NFL thing after our meeting. Sit down and eat something."

At that point I responded, "Mr. Snyder, you sound like my mother!" At that he chuckled (I think) and the ice was broken. I must admit I was a tad nervous meeting Mr. Snyder. After all, his reputation as a tough cookie preceded him ... by about one hundred miles. So that morning before I left the house—don't tell anyone, but—I availed myself of one of my prescription "calming pills," as I didn't know what to expect. Did I mention I was nervous?

Once we got started, I was pleasantly surprised as to just how congenial Snyder could be. Then again, I was with the father of the man who in my opinion was arguably Dan Snyder's favorite player of all time.

Since we were there at noon, a platter of assorted Asian foods was sitting on Mr. Snyder's conference table waiting for us.

As we all began to eat, I asked if Mr. Snyder would mind if I recorded his comments for this book since (A) I don't write very fast and (B) what I don't write or record I'd never remember, and I wanted to get it all down and get it right as with every interview I conducted. He agreed to my request.

During our initial small talk, Mr. Snyder asked how the project was going. I responded by saying, "It's good. Very good." And I offered to show him what we had done so far—the first two hundred pages of the manuscript that I printed off for the occasion. I handed the spiral-bound, unedited, raw version of our manuscript to Mr. Snyder. With his eyes widening, he began to read. "This is good. This is very good," Snyder said, looking directly at me. My internal smile turned outward just listening to his kudos. He continued to skim through, coming across some names from the past—those of coaches and players alike. Now looking at Pete, he said, "Wow! I haven't seen these names for a while." He then asked about some of those players, how they were doing, and whether Pete was still in contact with them. Taylor answered in the affirmative. Then Snyder said something like, "Great job!" and handed the manuscript-in-progress back to me.

❧

All psyched to begin, and without prompting, Mr. Snyder said, "Let's start with the first time I saw Sean Taylor in person. I saw him play with the U. In fact, I remember talking to all the coaches and scouts [about him] in 2002. In our opinion, we were talking about the best college team ever assembled, the Miami Hurricanes."

Mr. Snyder attended the national championship game in Arizona. The staff was actually scouting Willis McGahee, who would enter the draft the next season; but in that game, Willis hurt his knee.

Snyder recalled, "I remember watching Winslow at tight end; Andre Johnson at receiver; they had D.J. Williams; fourteen to fifteen players who could easily go in the first round of the draft. It was really exciting to see.

"I saw this safety, Sean Taylor, and I asked myself, 'How can a player that big run like that?' Wow. That was the first time we had seen him. Two years later, I hired Joe Gibbs and we had the fifth pick in the draft. In the off-season we traded for and signed a really good quarterback named Mark Brunell. We also had a pretty good defensive team, so the big internal debate was, do we draft Kellen Winslow, Jr., or Sean Taylor? I met and spent time with both here at Redskins Park, and I'll never forget Joe [Gibbs] coming down [to the office] and saying, 'You decide.' I said, 'No, you decide.' And we went back and forth, and it became a joke between us, because it was a tough call.

"Before the draft, C. P. [Clinton Portis] used to come by my office [open the door] and say, 'Seaaann Taaaylorrr. Don't be an idiot. Seaaann Taaaylorrr.' Then he'd close the door. There were two players we were coveting, and we had to make a decision.

Revelation

"We had two star UM players, and I remember that Winslow overslept a meeting, and that ended the debate; we took Sean."

●

The conversation transitioned to the organized team activities (OTAs) that were taking place on the practice field adjoining the building and visible from the large conference room picture window.

Resting on a table near the window were three gigantic pairs of binoculars that could have easily have been used by a lookout in the crow's nest on an old galleon or battleship. These no doubt got good use by Mr. Snyder and his staff as they scouted their own players during practice from behind the conference room's picture window.

While OTAs are not mandatory player practices, well, let's just say coaches don't take too kindly to anyone who misses them.

Next we chatted about summer training camp, which was moving about a hundred miles south to Richmond, Virginia. Would the new facility be ready in time? Snyder said he hoped so. It was, and in the summer of 2013, that's where practice was held for the first time.

Without mentioning his name Mr. Snyder also reported on the condition of his prized quarterback Robert Griffin III, who had knee surgery immediately following the team's playoff loss to the Seattle Seahawks in December 2012. Snyder said he was doing very well, running, and was at about 75% speed on the treadmill. He seemed excited about that.

Mr. Snyder asked us, "Did you talk to C. P. or Tana [Santana Moss] yet?"

"We've been trying to get a hold of them," Pete Taylor said. "They are either not answering the phone or they've changed their numbers. They do that a lot, you know."

At that point, Dan Snyder stopped eating and called his secretary to ask if Santana Moss was out on the field. "If he is, tell him Mr. Snyder wants to see him in his office," he instructed her. Since OTAs were in full swing, there was a good chance he was out there on the field.

When we were finished eating, Mr. Snyder began speaking about one of his favorite "sons," Sean Taylor.

According to Snyder, they had a quiet, reserved superstar in the beginning of the 2004 season. This was the first pick that Joe Gibbs and Daniel Snyder made together.

"Sean came in young, just very, very young, probably the youngest draft pick we had taken in the first round. What was he? Nineteen? Was he nineteen coming out or twenty?" he asked, directing the question to Pete Taylor, who was sitting at the opposite end of the conference table next to his wife. Actually, Sean was twenty-one in April 2004.

"Generally, that's very young for your first-round draft pick. Robert [Griffin III] was twenty-two when we drafted him.

Revelation

"Now, I'm not going to sugarcoat this, but after we drafted him, when Sean first got here, he had a seizure downstairs because he was taking supplements the guys gave him to lose some weight fast," Snyder said. "He got dehydrated. I was like, 'What the hell?' I don't know who gave him what, but he was out cold.

"If you try and lose a lot of weight quickly for training camp after holding out and you're late … put the recorder on pause for a minute," Snyder said. "Santana is here."

●

With the recorder on pause, Sean's former teammate, Santana Moss, knocked gently on the closed conference room door. Tony Wyllie let Santana in. When Tana saw Pete Taylor and the rest of us in the room, he breathed an obvious sigh of relief. Who knows? Maybe he thought he was getting cut by the big boss himself. (This was clearly not the case.)

After the Taylors and Santana Moss exchanged hellos and hugs, Mr. Snyder told Santana to take a seat. He told him about this book "we" are doing (referring to himself, Pete Taylor, and me).

I wondered if I had heard Mr. Snyder right when he used the word "we." Anyway, Snyder asked if he had any stories to share. Santana said, "Yeah. We played together, so yeah, I have stories."

Snyder then asked Santana to give Pete his current cell phone number so he could set up an interview with us. Santana agreed. I guess rank really does have its privileges.

After a few Pete-and-Santana pictures were taken and a few more "bro hugs" had been given, Santana left the room. Mr. Snyder was once again ready to continue telling stories.

With the recorder back on, Snyder said, "Sean was young and shy when he got here. He was so reserved until he knew you. You might say he was guarded. As he relaxed over the years, it was a lot of fun watching him grow up.

"He was the best defensive player I'd ever seen play football. I constantly get into arguments whenever I see guys like Ronnie Lott or other [high-profile] safeties. I always tell them I had the best safety to ever play in the NFL on *my* football team and he got taken from me."

●

"Sean got two fifteen-yard penalties playing against the Philadelphia Eagles. It was 2004 or maybe 2005, and Sean and Terrell Owens [a.k.a. T.O.], who was on the Philly team, were getting on each other. After the game, Sean and Gregg [Williams, the coach] were going at it [nose-to-nose] in the locker

205

room. Gregg said, 'What the fuck did you do?' We won the game, mind you. But he's screaming at Sean. T.O. had one or two catches for maybe eighteen yards ... nothing ... he was obviously scared of Sean, as most receivers in football should have been."

Gregg had a way of getting in a player's face, really on someone. He was pretty much on Sean, and Snyder was in the locker room, just watching.

"After continued badgering, Sean said, 'I hit the m-f'er in the face, okay? I hit him in the jaw.'

"I was dying, because at first when Gregg asked, 'What did you do? What did you do?' Sean said, 'Nothing. I didn't do anything.'

"'You did something,' Williams said. 'You got two fifteen-yard penalties ... personal fouls!'"

"'I punched the m-f'er in the face!' Sean sneered.

"He was fun to be with ... he was quite the character."

On personal time, Sean used to rip on Snyder about his eating habits. "He used to lecture me for eating crap food," Snyder said. "Yeah. He ended up getting very healthy with his food. We used to have barbecue Fridays, and I used to eat all these ribs, everything you could think of down there, and he was just harassing me ... 'Look at all the stuff you're eating. Ugh. It's not healthy,' Sean would say to Snyder.

"He was maturing, what with the baby, going to get married, studying football. It was fun to watch."

In Sean's rookie season there was an incident in Miami concerning Sean's stolen ATVs. You'll get the full story later. During that incident, Joe Gibbs, Sean, and Mr. Snyder were on a conference call. "Sean was still in Miami and mostly quiet during the entire call. I was pleading with him to just move up to Virginia and get out of any involvement with anybody wanting anything, doing anything ... just come up here. All he could say was, 'Okay, okay. Can you guys stop yelling?'"

About Sean's work ethic Mr. Snyder tells this story: "Sean practically lived here at the facility. He had an odd schedule when it came to his daily multiple workouts. We once spoke about how he always wanted to be ahead of his competition. He felt like if he could work at night while the others were sleeping ... he'd always get ahead. Have you heard this before?" Mr. Snyder asked.

Pete nodded.

"It was great to see. I would be on the treadmill, and I'd look over, and there's Sean. He took DVDs home. He worked. He just worked.

"He became less interested in hanging out with the guys and having a good time [a story corroborated by many]. He was much more focused on his career, his family … he was changing." (This too was repeated by many.)

Practices became a whole other story. "He took everything very seriously, but it was his teammates, [Fred] Smoot and [Shawn] Springs, who used to kid him and say, 'Stop knocking us out in practice! You're hurting the DBs [defensive backs] all the time. Will you stop?' The players said they got hit more in practice than they did in the games.

"He just loved the game. He was jacked to go out there, and he was the last to leave. He'd do gassers after practice was over. He was the real deal."

I asked what single Sean play stood out for Mr. Snyder—whether an interception, a hit, or a score.

"That would have to be the play Sean made that clinched our playoff spot in a game against Philly in 2005. At the time I said, 'Why did he do that? Why did he do that?' He went flying across the goal, and that's how you get hurt … like the guy that does a tumble that ends up hurting his back. So I was like, 'He's gonna get hurt … argghhh.' But he scooped it, scored, and changed the game for us, and we won.

"So we got in the playoffs after winning six in a row. If there was one play, that was it. But there were always plays. I thought he … ask Santana when you talk to him about the game against the Green Bay Packers in '07. We played Green Bay in the rain. After the game Tana was upset because he dropped a couple of balls. Sean was very upset because he had only two interceptions and he felt as though he should have had four or five. Everyone was upset for one thing or another, so in the locker room I said, 'Guys, we have to move on.' Those two were friends. Santana was really upset. Sean was upset, and he got everybody going [more about this game later].

"So many different plays—it was just the beginning of a career.

"One afternoon C. P. was at the whiteboard doing his thing, playing the role of coach," Snyder said. "He even had a headset on. 'The reason we have such great defense,' Portis said, 'Sean Taylor. When we call plays, we call Sean Taylor, because that's how we call plays.' It was very funny.

"Portis has a lot more stories. They were friends for a long time."

After a long pause, I broke the silence and asked if there was anything else he wanted to add.

"No. But whatever you want to know, I'll tell you," the owner of the Washington Redskins said.

So I continued. "I've heard you treat your players as if they were your own sons and they appreciate you."

"I try to," he responded. "I try to. Things happen."

For most of the interview Tony Wyllie sat quietly at the head of the conference table, kitty-corner from Pete Taylor. But now he had something to add.

"It's a business to some degree," Tony said.

Snyder added, "You're dealing with lives and families. It's a different thing. Chris Samuels just got married last January and he had his first baby; really cute, named Junior. A *biiig* baby." Everyone laughed. "That poor woman." Everyone laughed again. "He's a three-hundred-thirty-pound man. So they had a *big baby boy*. He's really cute. Beautiful wife. We went to the wedding last year."

Tony Wyllie wanted to remind us of this: "Speaking of being generous, how about the trust fund you set up for his [Sean's] daughter."

"There's still money going into it," said Snyder. "Anything that gets sold from his stuff, she gets. She should be set forever."

Changing the subject for a moment, Pete said, "There's something I want to say. After Sean's death, Mr. Snyder flew us up. He had everyone assembled in a room: his staff, his financial people—he made it so easy for us. We didn't have to go searching. We had all the assistance we wanted, and then I had the opportunity to talk to the team for a moment."

Mr. Snyder interrupted. "Do you remember the story of Sean never cashing his paychecks? He didn't care about the money. What he did was stick them in a drawer. He just wanted to play football."

That was a new one on me!

Taylor nodded and added, "I think he was one big kid. He just wanted to have fun. He just wanted to play."

"He was fun. Just fun." Visibly upset and with clinched fists Snyder added. "And they took him from me. They took him from me."

After another long pause, Pete spoke up. "Sean wanted to learn the tendencies of what the other team was doing and how he was going to defend against them."

"He didn't like wide receivers," added Snyder. "He would study each one of their tendencies on film and everything they've ever done. He worked hard."

"I'll tell you a little secret," Pete said. "I guess you were playing Minnesota the week before. I heard you had a turf football field. So we come down. We came to work out one night. We worked out in the gym, then we go to the field. There was a coach inside the gym working out, and he asked us what we were doing there at ten o'clock at night. So I said, 'Just working out.'

"We go to the field, and I start quizzing him. 'How would you defend Randy Moss?' We worked on getting a forty-five-degree angle on him. Then I said, 'What do you have to do when you get there?' So I think he got a pick in the end zone that game."

"I've never seen anyone that big," Snyder said. "I'd never seen Randy Moss in person before, and I said, wow, he is huge. He was gigantic. I was like, 'Daaaamn!'"

"The funny thing about that is," Taylor continued, "during Sean's eleventh grade, I took him over to the Chris Carter camp in Boca Raton [Florida]. Randy Moss and Chris Carter owned this speed camp. Chris was working out with Randy, and then they go to the field on Thursdays to do field work with the kids. And so all that came back. He remembered Randy's moves. Like you said, he wanted to know the tendencies."

Snyder asked, "Do you remember after the game what happened?"

Taylor said, "Uh, not really."

"Randy Moss left the field early, before the game was over."

"That's right. That's right," Pete and I said simultaneously.

"Randy was mad, and he did something I've never seen before. He just left the field. He just walked off. The Vikings got rid of him after that. They traded him. That was the game. I was scared to death of that guy. He was huge. Sean was a big man, but Randy Moss was the tallest, lankiest guy and he would run like ... oh my gosh ... that's a receiver? He just had a weird body. He ran like a gazelle with those long legs."

Changing the subject, Snyder said, "Sean would have liked Robert Griffin III. He would have said, 'It's about time you got someone like that to help us.' He would have been all over me."

"How do owners and general managers decide what players will fit their system?" I asked.

"They have one-on-ones, and they ask a lot of questions, primarily football questions, like, how long have you been playing? What are some of your highlight moments? There are personal questions, dinners, and introductions," Snyder replied.

Addressing the next question to Pete Taylor, Snyder asked, "Was Sean instantaneously relaxed, this reserved, at the U? Or did it take him a year or two [to come out of his shell]?"

Pete responded, "No. It's just that … it's about respect."

"It takes a little time for him," Snyder said.

"It's business. When you get to this facility, it's the owner that's right, the coaches that's right. I'm here for a job. Also remember this was really the first time he had been away from home. I'm not here to—"

"But before he could relax," Snyder interjected, "it takes him a little time. He would be guarded."

The topic of Sean's workouts came up again. "At the U, Sean would work out in the middle of the night. He would jump the fence with his buddies and run track," Taylor said.

"He used to run the stairs in the middle of the night [here]," added Snyder. "What happened to the U? They are terrible now."

"They're coming back," Taylor screamed. Everyone laughed.

"I was just talking about them in the draft room," Snyder shouted. "They said on TV that the first U player went in the fifth round this year. What happened to my guys? What the hell happened? It used to be four guys in the first round, a few more in the second. It used to be the whole draft was [imitating a sportscaster], 'We had eighteen from the U drafted and …' It used to be phenomenal."

"I just talked to the head coach down there just the other day—Al Golden—and he said, 'Make sure your son Gabriel is at the camp this year.' So I'm going to set him up. So we'll see," said Taylor.

"How old is Gabriel now?" asked Snyder.

"He's the same age as your son. Remember?" answered Taylor.

"My son is huge. He'll be 6'6."

"What?" Taylor exclaimed.

"And he's mine. My wife's father, who died of a brain aneurism, was 6'5", 280 pounds. He was a big, big man. On her side, my wife is the smallest of the family, but she's tall. So I have two huge kids and one little one. He's got a nine-and-a-half shoe at ten-and-a-half years old."

Taylor said, "We saw your son at the Dolphins game, and my son and yours were about the same size, so wow!"

"In Miami?" Snyder asked.

"Yes," answered Taylor. "And that's where I met [pointing to me] Steve [Rosenberg]. Gabriel was made player of the week, so his whole team was to be honored on the field. We got a chance to watch practice from the field, but what we didn't know was that we'd be on the side of the Redskins. Steve was on the field for pregame warm-ups with his sons [and his big group of Skins fans] too, and that's where he approached me."

Changing the subject, again, Snyder asked Taylor, "Were you at the Hall of Fame game, Sean's first game in 2004?"

"Yes," Taylor responded.

"He had the game-winning interception in the fourth quarter, and I remember Gregg Williams torturing him by not putting him in until the second half, and I was pissed. I was like, at practice he was the best player on the field from day one. He was awesome on defense. And Gregg was like, 'He's a rookie. I'm going to treat him like a rookie, and I'm not going to put him in until …'

"So I remember years later I told Williams, 'Do you remember that shit you did with Sean?'" Everyone in the conference room laughed. "I won't draft any more defensive players unless you play them. Not in the first round. I will not do that, because I know that if they were on offense, they would play right away. So I'm not playing with you." In a mock Williams voice, Snyder said, "'I got it. I got it. Yes, sir. Yes, sir.'

"He tortured Sean as a rookie. That's what Gregg was all about. In that [Vikings] game he got two interceptions. So in the locker room I said, 'Ayyyy, why don't we keep him on the bench?'" Everyone in the conference room laughed again. "Ayyyy …"

Taylor said, "Why don't you talk about your competitiveness? I'll never forget that."

"I want to win," Snyder said. "I feel really bad when I don't."

"You like to play racquetball," Taylor cut Snyder off.

"Yeah. I like to play racquetball and a round of horse with the guys; I used to tell the guys about Smoot. Smoot can't play. He was just terrible. Next time you see Smoot, tell him he sucks at horse. Tell him I'll take his money again."

Mr. Snyder became a little agitated, and with his knuckles turning a lighter shade of pale, he said, "I would have had quarterbacks on both sides of the field right now on defense and offense, ... and they took him from me." He was clearly pained. "They took him from me." And then, silence.

Snyder turned to Wyllie and said, "Why don't you take them around and see if there's anyone else they'd like to ... [speak to] here?"

Wyllie agreed.

At this point the interview was over. Pete Taylor asked Mr. Snyder if he could take some pictures with him. Snyder recommended taking the photos in his office.

On Mr. Snyder's desk was a picture of him with Sean Taylor just about to fist bump. When Pete asked Snyder about it, he said a fan sent it to him and it had been on his desk ever since.

19

Sean's Redskins Rookie Season

Pete Taylor

It was the summer of 2004 when Sean Taylor joined the Washington Redskins. "At first when I used to call Sean, he was either home or working out, because he really didn't know anyone up there in Virginia. Oh yeah— occasionally he'd run to the store to buy groceries," Pete said. "When we'd talk, he used to say, 'Dad, you don't know. They practice in the freezing cold. They trying to make us tough.' He also said, 'It could be raining or freezing cold, and we're still practicing.'

"I thought he was kidding, but he was dead serious. I thought they practiced in a dome, but that didn't happen until years later. They finally got one, but you know, sometimes you got to get ready for Green Bay or the Bears in midwinter at their house. So practicing outside makes more sense, since neither team played under a dome."

Pete Taylor on Redskins Coach Joe Gibbs

"When Sean first got to Redskins camp after he was drafted, we were going to meet with Coach Joe Gibbs in preparation for the news conference.

"Before the news conference, they put the Redskins Super Bowl trophies up at the front of the room—the ones won by the great Hall of Fame coaches

George Allen and Joe Gibbs. I must say, nothing says 'winner' like seeing those trophies.

"Sean was always aware of Coach Gibbs's accomplishments as far as being a Hall of Fame coach along with his championships. So it was a pleasure meeting him. We found Gibbs to be a man of character, high moral fiber, down to earth, and just a truly nice man.

"I hear people say coaches like Joe Gibbs are fossils and the game had passed them by. However, I think these coaches bring structure and leadership to the young kids coming into the league who have no clue about money, job relationships, life, or anything in the real world for that matter. They're twenty, twenty-one, twenty-two years old. How much life experience could they have had?

"Gibbs knew the game inside out. When he came back, he did have to relearn the personnel. But he made sure the kids [and the veterans] stepped up. He was the type of guy that allowed you to play. He put that ball in your hand. He was a hard-nosed guy. Coaches were going to beat you down, but that made you a better player. He trusted in himself, and players had to trust his style was going to work.

"As superior athletes, everything they've experienced all their lives was people telling them what they wanted to hear," Taylor remarked. "These people were sucking up to them as if they wanted something. They were used to having their asses kissed, but guess what, every player in the pros has had their ass kissed their whole lives. This is no way to grow up and become a mature adult. So the league needs coaches like Gibbs, Andy Reed, and Lovie Smith.

"You can be good, but the only way to be great is when you put great people around you. That's what Coach Gibbs tried to do. He was the focal point, the man of vision, but he also put together a great coaching staff around him, like defensive backs coach Steve Jackson. I remember him playing for the Houston Oilers. Tough guy. He used to call Sean 'the Hawk,' and I'm pretty sure he started calling him 'the Meast' [half man, half beast]," a moniker many of Sean's fans still use to describe him today.

"I also understand guys who bend and break because they're not used to criticism or people scolding or getting on them," Taylor said. "But at the end of the day, one thing I always heard Sean say was, 'I'm glad I had somebody that understood me and I could look up to. Dad, you're not always going to be around, but you have to have someone to be there for you when you're not at home.'

"If a guy like Joe Gibbs says something, you know it's going to be true. It has meaning. It has substance. With Gibbs you know what side of the fence you're playing on. It's like when you see a young guy coming into the work atmosphere and he's just starting his job. You say he may be looking to see how much he can get away with because he doesn't know much. But when you see a veteran, you know he's been there for a minute, so his voice stands out.

"For Sean it was important to have a great relationship with Coach Gibbs, because if you think about it, he'd never been that far away from home before. Even when he was at the dorms or the house he rented later on at the University of Miami, he was still home."

Jazmin "Jaz" Taylor

When Sean was at Gulliver, later on at UM and then the Redskins, his little personal cheerleader was right there with him—his half sister, Jazmin.

"I have a picture of me from a UM game covered head to toe with Hurricanes symbols. I was the cheerleader for every sport—everything. I was also the little support system."

So what was it like for Jaz Taylor to go to Killian, Gulliver, UM, and Redskins football games? What was it like seeing Sean on the field with everyone cheering him on?

"The fans would be different depending on the team and the game. That was the weirdest thing about it. At Gulliver games I would sit with the families, the moms, the sisters … and they would have paint on their faces. We would empty water bottles and put pennies and other loose change in them, and then we'd shake them, turning them into noisemakers. At the end of the game we were actually allowed to run on the field. I'd run to Sean, and he'd always pick me up.

"At UM games there were many more people. We couldn't run on the field, so we'd wait for them to go to the locker rooms and come out. At the NFL games, everybody would be dressed up. We sat in the family section, so all the wives would dress up. We couldn't go near the locker rooms, so we actually had to wait by Sean's car in the players' lot. The fans were there too, and that's where they'd get their autographs and pictures.

"It was weird for me to experience the different kinds of fans at different levels of his career. At Gulliver and UM, [to me] those were the most emotional, because we're not sectioned off with family or friends. You're in a section with anybody and everybody. You could be sitting with fans of the other team. They may or may not be fans of Sean, and if Sean messed up, you could hear the fans say, 'Hey! You shouldn't have done that.' You could hear fans cursing him out. And I'd be like, 'Hey, that's my brother you're talking about. You better shut your mouth.'

"My mom would have to remind me that it was 'just a fan' and to 'pay him no mind.' What was crazy was that same fan that cursed him would cheer him when he did something good. I didn't care. I was proud of him no matter what he did.

Life Lesson

"It was my father who had to explain to me that these people could love Sean. They just loved him in a different way—as fans. 'It is a different type of love that you have for him,' he'd say to me. 'So when they come up to you and express their love, you have to be appreciative of it and not get mad even though they didn't know him. They still love him because they spent their money to watch him play every Sunday. That is the kind of love that could only be appreciated by fans.'"

"Sean loved his fans for believing in him. So when all of this happened, I didn't realize how many people loved him. I was getting messages from numbers that weren't even saved in my phone tellin' me that they loved my brother and they were 'so sorry for my loss.' So I had to do what Sean did and learn to love them back.

"They watched him on YouTube and followed him throughout his career. You can't do anything but appreciate fans like that [those that would stick by him win or lose]."

The word "fan" is a shortened version of "fanatic." If you think about it, many fans are just that. They're fanatical followers of their favorite player or sports team.

"On the ride home, if the Redskins lost, it was a looong ride home," said Jazmin Taylor. "There's mostly silence, then Sean would just randomly talk about what he did during the game and what he could have done better. He talked about what happened and what should have happened. Then he would stop talking. Then a few minutes later he'd talk about the game some more. So in his head, he was replaying the game over and over again, and when he messed up he'd be like, 'Yeah, I should have done this or I should have done that. It could have been better if I did this. We could have won if I'd done that.' However, if the Redskins won, he'd be like, 'Okay, where do you want to go eat at?' So if they won, it was a totally different kind of car ride home."

When visiting the Washington, DC, area, the whole family stayed with Sean. But there was this one unusual thing about his home: the stairs. "Let me put it this way: every single person fell down those stairs," Jazmin said.

It was a three-level townhouse. The master bedroom was on the top floor. The second floor, which was the main floor, held the living room. In addition, there was a finished basement. Going from the master bedroom to the living room, one had to come down the stairs and make a turn. "Everybody slipped on that turn, especially when it was cold outside," Jazmin explained. "I don't know how, but when it was cold the stairs would be slippery, and everybody would slip at that turn. Maybe it was the moisture. My mom, Joseph, even Sean admitted to falling down those stairs. Nobody liked those stairs in that house."

"When Sean was alive, I used to call him 'my brother who played football.' In my eyes, Sean was never a professional football player. To me it was, 'Oh, that's my brother.' And people would say, 'No, that's Sean Taylor.' So they didn't see him as I saw him. He was just my brother who played football, not a football player. There's a big difference.

"Sean didn't do many interviews ... so [this is what] I want you [the readers] to know: he was all about God, his team, his family, and his fans. The crazy thing about Facebook, the Twitter world, and all these crazy social networks is, I have my moments where I miss him and I think to myself it could be so different if he were still here. My life would be so different. I would have somebody who was there for me, someone who knows what I'm going through and who could talk to me and give me insight and advice. Then I'll go on Facebook and see a picture of him and it's just like ... a perfect example ...

"One time I was going to school, working forty hours a week at a job and applying to nursing school all at the same time, and I said to myself, 'How am I going to do all this?' So I go on Facebook to clear my head, and I see someone put up a picture of Sean, and it all just came to me. That's how I'm going to do it. Sean did it forever. Sean would go to school, have practice, come home, do homework, and then work out some more, barely getting any sleep. If Sean could do that, I bet I could do whatever is thrown my way in life.

"So yes. The fans, we love them," Jazmin explains. "But now these fans are also my inspiration. Sean was my real inspiration, but the way these fans love my brother and have kept him alive for so long—that is now what inspires me. How many people remember him—it's just amazing."

"I just lay in bed sometimes, reminiscing about the time we spent together. There was this one incident that has gotten me through a lot. I had surgery on my foot. Everybody knows if you come home and something falls on that foot, it's the worst pain ever. I hit my foot right where the cut was, and I was in bed crying. Sean walked in my room and said, 'What are you doing?' I was just crying and crying. Well, he looked at me and said, 'Man up.' That's it. He said 'Man up' and walked out of my room. Every time I feel like crying or getting emotional, I always hear him in the back of my head, saying, 'Man up.' That was crazy, because I was the only girl, and he told me to man up? I was like, 'What?' So everything that I go through now makes me think of that moment. 'Don't worry about anything. Just man up,' Sean said.

"But I have another scar on my foot because of Sean," said Jaz.

Like a little puppy dog, Jazmin followed Sean everywhere he went. "So one day I was following him outside, but he didn't see me behind him and he closed the door on my foot."

Ouch.

Redskins Defensive Coordinator Gregg Williams

Mention the name Coach Gregg Williams, the former defensive coordinator of the Washington Redskins (et al.), and you'd most likely conjure up a hard-nosed, no-nonsense kind of guy that got the job done.

However, something else could easily come to mind. It was that same hard-nosed coach who was accused of putting a price, or a bounty, on opposing team's players' heads while with the New Orleans Saints. The job? To take them out for a few thousand in a player's pocket. This became a major NFL scandal called "Bountygate" in 2011-12, and when it was all over, Coach Williams was banned for life from the NFL.

After a very lengthy investigation, Coach Gregg Williams's suspension was lifted, and he was reinstated into the league in 2013, finding employment as the senior defensive assistant with the Tennessee Titans. That lasted all of one year, until the Titans released most of their coaching staff. Williams was hired by the St. Louis Rams in February 2014.

Sean played for Coach Williams while he was defensive coordinator with the Washington Redskins. It's Williams who constantly tells others he considered Sean one of the best safeties to ever play in the NFL. Their work together could become a blueprint for keeping offenses out of the end zone and winning games.

"I've had Hall of Fame coaches and players out there, but Sean is the best football player I have ever coached," Coach Gregg Williams told me as we began his interview. "The 'measurables': height, weight, speed, strength, instincts, and just being a football player—he was the best. I say that in most of my speeches when it comes up; I'm not embarrassed to say that. There are lots of great players that I've coached, but Sean Taylor was the best."

It's been said that Gregg Williams used to call Sean "fat boy." Williams admitted it. "Basically, that was a way to get inside Sean's head," said Coach Gregg Williams. "Sean was extremely prideful, and I had to figure out a way to push him.

"I will tell you this: his last year there he carried [his weight issues] to an extreme. He had gone to the Pro Bowl, and he had gotten some advice by the other players about dropping some weight, and I thought he had dropped too much weight. So then I was being hard on him for being anorexic. He really needed to put some of it back on.

"In the first two years I coached Sean, he knew I loved him. He probably never had anybody talk to him the way I talked to him. I challenged him. People would walk by my closed office door, and we would be in there just yelling at each other, almost coming to blows. Times changed. Attitudes changed. Thought processes changed." It became an individual versus teamwork thing. Sean was the individualist. Williams had a team to coach.

"Right off the bat, as he was juggling to get into it that first year, he had some off-the-field issues trying to get settled, and there were some other things going on down in Miami where he missed a few days. So I had sent word out, whoever sees him first to send him to me. I said I need to talk to him to rip his ass.

"Anyway, we were in a staff meeting, sitting there looking at some film, going over things, and Sean pokes his head in and smiles real big because he already knew he was going to get his ass ripped. And right there in front of the whole staff, I said, 'Come in here, and close the door.' Then I proceeded to just undress him about where he was and what was going on. I told him this wasn't a full scholarship anymore and he had to be accountable—'You gotta be in here' and he had to get to work, blah, blah, blah. He just looked at me and took it. I was done with him.

"All of a sudden he opened the door … began his exit … came back in, looked at me, and goes, 'I can't help this, but that's a nice haircut.' And he left! I had just gotten a very short, almost US Marine style haircut, and my hair was different from the last time he saw me. He had just taken an ass chewing, and he had enough of a sense of humor to turn back around and put me in my place by making a comment about my hair before he went out the door.

"Well, the coaches thought I was going to erupt, but instead I turned to them and I said, 'You know what, fellas? We got a very special cat here. He can dish it as well as take it, and that's just what we need.'"

Remembering what Dan Snyder told Pete and me when discussing coaching philosophies, when Sean first burst on the scene, Williams was hesitant to play him despite Sean's coming in with all that talent. Sean was getting pissed because he thought he should be playing. So why was the talented Taylor sitting on the sidelines?

The answer lay in Coach Williams's core beliefs. "Here's the deal on that. There's a travesty in our league, and scouts, owners, players, and everybody should understand this. You have to earn everything. It was preseason, not a regular season game, and just because a guy is drafted, it doesn't mean he is anointed at his position. The worst thing coaches and owners can do—and they have a hard time with this—when you anoint a guy just because he was drafted and he hadn't played a snap in this league, it spreads through the locker room like wildfire. It can be a cancer, because you're treating somebody special. I learned this from Joe Paterno a long time ago: morale will stay high as long as everyone at your company, your team, your school, believes they are being treated fairly. When one person is being treated better than everybody else or worse than everybody else, you got a problem."

Williams actually told the owner of the team, Dan Snyder, Head Coach Joe Gibbs, and everybody else that Sean Taylor or anybody they brought in had to earn his position. Positions were not given to players. He didn't want his players looking at any new guy in the locker room "cross-eyed."

Coach Williams's tone took a very serious turn. "What we would do was change things, game by game by game; a guy would play more and more if he deserved to. By the way, I did the same thing with other players ever since I was given the defensive coordinator position. When the players come to you and say … 'We're better when Sean Taylor is in there,' I'd say, 'Well no shit. Maybe he needs to be in there and play a little bit more.' But then players become empowered and we are in this together. There was an acceptance of Sean Taylor because he earned it.

"I've taken Sean out of games. That's when he'd freelance and do his own thing, but I had to be accountable to the defense. I can't cut ya, but I can dictate when you're gonna play. And if the owner wants me to go, I'll go. I was hired to make sure the best guys play. Sean bought into that real quick.

"There are some great stories; no matter who we would play, whoever the so-called best player was on the other team, Sean was going to go get a piece of him at some point in time. It was a battle of wills. It was almost like a dog peeing on his territory. He was going to go after whoever was the so-called best player on that team and test him. He'd make sure he asserted his will and his strength on them."

When asked about huge contracts and the "new league normal," Gregg Williams had an interesting take. "Believe it or not, coaches and players just look at all of that as a benchmark for the next guy to make more money. But it does affect them. So because I am a realist, I am going to make sure everyone is held accountable outside of the contract. One of the things I've told players I've coached, Sean included, is that I'm going to be a certain way and it doesn't make any difference to me how high you were drafted, how much money you make, who your mom and dad are, how many honors you had before, how many Pro-Bowls you've been to, how many times you've been an All-American. I don't care about any of that. Every day is an interview. If you interview well today, maybe you'll play more today, tomorrow, or next week. That way I can be as demanding, as hard, as I need to be to make us as good we can be."

Williams said he'd never mess with a player's money, as that belongs to the player. He doesn't care what's in the contract. He doesn't care about incentives either, because that's not his world. "My world is playing the best players all the time. The NFL is a production business. Two words that begin with the letter A that a professional football player has to own and understand is 'accountability' and 'availability.' And if you're not accountable to your teammates, to your position, to the demands of an NFL player, you won't play. Or, if you're not available and healthy, you won't play."

Williams actually worried about the way Sean practiced. He's the only player that could "light up" a teammate. "I worried about him going after other UM guys like Santana [Moss], and they were really good friends—but he'd knock Santana Moss out of practice if the competition was elevated enough.

"One time there was a big fight in practice, and he wasn't in it at first, but when it came time to protect his teammates, I saw him pick up Casey Rabach, a 300-pound man, by the belt loops and the shoulder pads because he was on top of the pile and throw him like a bale of hay, three yards away. And I'm thinking, 'Wow.' Then everybody jumped up and started running toward Sean, and when they saw it was Sean who did it, they all avoided him, because no one wanted a piece of Sean."

Williams remembers Sean's legendary workouts and practices: "I had this thing where I wanted to be the first guy out at practice. I wanted to be that way when I played and I wanted to be the first one on the practice field when I coached. I want to be the first one out because I'm an expert on body language. So much of who you are can be determined through visual keys as well as verbal keys. A lot of people can con you with their words, but your body language tells the story. So I love being out there early."

Sean, with his competitive nature, wasn't having any of that. His mission was to beat Williams to the practice field. Williams said Sean would be out there during the hour between meetings and practice. Some days he'd "get his business done" and then jog a mile even before practice started on the

Redskins Park practice fields. "He was always out there getting himself ready both physically and mentally. Ready to go. Ready to be the best he could be," Williams said.

Sean and Williams were both "competition addicts." Sean would run two conditioning workouts, go out and practice the spring practice, and jog home.

"One of the other things he would do at practice that was absolutely amazing, was his little battle of wills, where he would pick up a fumble or intercept a pass and would make sure you knew you couldn't tackle him and scored with every play. If it was an eighty-yard run, he'd run the eighty yards. Then he'd make everybody else wait for the next play in practice. He was not going to let you tackle him.

"You know he was a better running back in high school than he was a defensive player? So when he put his hands on the ball, that was a miraculous thing to see. The whistle would blow, shutting the play down, but not him. If the offense brought thirty people off the sidelines to tackle him, they still couldn't do it. He would do that every single time. I'm tellin' ya. He's just the best football player I've ever coached."

Coach Williams described their off-field chats this way: "Early on we'd talk about his conformity to team discipline. A little bit of the University of Miami stigma got put on me because I drafted and had more of 'them' play for me than any other team in the league. There's a little bit of individualism that came from there, and you had to get people to 'buy into the team.' So we had him do things the way we wanted from a discipline standpoint. However I would give him individualism within the position, within the scheme of the rules of the team defense. How he played his position was up to him and his individuality. The techniques he used."

As for the rest of their conversations, "the *big* ones were along the sidelines. All of a sudden he'd want to freelance and not play the specific call, and I'd be ripping his ass on that," Williams said.

Playing against the Detroit Lions in one game, Sean wasn't in the designed double coverage. He had his own ideas. Sean and Williams ended up in a battle of wills and heated 'discussions.' If he got a penalty for a late hit or the like, they had more 'discussions.'

During a game versus the Philadelphia Eagles, he took a shot at T.O. This gave T.O. and the Eagles another series of downs.

"We were getting ready to force a field goal, and all of a sudden they got another set of downs on a late hit penalty, and they ended up getting a touchdown when we had them stopped for a field goal," Williams remembered. "We would have arguments about those types of things."

Williams remembered another incident that took place when the Redskins were playing the Cincinnati Bengals. Sean was supposed to play the middle of the field. "Suddenly [I see that] he's up on the line of scrimmage, right next to the defensive lineman on a short-yardage call, and he stuffs them for a loss. Now I am ripping his ass coming off the field about what he's doing. He said, 'You know what, you made that call, but I knew where to play. I made the play and I got us off the field.'" He was right. "There were moments like that which were so remarkable."

So basically, Sean checked off his coach.

"He checked me off. That's exactly what he did." They'd argue, but inside they'd both be smiling. "I enjoyed that chemistry, the verbal and mental repartee; I enjoyed that with him. All great players have instincts beyond coaching. That's how Sean played."

Sean was very physical—an understatement, to be sure. In Sean's rookie season, Washington played the Philadelphia Eagles, who are a "deep shot" team. "Two or three times a game they're going to take 'max protection' and they're going to take shots down the field. The Eagles and the rest of the league stopped that game plan for several years versus the Redskins after Sean aborted the called play and just lit the receiver up. There was a pass-interference penalty, but he blew him up so much people stopped trying that [downfield play] against us. On deep routes down the field, if he couldn't make a play on the ball, he was not going to let anybody else make one. Instead he would make a play on the man. He also trash-talked to them and said, 'You don't want this anymore. I am going to be here all day long, and it's just going to get worse and worse and worse.'" Then they'd take that back to the huddle and let the quarterback or the play caller know not to run that play. "It's amazing how few shots down the field we had after that because of his physical and mental presence on asserting his aggressive toughness on players. People were just afraid of getting hit down the field," explained Williams.

There was a spitting incident, and after Coach Williams stopped laughing about it, he said, "I just told this story a little while ago! Let's go back to the Cincinnati game we spoke about before. We didn't play very well on offense in that game, but we battled our tail off. I think we got beat 19–16, something like that. We gave up a lot of field goals because they couldn't score a touchdown. At the end of the game, the Bengals are trying to run the clock out with three wide receivers, one tight end and one back. What we did was challenge the line of scrimmage, getting after them. Sean is up on the line, and he's just manhandling T. J., Touraj Houshmandzadeh, Jr. Well, T. J. mouthed off to Sean, and well, he [Sean] spit on him. Wait! It gets better. So this was Sean's rookie year. Well, those are the types of things I'm saying you just can't do.

"So I would say, 'You have to hate to lose more than you love to win.' I would say that all the time. Well, I didn't need to tell Sean Taylor that. He hated to lose *much* more than he loved to win.

"After the ballgame, I'm coming off the field, and T. J. comes running up to me and gets in my face and says, 'Hey! Your number 36, he spit in my face. You tell him to come down here. I want to see him right now.' So I grabbed him by the shirt and pulled him in close and I said, 'Look, you need to go to the locker room as fast as possible. If he comes back down that ramp to finish this with you, I can't help you, security can't help you—nobody can help you. Do not bite off more than you can chew. Take your ass to the locker room *now*!'

"So I let go of him and, he looked at me, and I said, 'I'm dead serious now. You don't want any part of this young man. Whatever happened, happened. But you need to bury it and get out of here right away before he tries to take it to another level.' So yes. This took place."

Redskins Teammate Clinton Portis—Being Bad

It took a while, but Clinton Portis and Pete Taylor finally met at C. P.'s downtown Miami high-rise condo to do an interview. Clinton had some great Sean stories, and as Pete said, he wants to give you—the readers—the good, the bad and the ugly. And that's exactly what you'll read next:

Clinton Earl Portis [C. P.] was known just as much for his hard-nosed rushing style as he was for his off-the-field, sometimes off-the-wall, fashion and style.

In 2004, in a controversial trade panned by many Redskins fans, the team sent shut-down cornerback Champ Bailey and a draft pick to the Denver Broncos for Portis. In the end, Clinton Portis had seven very successful seasons with the Redskins, which lasted until 2010.

In college, Portis was a star running back for the Miami Hurricanes, and alongside Sean Taylor and crew, he was part of the 2001 BCS National Championship team. On April 10, 2014, Clinton Portis was inducted into the UM Sports Hall of Fame.

●

"It got to the point where the only way the coaches could get in touch with Sean was callin' me," Clinton Portis said regarding Sean's avoidance issues. "You know, I remember on so many occasions Coach Gibbs or Coach Williams would call me, even during off-season workouts. I guess Sean hadn't come in. Everybody would be like, 'We haven't heard from Sean. Have you heard from him? What is Sean doin'?'

"Coach Gibbs called once and said, 'I can't get in touch with him. I just wanna make sure he's all right.' I'm like, 'Hey, I'm sittin' here with Sean right now. I mean, do you want to speak to him?'

"He's like, 'Yeah, man, I'd love to speak to him.'

"I tried to give Sean the phone, and he's like, 'Man, I don't feel like talking to them.'

"I'm advising him, like, 'Bro, that's Coach Gibbs.'

"He's like, 'I don't feel like talkin' right now, C. P. I don't want to talk to them right now. I'm enjoyin' myself.'

"I'm like, 'No, bro, you just gotta do … you know, I mean you let people know you all right and that you handling your business.'" Reluctantly Sean just took the phone to let Coach Gibbs know he was okay.

"Sean told Gibbs, 'Here's what's goin' on, Coach. Everything is all right. I'm workin' out on my own. I'll be ready.'"

Clinton gets very introspective and begins to speak a little more slowly.

"I just, like, remember those times. You know, when Sean first got to DC, he was stayin' at the house with me. He would always go to sleep around nine. He'd go in the room and shut the door. You know, I figured he was going to sleep, watch TV, [or be] on the phone."

After about two weeks, C. P.'s friend Derrick, who upon occasion would also stay at the house, noticed Sean leaving the house early in the morning.

"I was like, 'Yeah, he go work out early,'" Portis told his friend.

"He'd be like, 'Man, nah, Sean be leavin' like one, two a.m. Where the hell he be goin' to?'"

It turned out Sean's girlfriend Jackie was playing soccer for the University of Miami, and when they played the University of Virginia (a 2-hour drive) or Virginia Tech (a 3-hour-and-50-minute drive), Sean would leave early in the morning to see her and make it back in time for workouts.

"'Sean, what are you doin? Man, you're crazy; you're drivin' [four hours] to Blacksburg?' You know, I mean ... it was just like something he had for her," Portis exclaimed.

At one point, Portis spoke candidly about Jackie to Sean: "I think him and Jackie had went through a situation that I kinda exposed him to, not knowin' what was happenin' way before me, you know? I had no clue. I'm thinkin' like, *'Bro, I'm gonna just put you up on somethin' so you can just pay attention.'* I think that was the only time we had strain among us because it's like when somebody bring you information about your people, I think that's kinda hard to digest, knowin' somebody else know what's going on in your household. [But] I remember clearin' that up with him and Jackie."

Portis told the two of them, "'I got in y'all's business, and I should have stayed out. I apologize to you both. If this was for y'all, then don't let somebody else mess up that situation.'"

Pete said to Portis, "He was really private."

Clinton continued, "Yeah, he was real private about his personal life. There was another incident where, I forgot these girls' names, but one of them was from Houston and one was from New York. The one from New York, she went to school down here [in Florida]. She came to DC to visit me with a homegirl, and you know, they came and stayed up for a couple days. It just was an awkward time. We really didn't hit it off. A couple weeks later I go to visit Sean, and she was there. You know, when he tried to introduce her, I'm lookin' at her like, 'I know this girl.' You know, I mean, I think it was Sean tryin' to move on from Jackie. He thought he had found a replacement, and I remember deadin' that so quick. The next day I think he kicked her out and put her on a bus to New York.

"I just remember talkin' to him, sayin', 'Don't be in a rush to fall in love. You're gonna be exposed to so much stuff and so many women; like every woman gonna love you because of your fame and status. When you find that woman that loved you when you didn't have nothin', before the fame and status, well, you know what I mean? I think it was at that time when he realized Jackie was his old lady and kind of went back to her.

C. P. goes on to tell this story: "When Sean first got the 760 [BMW 7-series], I bought a Ferrari. We're down in Miami, and I call him. 'Sean, what up? What you got goin' on?'

"He was like, 'I ain't doin' nothin'.'

"I'm like, 'I got these girls in town. They want to go to the Keys. Let's take 'em to the Keys.'

"He was like, 'I got Mike with me.'

"'Y'all cool. Come on,'" Portis said.

"So we go down to the Keys, and me and Sean race from—what's that last town in Miami … Homestead? [Pete corrects him and says it is Florida City.] Yeah, Florida City. We race from Florida City to Key Largo in a Ferrari and a 760, and nobody ever knew it. Man, we went down this two-lane highway haulin', man, just wide-open. I'm talkin' about coming around each other, passin'. Wide open, just kickin'. I remember we pulled up to the little resort we was stayin' at. I tried to do donuts in the Ferrari. It was tech shift. I'm thinkin', *'Push the brake, cover the gas, and spin out.'* I was actually messin' up all the mechanicals—I mean, all the computerized stuff.

"We get there. It's me, Sean, Sean's friend Mike, and Derrick. I think I called another one of my partners—Rod. So we were five dudes and like eight or nine girls." All the girls were interested in Sean. Portis continued, "You know, we down in the Keys, we swimmin', we playin' volleyball in the pool, we havin' a blast. You know, enjoyin' life.

"Sean chose the one girl that got a boyfriend, which all of us probably woulda chosen. There was two more girls who I would have chose before her. But he chose to lock up on her. Sean invites her up to his room and she claimed like she can't do nuttin', but she was just in it for the competition with all her homegirls. Really? We didn't know this. So Sean ended up gettin' mad. He left in the middle of the night and came back to Miami because she didn't want to shake dat.

"I'm wakin' up the next day, and everybody lookin' for Sean. 'Man, where is Sean and Mikey?' Nobody can find him." Portis chuckled. "We tried callin', and finally he answered the phone.

"He was like, 'Man, that girl was nothin' but bullshittin', so I came back home.'

"I'm like, 'Man, you crazy; why you didn't just stay, you know, go to another room?'

"He was like, 'Man, I didn't have time to play her games.'"

Clinton changed the subject suddenly, remembering that was the year both of them were on a losing team. So during their bye week, C. P. and Sean decided to take a flight down to Miami just to let off some steam. They got on a plane out of Dulles International. Before heading for the airport, they stopped at Dulles Town Center to buy liquor.

"They had Hennessy Paradis," C. P. said. "I had never seen Hennessy Paradis. Sean and I used to drink Hennessy. But this was four hundred or five hundred a bottle. I said, 'Man, I'm getting that.' So, we bought a bottle."

On the plane, they popped the bottle open. (In case you're wondering, the FAA TSA liquids ban took effect in 2006.) "So people wouldn't complain about us bringin' our own bottle, every time the flight attendant passed by, we would buy all these small bottles of alcohol they had and gave them out to everybody around us. So that kept everybody happy," said Clinton, grinning from ear to ear.

"We landed about five in the afternoon, and we went straight to KoD, King of Diamonds [a well-known Miami gentleman's club]. When we got there, there were probably only five or six women working, and me and Sean. That was it! We were already out of it because we drunk that whole bottle of Hennessy on the plane. We went to KoD, and I guess we probably spent fifteen or twenty thousand dollars that day. We called Sean's homeboy Mike and my friend Rod, who came and met us. Probably about seven thirty the owner of the club walked in and asked us, 'Hey, y'all want me to just close down?' And we said 'No, we'll stay.' He said, 'No, I meant close it down for just you guys. Y'all got the club.'

"So then we were like, 'Yeah, yeah, yeah, don't let nobody in.' I guess they called in all the dancers. So the four of us guys had a blast. We partied the night away, and by the time we walked out, it was two o'clock in the morning.

"For one, we done flew from DC to Miami drinkin' Hennessy Paradis. Then we get to the club, just me and him, and we still drinkin'. So from two or three in the afternoon till two in the morning, and we don't realize how much time done flew by. When we leave out, we're pullin' out from the parkin' lot. Mike was drivin' him, and Rod was drivin' me, because we called them to come pick us up because we couldn't drive. As soon as they pulled off, the car stopped. I just see Sean leanin' out of the car and he throwin' up. I'm laughing. We pass by and pull up beside him. I'm sayin', 'Sean! What— you can't handle your liquor?!'

"He's all, 'Yeah, C. P., you know,' and he's talkin and pukin'.

"I remember goin' home and tryin' to get in my house. I couldn't even stick my door key in the hole, and I probably dropped it thirty-five times."

Clinton's friend Jamilla was in the house and thought someone was breaking into it. "She's inside, scared shitless, and I keep droppin' the key, droppin' the key. Finally I get in and she like, 'What the heck?' She didn't know I was comin'. So it was like I was surprisin' her. I walk in, and I'm out of it. The only thing I can think of is, *'I wonder if Sean done made it home.'*"

Sometime later, Clinton ran into Sean and Jackie, who remembered Sean coming home that night and doing the same thing. "Jackie was like, 'What did you *do* to him?'" C. P. laughed really hard at this, as did Pete. "I didn't do nothin'! What did he *do* to me?"

Another time, C. P. and Santana Moss were sitting together on a team flight. Sean was sitting behind them. "… so we go back to talk to Sean and he got his earphones on," Portis said. "Everybody got iPods, and Sean got a old CD player. So me and Santana be crackin' jokes and makin' fun. You know, everybody got the big headphones. He got regular headphones on. Everybody go back and say, 'Sean, what you doin'? Why ain't you got no iPod?'

"He'd take his headphones off and say, 'What y'all sayin'?'

"We're like, 'Man, we're gettin' you a iPod.'

"He said, 'Man, I don't need no iPod. This is all I need.'

"I'm like, 'What are you listenin' to?'

"He caught everybody on the plane off-guard. He said, 'Man, y'all never heard of T-Pain?

"We like, 'What?'"

Speaking increasingly louder, C. P. imitated Sean when he said, "'Y'all never heard that T-Pain CD?' He really couldn't hear how loud he was talkin'." C. P., mocking Sean, spoke even louder. "'You mean you really never heard that T-Pain CD? This CD got heart.'

"Everybody on the plane laughin', sayin', 'Sean Taylor listenin' to T-Pain!' Like, 'That's your type music? T-Pain? Lemme buy you a drink.' T-Pain?

"I remember me and Santana makin' fun of him over that."

Pete asks if it wasn't Tupac Sean was talking about, because he used to listen to him at the house.

"No, he was listenin' to T-Pain. Everybody else would have been listenin' to Tupac. He was listenin' to T-Pain on the flight."

Next Portis recalled an episode with Sean's least favorite wide receiver, Terrell Owens.

"I remember walkin' with Sean, comin' out of the tunnel, when he runs into T.O. 'I'm gonna fuck you up!' Sean said to him. 'I'm gonna hit you every play, 'cause I don't like you.'

"I'm like, 'Man!'

"Sean was like, 'Arrrhhhhh! You know me. I'm rabid. I'm gonna hit somebody every play!'"

Portis said, "That game, first play, I think T.O. dropped a seventy-yard touchdown just because he was lookin' for Sean, like he had alligator arms—didn't even stick his hands out. And that was the one time that Sean didn't hit him. Every play—man, Sean tackled T.O. every time. Whether he had the ball or not, he hit him."

C. P. began speaking thoughtfully and slowly again. "I just remember, like, you don't find a teammate like that; you don't find somebody who raise your level of play. In my career I was fortunate to have Al Wilson and Shannon Sharpe [on the Denver Broncos] to guide me and show me how to raise my level of play. All of a sudden I came to the Redskins. When I first came, I had Marcus Washington, who played football the way it was supposed to be played—not for accolades or fame. He told me, 'When I get out on this field, I'm gonna demolish something,' and then all of a sudden you bring in Sean T. and ignite everybody and everything around you.

"I remember me and Sean used to argue over who had the hardest hit during the game or who going to get the knockout blow. And I can't wait to tell you it was me, you know what I mean?" Pete chuckled. "That was our argument—not about interceptions, not about touchdowns. It was, 'I'm gonna take the fight out of somebody.'"

Playing with UM alums, Sean Taylor and Santana Moss represented the good old days for Portis. "I think so much of me, the competitive side of me, left with Sean. The moment after that playoff run and we finally lose to Seattle—we were a team comin' together. Everybody was playin' for one cause. After that I was so drained and empty—missin' out on family, missin' out on friends. After that, the game wasn't the same to me."

Changing the subject a bit, Pete asked, "What about that tribute that you did when they put Sean up in the Ring of Honor? I know they had you bring out the flag."

C. P. responded, "You know, when they told me I was going to carry the flag out, that was an honor."

After Sean passed, the Washington Redskins honored him with a special flag. It was Clinton Portis who came tearing out of the tunnel to a huge ovation, carrying a red flag with a center burgundy dot surrounding a gold 21. Clinton appreciated even being asked. He said that was a great moment for everybody.

"But for me it was like hoisting that number for the last time—like I was sayin' good-bye, you know what I mean? After runnin' out, I don't even know who played that game. I don't remember stats or anything. I remember runnin' so hard I was tired when I got to the sideline. Like, I don't know. Like, football disappeared for me after that. You know," he said with a slight chuckle, "like, stats didn't matter to me no more. It's like, what am I doin'?"

When it came to Sean's legendary work ethic, everybody took notice. Portis recalled one particular workout after he hurt his shoulder: "I guess this was 2007, during OTAs. I had to take my running test. When I got there, I was not ready. Sean had on some cut-up jeans, flip-flops, and a thermal shirt. He comes over and says, 'C. P., what you about to do?'

"I told him I had to do my [running] test.

"He said, 'I'll run with you.' You know, he beat me in jeans. Man, this dude, he carried me, saying, 'Come on, come on! I got you!'

"I remember bein' so exhausted, and Sean just walked off the field like, 'All right, he done.' He'd leave and kind of disappear into thin air. When I finally came to, I remember bein' like, 'Man, this dude just ran my conditionin' test.'

But wait. There's more.

"The strength coach was sittin' there sayin', 'Man, what in the hell he been doin'? That was his third time running the test today!'

"I'm like, '*What?*'"

That day, Sean ran three conditioning tests [the defensive back test, the receiver test, and the running back test] and beat everybody. That was just Sean's way. Portis said, "Sean went defense, scout team, full speed, all out, every practice. If it was hot outside, he was in jogging pants and hoodie, just killin' it. If it was cold outside, he came out in some shorts and a jersey—no gloves, freezin'—and it was just a mindset. I have never in my life seen anything like it. I used to think Frank Gore was the toughest 'cuz he played with no socks. I thought that was amazin', like it's impossible, and he [Sean] played with no gloves. I can't even take a handoff with no gloves."

C. P. speaking very slowly, yet with much emotion, said: "You know, just to see Sean in the condition that he was in, you never would have known how hard he prepped and primed. On top of that, when he left the building, he would carry film with him. He was a football fanatic! You don't find that. The football fanatics are the people who do all the ins and outs and study them. They are usually the people who don't have as much talent, so they gotta compensate for it by knowin' where to be and how to be—know all the signs. You don't see somebody with all the talent in the world, all the heart in the world, the speed, the size, and then he's still a student of the game. Like, you don't see that!

Revelation

"If I look back at my career, I was never a student of the game, and I think I had a hell of a career. But if only I would have watched him, if only I would have practiced or participated, I probably would have been the leading rusher of all time. But I wasn't pressed to perfect my craft because I looked at it as a game, and it gotta end one day."

Continuing his look back, C. P. said, "To take Sean under my wing was the easiest thing to do. It was like, 'I'm guidin' you in the stuff that I'm doin'. I'll try to show you how to have fun without gettin' in trouble.' You know what I mean? Just be 'stand up' about it, about whatever you doin'. That was the only thing I seen myself teachin' Sean compared to how much Sean taught me. It was like big brother, little brother. The crazy thing is I had that same exact relationship with E. J., and E. J. like big brother and I'm little brother."

Pete said, "E. J. is Edgerrin James?"

C. P. said, "Yeah, Edgerrin. When I think of my relationship with Edgerrin, it would always remind me, like Edge took me under his shoulder, like little brother, the same way I did with Sean.

"I was havin' this conversation with some people, and I said I didn't get money and find new friends. The people that know me, the people that I roll with, the people that I rock with, my best friends, are all from high school. My partners from the league all went to UM: Roscoe Parrish, Reggie Wayne, Phil Buchanon—you know what I mean? Like day're my peoples, day're my partners. I didn't get no friends when I got to the NFL. I don't hang with nobody else from the NFL now. Like, if me and you wadn't playin' ball, I wouldn't hang wit' you. The crazy thing is, I think my last friend might have been Sean. I cain't name nobody that I've met after Sean that became my friend."

Renaldo Wynn: First Impressions Aren't Always the Right Impressions

Renaldo Wynn played defensive end during his two terms with the Washington Redskins. In a league full of prima donnas and misbehaving NFL players, Renaldo Wynn charted his own course. He's a stand-up, community-oriented guy involved in charity work and a ministry of his own.

Just prior to this interview, Wynn moved from Las Vegas to Charlotte, North Carolina, as he had accepted a position in sponsorship servicing with Joe Gibbs Racing. He also works on Gibbs's ministry site, *Game Plan for Life*.

Back in Northern Virginia, where he lived while with the Redskins, he still runs a charity for underprivileged youth.

"The Redskins drafted this kid, Sean Taylor," former teammate Renaldo Wynn recounted. "My first experience with Sean was really ... it's not fair, but sometimes you stereotype guys. Sometimes people go off of what they see on television, and let me say that many times what you see in the media is not a true depiction of who the person is. It's all I had to go on. Not only that, the Miami label that comes behind that, and immediately it's 'Hey, this guy is from Miami; he's gonna have swagger, he's going to be arrogant and all this'—and it turns out to be just the opposite.

"Sean wasn't a mouthy guy [in the locker room]. In fact, when he came in, you knew this was a guy who was serious. Not too many guys messed around with him at all, but you respected him because he didn't mouth off. He did his talking on the field. And when I say talking, I mean grinding, putting the work in, trying to be a better player. There're not too many guys who can come in and make an immediate impact.

"Now obviously he's a young kid, and he's going to make mistakes. Everybody makes mistakes. Just seeing that young kid come in and seeing him grow and mature over the time I had the opportunity to spend with him was amazing.

"I had the privilege to see it firsthand," Wynn said. "I'll never forget, before the 2005 season there was my locker; Santana [Moss] was to my left, and Phillip [Daniels's] locker was two to the right. The locker right between Phillip's and mine was an empty locker. It was actually a locker that nobody wanted. Everybody that had that locker got cut. The player who had it never lasted more than two months. If he was in training camp, that guy wasn't going to make the team, so it was kind of a cursed locker. So guys were like, oh man, I don't want that locker!

"I don't think Sean knew what we were talking about in relation to that locker, but he said, 'Hey, man. I gotta make a change.' We weren't thinking about what he was talking about. So we were like, 'Yeah, man. Whatever you say, man.' He said, 'Yeah, I gotta get over with you senior citizens.' So yeah, he took a little jab at us. But he said, 'I could learn some wisdom and some knowledge. I got to change up what I'm doing.'

"I thought he was just talking. Talking about change. I didn't know he was going to actually move his locker. He wasted no time, because sure enough, the next day, he moved his right next to mine. So I'm like, 'Ooh, this guy was serious.' He said, 'I wasn't playin', man.'"

Perhaps the jinxed locker was another case of predestination?

The two locker mates spoke on a variety of subjects, but according to Wynn, "He loved talking about his daughter." The two of them discussed family issues, being a father, just doing what it takes.

"Football came easy for him, but he wanted to get to another level," explained Wynn. "He busted his butt to see just how good he could be. He started going on that journey. He stayed after practice, working but having fun. He'd work with the scout team. He'd ride his bike to practice from his house, to the facility, and back home again.

"So here's a guy who came in young, free-spirited, who turned into someone focused, dedicated to work and his family, just wanting to be the best in every category: father, football player, person."

Sean's relationship with God got even stronger when he started his family. Was Wynn aware? Did they have conversations about church, Jesus, the Lord, anything like that at all?

"I did notice that Sean went to the chapel the night before games. At that time Coach Greg Blache coined me 'the Rev,' so the other guys picked up on it, and they started calling me the Rev, and even if I called Coach Blache today, he'd call me Rev. 'How are you doing, Rev?' he'd say. So that started spreading like wildfire. I'm going back a little bit, but Sean once told me, 'God is calling me to play football, and that's what I'm going to do; I will play football to the best of my ability.'

"Sean was just a doer, not a talker. And that's how he lived his life. He didn't have to say, 'I'm growing in my faith.' He would have his Bible with him, and he'd go to chapel."

Renaldo then spoke about Coach Joe Gibbs and an environment where one could rely on one's faith for strength and substance. He said Gibbs had three chaplains, whereas most teams had only one. "There's only so much one man can do," Wynn said. "There's sixty guys plus coaches. Coach Gibbs was a visionary and produced such a fruitful environment with an atmosphere for success.

Renaldo said, "Sean just thrived in it. He needed direction, and he received it." Right before their eyes, they saw a youngster enter and a man leave. "At the end of the day, if you're going down a dark alley, he's gonna have your back. He went out there committed to what we were doing and made us all better. He made me better.

"He actually loved the game of football. He even loved practice. I never met anybody that actually loved to practice. Even when it was tough—I mean like training camp, right now, this time of year [August]. I get nightmares just thinking about [it]. I can feel the heat, smell the grass. It's a nightmare for me right now because I'm just thinking about how it was for *this* big guy at training camp."

🏈

"I'll never forget in the January 2006 playoff game where we beat Tampa Bay. It was in that game I broke my arm. As I'm going to the locker room in excruciating pain, my wife, my mom, and my daughter were there, and they were just devastated.

"Right after that, Sean spit in the face of Michael Pittman, and he got kicked out of a nationally televised playoff game. Now mind you, I'm already in the back of the locker room trying to get situated and minimize the pain, and within minutes, here comes Sean. I didn't know he got ejected, and I certainly didn't know why [he was back in the locker room], but I'm in pain.

"He comes into the locker room like a tornado, and he's throwing his helmet ... mad as heck ... it sounded like a hundred bulls back there, just throwing stuff, just upset. My mom? She disappeared. Turns out Mom went to the back and started talking to Sean ... and all of a sudden I hear a soft voice saying, 'Baby, it's gonna be all right.' In the midst of all of my pain, I hear my mom talking to Sean and trying to console him ... and I still remember her saying, as clear as day, 'Baby, I know you didn't do that, baby; don't worry about it.' And I just started hollerin', '*Mom! Get out of there ... Get out!*'

"Now my wife goes to the back, and I hear her say, 'Ms. Wynn, come out from back there. Leave Sean alone.' And I'm thinking, '*He's gonna kill her.*' Figuratively speaking, of course. But you know ... nothing happened."

That night Mr. Snyder was gracious enough to fly Wynn back on his private plane because he didn't want him having surgery "in enemy territory." Upon arrival, Wynn went straight to Reston Hospital in Northern Virginia.

After some healing time, Wynn finally went back to the locker room at Redskins Park, where he was met by Sean Taylor. "He came over to me and said, 'Please tell Ms. Wynn how sorry I am. Your mom, man—she's awesome, man.' Every time he'd see me after that he'd ask, 'Hey, how's your mom doing? Tell her hello.' So I looked at this as a connecting key for him and me from that sense. That's one of those stories Mom and I always tell."

In the locker room, Sean was friends with the UM guys, such as Portis, Moss, and a few other guys, because there was a strong bond among them coming in. However, was there anyone in the locker room that Sean didn't get along with?

For some reason, Renaldo Wynn thought that was a funny question and started laughing.

"Gregg Williams had a very good rapport with Troy Vincent. And I'm sure Gregg felt like Troy would make a great mentor for Sean. Now, it was nothing against Troy, but Sean just didn't take to him. It was one-sided, and I don't know why, but he just didn't."

Wynn went on to describe a situation that happened in practice, where Sean was like a cute little Chihuahua with everybody else, but like a pit bull with Troy. "I know there was this one incident where Troy got ticked off," Wynn remembered. "I think he felt disrespected in front of his peers. Most guys looked up to Troy. He was our union president, and Sean said something to him that just ticked him off. It was something like, Sean was supposed to go in and sub for him, but Sean kinda waved him off in a disrespectful way. It just went on from there. I'm not even sure Gregg Williams even knew about that, because sometimes these are subtle signs where the coaches are not aware [of issues] but the players are."

Gregg Williams is famous for saying he was going to play the guy that gave the Redskins the best chance of winning. "Now, if he felt that was going to be Troy, that's who he would play," Wynn said.

"I'll never forget, but when the stuff hit the fan, I don't remember what flight this was, but it was on a long one. We were coming back from a game, and Troy was sitting right next to me. I think Griff [Cornelius Griffin] was on the plane right near us. So Sean said something to Troy, and I saw a side of him [Troy] I had never seen before. I saw the Trenton, New Jersey, part come out. Man, it really got to him, and I'm like, 'Troy, you gotta relax, man. Just calm down.'

"Troy said something like, 'This is some ghetto stuff,' and a few other choice words, and I'm like, 'Wow.'

"Now here's Troy, talking about how he was going to have someone waiting for Sean at the plane once we land. I said, 'Come on, man, you're the president of the union. Chill.' So for whatever reason, this would be the one guy that Sean did not get along with."

Sean always felt as though he had something to prove. He wanted to be bigger, faster, and stronger than the next guy. He wanted to be the one on the field at all times and wasn't going to let anyone take that away from him. So maybe it was Sean who felt disrespected, insulted, or challenged when the Redskins brought Vincent in, in 2006.

Nevertheless, in the camouflaged words of Renaldo Wynn, "when Sean said something like, 'N-word whatever, F-bomb you,'" in a gritty way, he saw the Miami come out of Sean. Despite Troy's being union president, and despite his being as eloquent as he was, Wynn saw the Trenton boy come out of him as he held his own against Sean.

Renaldo wants people to know about the softer side of Sean Taylor. "I just want people to know about the whole transformation. We were dealing with a gentle giant, bro. He wasn't perfect. Nobody is. I had an opportunity to see firsthand how he played the game, how he loved the game, and how he gave 120 percent. He was a person that cared about family and his teammates. When he spoke, he spoke in a profound way with meaning behind his words."

On the other hand, Coach Gibbs used to say to Sean, "Slow down. This is only practice." Then all of sudden, on the next play—*bam!*—he would take out a teammate, to which Gibbs would say, "I don't think he heard a word I said."

Renaldo continued, "There are some guys who become bigger than life. Some are even unapproachable. Sean, on the other hand, was very approachable because he didn't have an ego! I never saw him blow off anyone. Maybe there's someone who wanted an autograph—he signed to the last fan.

"That was another unique side to him that was just amazing. He had a great disrespect for arrogance. I really think he was at a point in his life where he wanted to give back and have an effect on kids in his area, and to some, give them hope."

🏈

If you'd like to learn more about Renaldo's ministry, please visit http://familyoffaithfoundation.com. To learn more about Coach Joe Gibbs's mission and ministry, visit www.gameplanforlife.com.

Redskins Coach Steve Jackson

The Washington Redskins safeties coach, Steve Jackson, spent more time with Sean Taylor than anyone else on the Redskins staff. He coached free safety Sean Taylor from 2004–2007 and considers himself fortunate to have done so. Coach Jackson remained with the Redskins until 2011.

Revelation

"Early in the 2004 draft process, people were saying all kinds of stuff … negative things about Sean," began Coach Steve Jackson. *"There were different opinions about him in the building, but everyone knew that he and Kellen [Winslow, Jr.,] were good prospects. Gregg [Williams] was selling Sean from day one. Everything negative that was said—well, it was Gregg who was pounding the table, saying, 'This is the guy we need.'"* Coach Jackson also offered this: *"It was Coach Gibbs that made the final decision."*

It was the offensive staff who were really pro Kellen Winslow, Jr., because he reminded Coach Gibbs of his tight ends from the past. Gibbs thought Kellen could be the tight end that could stretch the field. He was everything Gibbs could possibly ask for, "but Gregg did one hell of a job selling Sean over and over and over," *Jackson said.* "Vinny Cerrato liked him, but it took selling Sean to Coach Gibbs, saying he was going to help the entire team and not just the defense. He had to make the whole team better."

Coach Jackson's first memory of Sean after the draft was when he didn't show for OTAs. When he finally came in, Coach Gregg Williams just blasted him. "We're thinking Gregg was just going to rip him a new one, and I'm thinking I'm going to have to bring him back after Gregg pissed him off. I was the one who was going to have to deal with him. I mean, Sean just shrugged it off and, as he left the meeting room, said, 'Nice haircut.' The interesting thing was, Gregg was like, 'You know, none of you other sons of bitches said anything about my haircut.' And that's how it was with those two.

"You know, Sean Taylor was a fierce competitor, and that's what made him so much better than everyone else. He had the athletic ability, he had the size, but Sean would compete against all of his teammates at practice every day. Sean was going to try and be the best of everybody out there. I mean even if a new guy came in, he competed to beat him too. I have never seen anything like it before or after him.

"If there was a guy with a new contract making more than him, Sean would never say anything. But all of a sudden you'd see Sean going one hundred miles an hour at practice."

How many times has it been said before that Sean had only one speed? Full!

"You know, we would tell Sean and everybody else in practice, 'Hey, nobody dive for any balls,' because we didn't want to get anybody hurt. 'Okay, Coach,' Sean would say. But as soon as a ball came near him, Sean would be diving for it."

Remembering a certain practice in Sean's rookie season, Coach Jackson said, "We were three and thirteen, I think, or four and twelve—something like that. We had no chance of going to the playoffs. So on the last day of practice, a full-pads practice, in the last week of the season, Sean is out there going *full speed*. Everyone else has pretty much shut it down, getting ready for the game or worse. Some were getting mentally prepared for the off-season. Not Sean. He is chasing people, intercepting everything, going after the scout team; it even made an impression on the better players."

Revelation

When asked about Sean's relationship with his teammates, Jackson unexpectedly followed with this: In the beginning, "he and LaVar Arrington didn't really get along. It all started with this incident during Sean's rookie year. I don't think Sean ever forgave him for that either.

"Sean was a very high-profile player. LaVar was a fading high-profile player. There are initiation things that veterans do, and LaVar felt it was his duty to do one of those things to Sean." What happened was this: Arrington bought an aluminum pie pan and filled it with shaving cream. During one of Sean's rare interviews, LaVar smashed the shaving cream pie in his face. "Well, it got into Sean's eyes, and it burned the hell out of them. And Sean was like, 'What the hell are you doing?' Sean couldn't see. He couldn't go to the meeting after, and I think he couldn't see for two days," Jackson said.

"Coaches Gibbs and Williams had to address the situation. Sean didn't talk about it much after that, but he was angry for a long time. Sean just thought it was stupid [not to mention it could have ruined his eyesight—or worse, his career]. After that he never had anything good to say [about LaVar]. He didn't say anything like 'I can't stand him,' but there was never any praise for him either."

LaVar Arrington was with the Redskins until 2005, and in the end, reports were that he and Sean did make amends.

It's been well documented that Sean did not like Terrell Owens. But were there any others on his "do not like" list?

"Terry Glenn of the Dallas Cowboys," Coach Jackson exclaimed. "Yeah! It was those two Cowboys—T.O. and Terry. Parcells had them both there. They … would … not … go … anywhere … near … Sean! The way they played, it was almost like a game to see who could get the furthest away from him [Sean].

"I'm trying to think of anybody else. T.O. was a special case, because Sean's hits on him were recorded and memorialized on TV … how Sean intimidated him." (There were no imaginary Sharpies being pulled out of a sock for autographs after one of Sean's hits.)

"I have some other people in my mind that would definitely not catch the ball [when thrown their way], like Todd Pinkston of the Philadelphia Eagles. He wouldn't make a catch unless he was on Ryan Clark's side. If Sean was anywhere in the vicinity, it would probably be a dropped ball.

"I mean, very rarely would players go down the seams, and the only reason they would was they were hoping Sean would be asleep. If you were to go through all of Sean's highlights, you would see the ball being thrown down the middle of the field more than you would expect. Then he'd either pick it or knock somebody's helmet off. You would think that part of the field was off limits. But QBs would actually still try and throw the ball down there. As a defense, we eventually got so used to people not throwing it there, even if players looked wide open. Sean would come out of nowhere and just decapitate them," Jackson said. "He covered so much ground and was so quick at the moment of impact, there was no way. I mean, a guy, 6'3", with that kind of explosiveness—no way he would 'cool off' when the ball was coming and wait for a guy to take two steps. He either goes through him or he lets him go."

Sean played like there was no tomorrow because he never knew when his last play was going to come. "You may not get the chance to come back next week or next year and do it again." Jackson preached. "Hey, we got a good team and everybody is coming back, but they may say, 'Everybody is coming back but you!'"

"It was a real joy seeing Sean develop," Jackson said. "He went from a guy who really didn't care about the inner workings of the game to learning as much as he could about it. He took the mental part of the game to another level. Not only would he want to crash people at a hundred miles an hour; he became a student of the game. In the beginning we would put things on the board, like certain formations, and Sean would say, 'Coach, I don't know what that is.' Or he would just mess up a coverage."

By 2007 Sean was able to go up to the board and draw in the formation and explain what everyone was supposed to be doing. He had had the physical ability down for some time, but he took his mental attitude to an entirely new level.

20

The DUI That Wasn't

IMAGINE IT'S OCTOBER 27, 2004, AT TWO TO TWO THIRTY IN THE morning and you're new in town. You're driving back to your house from a party with a friend in a car you just bought with your own money. Now imagine you're a young African-American man, a professional football player, and you get pulled over by the Virginia State Police on Route 66. What do you do? WWSD? (What would Sean do?)

Now imagine you're home watching television and a news report about your son comes on. That's how it was for Sean's father, Pete Taylor, as he saw the report of his son's arrest on the charge of DUI (driving under the influence) on the local Miami television news.

"I was sitting at home in Miami, and I see on the TV news Sean Taylor got arrested for driving under the influence," Pete Taylor says, beginning to tell of the story of this incredible ordeal. "Needless to say, this was news to me," Pete Taylor said.

Initially Sean got stopped by a Virginia state trooper for speeding on Route 66 in Fairfax County, Virginia, at about two thirty a.m. However, the trooper had something more in mind,

There is a part of Route 66 where the speed limit suddenly drops from 65 mph to 55 mph without warning. Anyone who has ever extensively traveled that part of the highway knows exactly where that is. Troopers set up very close to the 55 mph sign, waiting to catch anyone who doesn't react quickly enough to the posted reduction in speed. Generally people drive 5–10 mph over the limit, so if you're doing 70, which is 5 over in a

65 mph zone, and miss the sign, that means you're driving 70 in a 55 mph zone. Sean, being a Redskin rookie and new to the area, missed the 55 mph speed limit sign.

When Sean got pulled over, he remained calm and in his vehicle until he was asked to exit. A few moments later, Sean was asked for his driver's license and registration, which he produced post haste. The trooper retreated to his cruiser, where he ran a check on the man and the car. Sean was left standing outside by his car with only a long-sleeved shirt on in the chilly October early morning. We know all this because it was revealed on the officer's dash cam video, captured by a little camera mounted on the cruiser's dashboard which recorded the traffic stop.

The speculation is that the trooper was waiting for Sean to make some erratic gesture, stumble, or fall down. Instead Sean remained calm, and while waiting for the trooper to return, called his agent, Drew Rosenhaus to let him know he had just been pulled over. Drew advised him to stay there and not move.

Five minutes went by. Ten minutes went by. After twenty minutes, the trooper was still in his vehicle, while Sean was standing outside. On the video one could see Sean's breath steaming out of his mouth in the cold air. About twenty eighteen-wheelers flew by, each ruffling Sean's clothes. But Sean remained calm and steadfast.

Finally, the state trooper exited his cruiser and approached the frozen Taylor. When Sean tried to get on the phone again, presumably to call his father, the trooper demanded (in an elevated voice) that he immediately get off the phone and stand still. And he did, like a soldier.

"Do you know why I pulled you over?" the trooper asked Sean.

"Not really," Sean replied.

"Suspicion of DUI. That's driving under the influence!" the trooper screamed.

Respectfully, Sean responded, "Sir, I had one drink tonight," (and that had been hours before).

The trooper lashed out at Sean again, and with the harshest of voice said, "We'll see about that." He then had Sean perform a field sobriety check (FSC). He had Sean perform the standard tasks: walk the straight line, walk heel to toe, tilt the head back and don't fall over, touch your finger to your nose, etc. Sean passed all of his tests.

Despite all of that, the trooper decided there was probable cause and wanted Sean to take a breathalyzer test, which Sean refused.

Upon Sean's refusal to take the breathalyzer test, he was immediately arrested and taken to jail. There he was fingerprinted and had a mug shot taken (which was released to the press). He was then put in lockup overnight and didn't get out until the next morning. And the story continues from there.

Clinton Portis

Clinton Portis was at the same party as Sean. "I remember when Sean left the house. Probably five minutes after I leave, my friend Derrick called me. 'They done pulled Sean over,' he said.

"So Sean was pullin' out from my house, and the police jumped behind him [on Route 66]. I'm like, 'Damn!'

Next, Derrick called Sean's lawyer Robert Bailey and agent Drew Rosenhaus. He said to them, "They took Sean in." The next day, many people, including the coach, called Clinton for an update. "I'm like, 'Bro, I don't know. He was at the house and he left. You know, like, I can't make him stay.' You know, he was leavin' the house, and he ended up gettin' a DUI," Portis said.

Redskins Teammate Fred Smoot

Another one of Sean's Redskin teammates, Fred Smoot, was at the party. He recalled the events of the evening this way: "The night Sean got stopped for the alleged DUI was a classic DBs [defensive backs] guys' night out. We did this every week. That night there were maybe twelve to fifteen of us going out. We usually started with dinner, and sometimes we had drinks afterward."

According to Smoot, Sean may have had one drink at dinner, but after that, nothing. "So now we're trailing each other back home. That's one thing we always did. We come together, we leave together. We're coming down Route 66 in Virginia, and a state trooper ended up pulling Sean over. All of us start to veer off, pull over to the side of the road." Smoot went on to say, "There must have been four carloads of guys just sitting on the side of the road, watching things go down. They were about four or five car lengths behind Sean's car when a second cruiser pulled over next to the caravan. When the trooper from that car approached them, he told them they had to move because they could be charged with obstructing justice if they didn't.

"So we see Sean getting out of his vehicle. If you know Sean, and if he feels like he ain't did nothing wrong, he'll speak to ya. He's going to stand up for himself. Next thing we know, they're putting him in the police car. So we all know what time it is."

⬤

Sometime early in the morning, Sean was released from jail. Joe Gibbs and others were calling Sean nonstop to find out where he was. When he got out, he made phone calls to his team, his agent, and his father. Because he had been up all day and night, the team advised him to go home and not report for practice until the next day. They were afraid of throwing him to the lions of the impending media circus. The Redskins wanted to protect Sean and avoid any team distractions. For what *that* was worth.

Sean was already making an impact on the team. Some good. Some not so good. Regardless, when Sean was released, a lady working at the police station asked for and received an autograph. Figures. Right?

When he finally got to speak to his son, Pete Taylor asked him, "You okay?"

Sean responded, "Yeah. Dad, I got stopped last night, but I wasn't drunk. But the guy took me."

The damage was done. The news of the DUI arrest went national, and once that cat is out of the bag, it can never be put back in. Some media outlets wrote the story as if Sean were a thug; they didn't wait for a trial or the presentation of any evidence, allowing him to prove his innocence. A rush to judgment in a twenty-four-hour news cycle is the norm rather than the exception these days. Plus, if a suspect is proven innocent, retractions are few and far between or just buried.

Clinton Portis

Clinton Portis continued. "Coach Gibbs was like, 'Have you heard from him? Have you heard from him?' Ridley and Derrick was with him the whole time. Derrick is the one who picked him up from the police station. So, you know, I'm in communication with Derrick, and he tellin' me everything that's goin' on."

Clinton said to his friend Sean, "Man, where you all at? Y'all should be here [meaning Redskins Park]." On the other hand, whoever initially spoke to Sean from the team told him to go home and avoid the media circus.

"Derrick responded, 'Man, Sean told me to bring him home.'"

"I was like, 'What? Y'all need to be here!'

"Derrick was like, 'Man, I'm over at Sean T. crib, man.'"

Sean told Derrick he wouldn't be going to Redskins Park, as the media was going to be there and he needed to brush his teeth and hadn't eaten in a while. Chuckling, Portis said, "Sean went home and started cookin'! Everybody callin' Sean, like, 'What's goin' on?' I remember callin' Sean. I'm talkin' to him, like, 'Bro, what are you doin'?'

"Sean says, 'C. P., I'm not gonna come over there and talk to them people. Like, I'll talk to 'em tomorrow.'

"I'm like, 'Naw, you cain't talk to them tomorrow. You gotta come in and see Coach Gibbs, talk to Mr. Snyder or Vinny Cerrato.' I'm like, 'You gotta come talk to them.'"

Sean refused and said he'd see them the following day when he came to practice.

"I remember havin' to leave practice," Portis said.

Then he went to meet Sean at his house. "We just sittin' over there playin' video games. I look at him like, 'Man, this dude crazy!'" Portis laughed and repeated, "This dude crazy!"

There are certain advantages to being a chief of police. For one thing, within minutes he or she can tell if a traffic stop is legit or not.

In an attempt to help out his son, the Florida City, Florida - Chief of Police Pete Taylor flew to Washington, DC, to meet with a few attorneys and with Sean. There were many questions to be asked. Since the traffic stop had taken place in Virginia, which is a commonwealth, the laws were just a little different than those in Florida. For example, the rules of disclosure were different.

Sean's lawyers couldn't get the charges dropped by the Virginia district attorney. Luckily the court date was scheduled after the season was over.

The DUI Trial

On March 10, 2005, Sean and his father Pete entered the Virginia courthouse, ready for trial. The first person they ran into was the arresting state trooper. He was about 5'8", had a muscular build, and was dressed in his trooper uniform.

"I don't know his name, but he said, 'Hello' to us," said Pete. "Sean says to me, 'Dad, that's the guy who arrested me.'

"I said, 'Really?'"

Pete spoke to Sean's lawyer. "Get the cruiser video. Get whatever you can because he must have run video."

Sean turns to his dad and says, "Dad, I am not guilty. I am telling you, I am not guilty. I wasn't drinking."

Finally, court was in session. The judge asked if both parties were ready. He asked the officer if he was ready. "Yes." He asked Sean's lawyer if he was ready. "Yes."

In the courtroom, some of Sean's fellow teammates came to testify on his behalf. There were Clinton Portis, Laveranues Coles, Fred Smoot, Shawn Springs, and LaVar Arrington. They were at the party that night and came to testify that Sean wasn't drinking.

Sean's lawyer called his first witness, Laveranues Coles, who took the stand and testified that Sean hadn't been drinking during the party on the night in question. When the judge asked how he knew Sean wasn't drinking, he said that at the time he thought his girlfriend liked Sean. He wasn't sure, so he kept watching Sean out of the corner of his eye all night. It turned out that Sean left before Laveranues, so he'd know if Sean had a drink or not. "In spite of how he felt about his girlfriend and Sean, nobody would ever go and testify on their behalf if it wasn't true. That shows that Laveranues was the bigger man," said Pete Taylor.

Fred Smoot

Fred Smoot got to testify on Sean's behalf as well. Smoot said, "When the trial came up, everybody that came spoke the truth—the same story. I'll tell you this right now. There's no way he should have been accused of DUI. He didn't even drink at the party. Not to mention that Sean even passed the roadside sobriety check and did everything the state trooper asked him to do. But the trooper still wanted to take him to jail, so he did. And he did this without regard to the future of this young, budding NFL star.

"It was a case of wrong place at the wrong time with the wrong police officer. But we went through it as a team, and that's the point here. We didn't let him go through it alone. When Pete called and said he needed some people to testify, it was eight of us, the same people who were out … yeah, we there," said Smoot.

Sean's team rested.

The judge then asked if the trooper was ready to testify. He was. A videotape player and monitor were already set up in the courtroom. So first the trooper offered this: "Let me show you the video of my stop."

Pete shared what happened next. "The judge comes off the bench to watch the video, and now he's sitting in a chair with his arms folded. He's on the same side of the room as us. The video is going, going … you see the car stop; you see the brake lights come on; you see [about nineteen to twenty] eighteen-wheelers come blowing by. You also see Sean getting out of his car and left standing on the side of the road for some time, trying to keep himself warm by putting his hands in his pockets."

From the audio one could hear the trooper scolding Sean, telling him to take his hands out of his pockets. "You see Sean blowing into his hands to keep them warm. Then Sean gets on his phone and tries to call his agent, Drew Rosenhaus," remembered Pete Taylor.

According to Clinton Portis, "That trooper was being a jerk; a real asshole."

On the other hand, the trooper could have been a little nervous at this point, seeing several carloads of Sean's friends show up and pull in behind him. The trooper in the second cruiser arrived and demanded they leave, which they did. No one wanted to get in trouble.

The video showed the trooper keeping Sean outside his vehicle. The seconds and minutes were ticking off the video time code. It was a dewy night, about thirty-five to forty degrees, which is unusually cold for late October.

Pete further described the scene: "Sean was standing in front of the cruiser and behind his own car, straight up. When the judge looked at the video, he saw Sean remaining perfectly calm. The trooper's demeanor is far from calm. He seems quite upset and agitated. Sean spoke calmly and clearly, but the trooper did nothing but scream.

"The trooper didn't get what he wanted from Sean, so his voice became even harsher," Pete said. "When the judge saw all this, plus Sean passing the FSC, he became very upset, because he sees the trooper, who he thought had class, yelling like a maniac and crazy as hell. He just put his head down in his hands.

"Halfway through the video, the judge asks both attorneys, 'Do you need to see any more?'"

The judge returned to the bench and asked if there was any additional evidence. There was none. So both the defense and prosecuting attorneys said no. Sean's attorney then made a motion to dismiss the case, saying there was no apparent DUI.

Based on the evidence, the judge dismissed the case, and that's exactly what the Taylors wanted.

But the trial(s) didn't end there. During the first court trial, the judge could have thrown the entire case out. He didn't. He had Sean reappear to face the charge of failing to take a breathalyzer test. So once again, more damage done.

According to Pete Taylor, and without going through all the details, "At the second trial, all charges were dismissed. We eventually filed a complaint for misconduct against the trooper. When you file a complaint in Virginia, if they take action, they don't have to tell you the results of the action, and in my opinion his actions were unbecoming of an officer.

"Don't get me wrong. Officers do have a difficult job and sometimes get upset, frustrated, and even sometimes exhibit poor judgment. But to take a guy in when there's no slurred speech, no staggering, no bloodshot eyes, no signs of the usual DUI, suggests the officer may have had another agenda.

"So here's what I tell my people at the FCPD [Florida City Police Department]: 'You only meet resistance with resistance.' This kid was not resisting; he didn't do anything.

"During the entire incident, I felt like crap. You always want your kids to be honest with you and tell you the truth. When I spoke to Sean, he was completely honest with me and told me he wasn't drinking. Of course I want to believe my own son, but there's always some doubt because I wasn't on the scene."

Sean and Pete had a deal. "When Sean moved in with me when he was eleven years old, we agreed he was never going to lie to me. We were going to be honest with each other. Whatever happens happens, but he's going to take complete responsibility for his actions. That's how children should be raised. And if there's a pattern of telling the truth, you're going to believe them.

"The [press] liked to make Sean a villain. Oftentimes, he wasn't the villain; he was the victim," Pete says. "Remember, bad news sells. In this case, the video proved that Sean was telling the truth."

Revelation

Sean's friend Mike said, "You know the reason Sean even changed his number from 36 to 21 was because after he won his DUI case, he asked me, 'Do I keep my number 36 or change it?' He thought 36 was his bad luck number. So I told him, the first thing you have to do is start new." So that's how he went from rookie jersey number 36 to jersey number 21, taking Fred Smoot's number when he left to join the Minnesota Vikings.

"I would say that's who Sean related to most in his rookie year was Smoot. Here's another thing. Smoot had a cousin named Sean, and the four of us would hang out. We would go bowling and do different things together. I would say his closest 'partner' who mentored him was Smoot," Mike said.

21

The Case of the Stolen Banshees

THE OFF-THE-FIELD PRESS WOES CONTINUED FOR SEAN TAYLOR. ON June 3, 2005, two of Sean's Banshee all-terrain vehicles (ATVs), used mainly for joyriding in the woods, were stolen. He had them stored at a friend's home in Perrine, Florida. Here's the story:

Attorney Richard Sharpstein

Richard Sharpstein was a Miami criminal defense attorney for thirty-five years. Before that he was a prosecutor for another five. Attorney Sharpstein worked on many famous cases, including the prosecution of Panamanian president Manuel Noriega and the drama surrounding a young man forcibly brought to the United States from Cuba, by the name of Elian Gonzalez.

More importantly, to the Taylors he was the family friend who helped out in some very difficult times, including the now famous Sean Taylor Banshee ATV incident. Sharpstein righted what could have been a huge wrong. The problem was that most in the press didn't see it that way. It was another case of "report and print first, ask questions later."

"I was Sean Taylor's attorney in the stolen Banshee ATV case," said Richard Sharpstein. "I didn't represent Sean right away; in fact, it wasn't until six months later that I even got on the case after a friend named Ralph Ortega, whose son played football with Sean at Gulliver, alerted me to what was going on."

Ironically, Sharpstein had known Sean's father, Pete, for thirty years, "since he was a young cop in [Florida City]. I think he was there by the time I was a prosecutor," Sharpstein said.

"I met Sean at Gulliver Prep, the same school my daughters attended, the school Sean helped win a state football championship in 2001. Both of my girls were cheerleaders; one older, one younger than Sean." According to Sharpstein, the cheerleaders would have fundraisers, and Sean always participated. The mothers sold refreshments at the games, but he would help out despite being a superstar—even in high school.

"I'll never forget his humility," Sharpstein said. "Sometimes people mistook that for arrogance since he was such a quiet, soft-spoken kid who was never self-absorbed."

Some thieves in the neighborhood spotted the ATVs as Sean and his friends were out riding them. Those four-wheelers became the target of their desire. The thieves eventually stole them from Sean's friend Mike's house in Perrine, Florida. According to Sharpstein, Sean kept them there to use in the off-season when he would visit.

Sharpstein said of the ordeal, "Sean and his friends T. J. and Mike went to confront these young men, these thugs, gangsters, these bad-ass kids, to get his property back. There was a confrontation with the criminals on the lawn of one of their houses in Perrine, Florida. These guys lied about not having the ATVs. There was almost fisticuffs and talk of getting guns, so Sean and his buddies left."

Mike McFarlane

Warning: This section contains the N word.

"This is how it started," Mike said. "Sean kept the Yamaha Banshee ATV four-wheelers at my house overnight because Sean went off to see some chick.

"In the morning I woke up to go to work. I was in the kitchen and looked out the window, and the bikes were missing. Even though they were missing, my first thought was, 'I gotta get to work and deal with this later.' So I called the police on the way in and told them someone broke into my house. Verbatim, what the police officer told me on the phone was, 'If you don't have proof that you purchased them, there's nothing we can do. We can't do anything for you.' So I hung up." (Mike may not have had the proof of purchase, but Sean did.)

Frustrated by the call, he thought about the situation a little more and decided it would be best to turn around and go back home. At that point he called work to inform them he wouldn't be coming in and then tried calling Sean to let him know what happened. As Mike was dialing, Sean was pulling up to his house. "I was like, 'All right, shit—you're here.'" So in front of his house, Mike told Sean that his ATVs were gone.

Sean and his buddies decided to pay a visit to the neighborhood where they believed the ATVs were. When Sean got to the house in Perrine, he was confronted by a guy who came over to him and said, "Hey, this isn't your area, and you shouldn't be here." But Sean didn't leave. Sean was still sitting in his car, just observing, when another guy came up to him and said, "You got to leave, *now!*" Sean said, "I'm not going anywhere."

Words were exchanged, and when Sean exited his vehicle, the two got into a little tussle. Separately Sean's friends arrived and witnessed Sean scrapping with the guys who they believed had stolen the ATVs. So they all jumped out of their car to help break up the fight. Some other neighborhood people came over to help their friends out in the fight. A gun was brandished, and at that point, everybody either started running or, as in the case of Sean and his friends, got into their cars and left.

Sean returned to Mike's house, and when he got there, he went inside for a few rounds of video games. Unbeknownst to them, the alleged thieves had followed them back to the house. About a half hour later, all hell broke loose as the alleged miscreants came to the house armed with an AK-47 and shot it up. Bullets entered the house, and everybody in it hit the deck and took cover. Thankfully nobody was hit. Someone in the house said, "Call 911." Ironically, the shooters were simultaneously dialing 911 to report that Sean Taylor had been at their house to confront them, and they said he had a gun!

According to T. J., Mike, Pete Taylor and Attorney Sharpstein—they all said the same thing—Sean didn't own a gun.

Pete Taylor followed with, "On the day of the occurrence, I was unaware of what was going down. I think I was at a restaurant, having dinner with the rest of the family, and then my cell phone started blowing up."

Attorney Sharpstein added, "The police now had two crime scenes: the home where the original confrontation took place, and the home that was shot up."

After the entire incident, Sean left Florida and returned to his Virginia residence. By that time the news had reported that Sean was being sought by the police for questioning.

Pete remembers calling Sean and leaving a message on his cell phone. "I figured he'd call somebody just to let them know he's okay and to let him know he needs to come back and turn himself in."

Appearing on the TV news, Miami-Dade Police spokeswoman Mary Walters said, "We need to speak to him [Sean]..." And, "We don't know if he's a victim, witness or suspect. Taylor was allegedly present at, and possibly involved in, an incident in which bullets allegedly were fired into a stolen vehicle." Not exactly accurate, but close enough, for the moment.

Soon after, Sean returned to Miami. There he and his father met with an attorney. "Then we took him over to the police station," Pete Taylor said. "I walked him into Miami-Dade Police Station Number Four and told them Sean Taylor was here. The detectives then spoke with him briefly. They then booked him and took him to Miami lockup."

On June 5, ESPN and the *Miami Herald* both reported that Sean Taylor, accompanied by his lawyer, had surrendered to Miami-Dade police at approximately 10pm EST on June 4 at the Cutler Ridge district police station, from which he was transported to the Turner Guilford Knight correctional facility. He was charged with aggravated assault with a firearm (a felony) and misdemeanor battery. Miami-Dade police issued a statement the same day confirming the earlier reports. "Taylor had allegedly pointed a gun at a person over a dispute concerning two ATVs that he claimed were stolen." The Associated Press reported that Taylor was released the evening of June 4 after posting bond of $16,500.

Pete Taylor continued. "The accusation was that he had committed a crime using a firearm. The guys who shot up Sean's friend's house tried to flip the story around from people who were trying to kill a high-profile football player to one where they had the AK-47 as protection and to defend themselves against someone firing at them."

Through their attorney, the thieves argued that there was a plot against them perpetrated by the Florida Highway Patrol (FHP). They also argued that since Pedro Taylor was with the Florida City Police Department, he was working out a deal with the FHP. Amazingly, they accused Pete Taylor of being behind it all.

In the meantime, while waiting on the court date, the thieves were being picked up again, this time at three o'clock in the morning with stolen cars and bikes in their possession.

Pete Taylor stated that an attorney came in the next day, someone who was trying to protect his own clients. Sean's "victims" had their case immediately dropped. Consequently, every time these guys got in trouble, which occurred about three or four times, the attorney would have their case dropped so there would be no charges against his clients. "That wasn't fair to the people who got their property stolen," Taylor said. "So the [state's attorney] keeps rewarding bad behavior all in an effort to make his department look good for their trial against Sean Taylor, the professional football player.

"Now, if Sean was in the wrong, I understand, but if he's not, this guy was about to jeopardize his career," said Pete. "But did he care? No! Florida has a mandatory three years in the penitentiary for a crime where a firearm was used. But if you're in a high-profile case, and they say you committed a gun crime, they want to hold you for trial.

"In a pretrial meeting, the prosecuting attorney says he's going for three years' probation," Pete Taylor said. Additionally, the prosecutor advised, "As you know, a lot of trials can go fifty-fifty. Some cases we win, and some we lose, and a lot of them seem to go on forever. If we lose, we just chalk it up as a loss. So we want to work out a plea deal."

"Since he wanted Sean to plead to a crime with a weapon, we said, 'No deal.' Sean didn't have a weapon," Pete Taylor said. "He didn't even own a weapon. Sean was adamant, and I supported him."

Sean said, "Dad, I'd rather do the time if I lose the case rather than admit to something I didn't do."

"When I heard that, I asked, 'Sean, are you sure?'" his father inquired.

Sean's response was, "I'm not going to admit to something I didn't do. If I did it, I would tell you and take whatever punishment is handed down."

So the Taylors said, "No deal."

"We sat there for a moment while [the attorney] went to speak to the powers that be," recalled Taylor. "When he returned, he offered a similar yet lesser plea deal of trespassing, battery with no weapon involved, and disorderly conduct, which were all misdemeanors."

The condition was Sean had to give up the names of the other people he was with. But Sean said he didn't know anybody, so the deal was taken off the table. The prosecution then stated they were going to go for three years for each of the defendants and that they were going to ask for forty-five years in prison. The Taylors said, "We'll see you in court."

On January 28, 2006, Michael Grieco, the Miami-Dade County prosecutor, announced that he was filing new charges against Taylor, which would have increased his potential maximum state prison time from sixteen years to forty-five years. The new charges were made by increasing the felony assault charges from one to three.

Incredibly, "there were some improprieties in the case that we knew about, and we tried to speak to the SA, as well as anybody in the state's attorney's office who would listen," Pete Taylor said visibly annoyed. But of course nobody really wanted to sit down and discuss the case.

Richard Sharpstein

When Sean's new attorney, Richard Sharpstein, began investigating the "victims" who allegedly stole the ATVs, it didn't take long to find out that every single one of them had been arrested before, with cases closed or pending; some of them were on probation. "It was kind of shocking to me," Sharpstein said. "We even found out that two of them had been arrested for stealing another ATV months after Sean's theft. None of this had been brought up in pretrial. I went to him [the prosecutor] and laid all this out and asked him, 'How come you didn't give us any of this? You should have had all this information.'"

His answer? Grieco responded with something like he just didn't have it. But all they had to do was look up their own records.

"Since we thought it was his obligation to give up the information, we filed an initial motion for prosecutorial misconduct and dismissal with Judge Mary Barzee Flores," Sharpstein said. "We then knew the prosecutor was just pushing this case, this garbage case that never should have been brought against Sean. Meanwhile he was basking in the limelight of all the publicity that came both locally and nationally."

As they got closer to trial it was discovered that Grieco had been moonlighting as a disc jockey in Miami Beach on the weekends. "So I told my associates to look into it, and we found what was to be the silver bullet, the so-called smoking gun," Sharpstein said.

According to Sharpstein, it turned out that Prosecuting Attorney Michael Grieco had a MySpace page under the name DJ Grieco, and on it was everything from a ten-year-old kid rapping to girls who were communicating with him, saying, "Thanks for the Captain Morgan the other night and oh by the way, I'm only 15." There were also pictures of the DJ booth, which was lined with ... let's call them very inappropriate pictures.

Amazingly his MySpace page had a link that said something along the lines of "Click here for my news coverage of the Sean Taylor trial." So Sharpstein's team made screen captures and downloaded that to a disc.

"We were coming up for court the next week, and like I said, we put together a formal prosecutorial misconduct and dismissal based on the fact that he was using his public office for private gain. We went to court for a status conference armed with a CD-ROM of the MySpace [page] and gave it out to all the media that was there: CNN, the *Washington Post*, ESPN, etc., and they were all on it.

"By the time we got out of court, they looked at the CD-ROM, and when Prosecuting Attorney Grieco came out, the media surrounded him and started asking questions about his MySpace page. Well, he completely freaked out and literally ran out of the back of the courthouse while we gave a press conference on not only this being ethically challenging but a violation of certain pornography laws."

By two o'clock that afternoon, the news media had gone crazy with the story, and at 2:01 the prosecutor was taken off the case. By four o'clock Grieco was fired.

"Katherine Fernandez Rundle, the state attorney, was particularly interested in his MySpace [page], where there were pictures of him on a Friday afternoon at the Fontainebleau Hotel on a chaise lounge with a couple of young ladies and a beer can by his side when he was supposed to be working. So he was fired, and a new prosecutor was assigned. It was Abe Laser, one of the chief assistants, who has since retired. Once I showed him everything, he agreed that if Sean were to do some community service, he would dismiss the case. Which he did. And which Sean did."

The trial was set to begin on July 10 in Miami, but on June 2, the charges against Taylor were dropped as part of a negotiated plea bargain. Taylor donated his time to various charities and made one-thousand-dollar donations to ten southern Florida schools in the form of scholarships. In exchange, he would avoid jail time and a felony record.

Sean had already been doing (non-court ordered) community service. On his own, he was already speaking to "at-risk" kids about not carrying guns, staying in school, and trying to make something of their lives.

Since Sean was a first-time offender, he accepted the court-ordered community service deal, which included speaking to fifteen schools and donating money to schools such as South Dade, Killian, Southridge.

"This whole thing took place during the summer, so Sean made it back to training camp unscathed, but it did take him through the muck and mire of the press for a year," Sharpstein said. "Everyone from the team to the fans were super concerned because of the accusations of violence [and gun crime, which is enough to ruin any career]."

Pete Taylor

"These were all schools happy to see Sean, and helping out their football/ sports programs financially was just a bonus," Pete said. "This was rewarding in a sense, but it also enlightened Sean on life itself."

In addition to the community service, Sean also had to check in with the courts every month for about eighteen months so they could keep track of him. This all took place during what's called a pretrial intervention. Since Sean accepted this deal, there was no trial and no conviction.

Revelation

It is a common misconception that when Sean defended himself during the breaking and entering event that would eventually take his life, he could not own a gun because of the ATV incident. But Sean did not have a gun, didn't even own a gun when the confrontation with the ATV thieves went down. The policeman that filed the report believed the thieves, who said Sean had a gun. That's how it got reported in the media.

"He could have had a firearm!" Florida City, Florida Chief of Police Pedro Taylor said authoritatively. But he didn't.

"Sean could have gotten a gun at any time. I tried to get him one legally so he could carry it anywhere he wanted," said Pete Taylor. "He didn't want to do it at the time."

Mike McFarlane

"But we was young and we wanted to take care of this ourselves," Sean's friend Mike said.

"The most important thing I want people to know out of the book is that Sean was not as bad as everybody thought he was," added Mike. "So the thing I want to get across is, of the wild and crazy things you may have heard about Sean, he made a complete 180 the moment Baby Jackie was born. This was a God-fearing, family-loving man. And when I say family, I mean anybody who was close to him. If you weren't in his inner circle, you were just more or less an associate. This was a person who was very private in everything he did. He didn't express a lot of things to a lot of people.

"It would be an easy decision just to call Pete. But at the end of the day, Sean said, 'Nah, these niggas are trying us.' So it was bigger than that. We still gotta walk around in these streets and we gotta keep walking."

So why didn't Sean just call the police when he found out the ATVs were missing? The ATVs were clearly his. He had the receipt, and on it were the vehicle identification numbers. (As stated earlier, when Mike called the police to inform them of the stolen ATVs, they told him that since *he* didn't have the receipts, there was nothing they could do for him.)

"If the ATVs were stolen, just call the police and let them deal with it," Pete said. "And guess what. If you don't find the ATVs and you don't have insurance, chalk it up as a loss."

Buck Ortega

Buck Ortega, Sean's high school, UM, and Redskins friend and teammate, summed up the ATV incident this way: "It was garbage. The reports [that came out after his death] about how he hung out with the wrong crew made my blood absolutely boil. When he was charged with assault and possession of an illegal firearm, what was he supposed to do? They stole his ATVs! What the heck? I would have done the same thing if someone stole my four-wheeler and I knew where they were. I might have gone to get them back too. That's the kind of kid Sean was. [He liked taking care of business on his own.] I don't blame him. That he was hanging around with the wrong crew was the furthest thing from the truth. Sean was a family guy. He was a guy who liked to laugh; a guy who just liked to spend quality time with his girlfriend, Mommy Jackie, and his child, Baby Jackie.

"When I signed with the Redskins early that summer, Sean missed a lot of time at training camp because he had to deal with the courts. When he got up to DC, he took me under his wing, took me out to eat, showed me all the good restaurants, and took me over to his house, and all he talked about was Baby Jackie. That's what he was. He wasn't anything but that. He was a quiet kid who liked to laugh. He was also blessed with an ungodly ability to play football."

🏈

Coach Steve Jackson

How did the Redskins deal with the intense media coverage of those things Sean was accused off? Coach Steve Jackson answered this way: "I was fortunate enough to play for nine years as a DB in the NFL. So the stuff he was going through I could really relate to. I didn't have the cleanest track record either, ya know? We all know what Gregg Williams was accused of, so there was this mentality there that we were all in this thing together. You won't get judged by your teammates. You won't be judged by your coaches. You will, however, be judged by what you do on the field.

"You have to do what's right. So we didn't have to lecture Sean about anything. He knew right from wrong. But just being the celebrity that he was, he was being accused of not always making the right decisions."

Jackson continued. "The stuff that came out in the press was … was … I don't want to say overblown, but since he was a celebrity, everything became sensationalized. But day to day, Sean just brought his lunch pail to work. He wasn't one of those guys with flashy jewelry, with flashy clothes … 'Look at me … look at me.'"

Side Story

T. J. Holten likes to talk about Sean's trips to Las Vegas to have a good time and play some cards. So here's this very large African American sitting at the card table with a huge stack of chips—not unusual in Vegas, mind you. However, every once in a while in conversations with the card dealers, they'd ask Sean, "Tell me, what exactly do you do for a living?" Sean was both shy and unassuming and did not want to be known as "that superstar football player," so he answered this way: "I'm a garbage man," T. J. said.

"What?" the flabbergasted dealers would say. "A garbage man? Then you must be doing pretty well for a garbage man."

Then Sean would say, "Yeah. I pick up a lot of garbage!"

22

Favre Breaks the Record!

Washington Redskins Teammate Santana Moss

Both Santana Moss and Sean Taylor came up playing football in the South Florida parks and high school system. Taylor played at Killian High School and then Gulliver Prep, while Moss played for Miami Carol City Senior High School. With this similar upbringing, few could relate to Taylor better than Moss. Like Taylor, elite receiver Santana Moss played for the University of Miami, where he was an All-American. He was a 2001 first-round draft pick by the New York Jets. In 2005 Santana was traded to the Washington Redskins from the Jets for Laveranues Coles. By then Sean was already in his second season with the Redskins. In 2014 Moss began his tenth campaign in Washington.

With the interview arranged by Washington Redskins team owner Daniel Snyder himself, Pete Taylor and I were set to have our phone conference with Santana.

●

Right off the bat, Moss said Sean T. reminded him of himself. Off the field both were shy, quiet, private guys. From the beginning, Moss liked how Sean carried himself and how he tried to stay away from all the attention he was getting from the press.

"The more and more and more I heard about or saw stuff that he did … I had the utmost respect for him," former Redskins teammate Santana Moss said. "Man. I just couldn't believe it. You watch this guy play … like … he was way before his time. That's why I say I was pissed off when the media tried to get on him about stuff that happened in the past. Everybody has a past. Everybody has miscues. You can't just take something and ride with it, because, you know, because you don't know the guy any other way.

"You know there's a time and a place for everything, so I wanted to conduct myself accordingly. It was time for me to be professional. It was hard to believe some of the stuff that they came at him with and how they ridiculed him just because of how he carried on with them or how he's seen through their eyes. That's why I said they ain't right.

"I feel like he was one of those guys that was very soft-spoken, so he didn't always have something to share with them [the media]. So that was their way of coming at him, by saying something negative about him. The only reason I say that is because I experienced it in New York."

Moss had major issues with people who posthumously put a label on Sean, based on his past. "I think it's disgraceful that, just like me, [because of] some of the things he went through earlier in his life, everybody tried to label him as 'that guy.' I didn't know him [back then], but when you met him, you're like, 'Come on, that's not the guy they portrayed him as.' I didn't have to know anything about where Sean came from. But I did, because we came from the same upbringing and, man, you couldn't believe some of the things people were saying. You could see the way I carry on and act, and yet you don't judge me the way they judged him."

Sean's reputation preceded him, so it's very easy to judge. "I remember when I got to the Redskins; there was this coach who went through that scandal thing [Bountygate] last year—Gregg Williams. When I got there, Gregg was on the field a lot, but I'm sure, based on his troubles, people judged him too. However, I can tell you he's a really cool guy. Gregg really liked Miami guys." [And he loved Sean Taylor.]

Moss alluded to the fact that all the Miami guys came with a reputation and the coaches had to develop a way to communicate with young, hungry, talented guys who liked to party. "You know, the kind of players we were on [and off] the field. So when I got there, Gregg, when he didn't see Sean or when he wasn't around, Gregg asked, 'Didn't you and Sean get caught up in stuff in Miami? Weren't you in charge down there?'" He was joking, of course. But that was Gregg.

When Moss came to Washington in 2005, he noticed the difference between Sean and his peers. For an NFL guy, "Sean wasn't big on hanging out, and that's something rare for a young guy who comes from where we came from. He would come out every now and then. That's kind of good, in a way, because when you're caught up in this game, caught up in the lifestyle we live, you know a lot of the young guys don't make it because they like to be out more than they like to work on their craft. That's what I found to be unique about him. He would rather be doing something pertaining to what he did for a living than be out with us. I used to tell him all the time, 'Come hang out. Let's go get a drink or something,' and he'd say, 'I'm okay.' We used to laugh about it. He'd say, 'That's for you guys. If I come out, I'm just going to drink too much.' So he stayed in and studied football. And I respected that about him.

"Another thing I can tell you is, me and Sean, we would have these talks. Real man-to-man talks, like on the plane going on every trip. I recall one time I was pissed off after we played the St. Louis Rams. Sean could see in me that I was pissed off about something, and he kept looking at me and finally said, 'Get off the chip.'

"I looked up at him like, 'Hey man, just leave me alone.' Sean repeated, 'Get off the chip.' I didn't say anything, so Sean said to me, 'Hey man, whatever you have to do, get off the chip. Get it out of your system now, because we got to move on.'

"I'm not sure if we won the game or if we lost, but I was pissed off about whatever happened in it. Sean said, 'You know what, man? The coach tried to tell me how to cover the tight end a certain way. He tells me the same thing after every game: "Keep your head up. Next time, head up, Sean. Head up next time." So what I tell the coach is, whoever that guy is who's going to catch the ball, I'm gonna bust his head.'

"So I looked at him and I was like, 'What?' So Sean, the 'freelancer,' said, 'Whatever coach says, we know how to play this game. We don't always do it their way. Do it the way you know how to do it, 'cause at the end of the day, you gotta be the one out there making that play; you the one out there running that route.' And the players are the ones who are going to be the hero or the goat.

"So here comes one of my peers that shared those words with me. It was like, I didn't expect it from him. That was the start of a great friendship between us. From that moment I never expected it, but I was going to change my game, because at the end of the day, if I was the one to take the blame, I may as well go out there and do it the way I know.

"I remember the Green Bay Packers game because it was one of my worst games ever," Moss related. "I had just come off a slight groin pull injury, and I tried to play, but I guess I wasn't ready. When you're a player, you want to be out there with your team.

"So when I came back, that was the first game up. It was a wet, crappy day, and if I'm not mistaken, Sean had two picks against Brett Favre, two interceptions, but he could have had six, as he missed three or four—I'm not sure. It was one of those games [where] looking at it, man, do you see how many times ... I think Favre underestimated Sean, because every time he threw the ball deep, Sean came from one side of the field all the way across and got after the ball.

"I don't have any recollection of what was said after that game, but I told the media myself—the game was over with—I think I fumbled the ball or something like that. We lost the game just barely, and I blamed the loss on myself. Sean came to me and said, 'You can't blame it on yourself. It's a team sport.' But I knew I [felt] like I had lost it because that last field goal came off of my fumble. That's one of the things we talked about. He was pissed off too about [his own] drops."

Moss barely spoke at all on that ride home from Green Bay because he was pissed off about the game. "I can live with myself if I'm to blame, because at the end of the day I feel I made the mistakes. If Sean made those picks, it would be a different story too. I just wanted to be left alone. The only one who could talk to me was him [Sean]. I just wanted to put my headphones on and try to go to sleep on that short ride back."

Redskins Coach Steve Jackson

Steve Jackson spoke about the same Green Bay Packers game, but with a different twist on the story.

"You know, Sean wanted it 'right now.' Case in point: a couple of weeks before he passed, we lost to Green Bay. Brett Favre was getting ready to set the record for most interceptions thrown in a career. Well, Sean had a lights-out game. He had two interceptions, but the weather was awful, and he dropped two or three more balls. They came right out of his hands, which was very uncharacteristic of him. He was player of the game, and one of the Brett Favre record-setting intercepted balls that he picked was supposed to go to the Hall of Fame, but they couldn't find it. Our guy got it and made it a game ball for Sean because he was the guy who intercepted it and was the one who helped tie and break the Favre interceptions record.

"Well, we never gave away game balls if we lost. So Coach Gibbs walked into the defensive meeting and said something like, 'I want to recognize Sean for intercepting two passes and helping Favre break the interceptions record,' and he gave him the ball. So everybody clapped, and da, da, da, da. After that meeting broke down, it was just the safeties in the room. We were finishing our meeting with Sean and LaRon Landry, and I said, 'We got this coming up, and we're going to have to do blah, blah, blah, blah. Sean, this week you had a good game, but next week we're going to need you to catch those balls that you dropped.'

"So as we're walking out of the room, Sean throws the game ball into the trash. He throws ... the Hall of Fame ball ... into ... the trash. LaRon and I look at each other, and I said, 'Sean, why did you throw the ball into the trash?' And he said, 'Coach, because we didn't win.'

"All I could muster was a 'Daaamn.'

"So me and Landry made a mad dash to see who could get to the trash can first! And by the way, Gibbs never found out [until now]."

❦

NFL.com reported that *"the difference in the game proved to be each team's ability to recover fumbles. The Redskins lost two of their four fumbles, including the one that was brought back for the Packers' winning score. Green Bay, meanwhile, managed to recover all four of its fumbles."*

Also from NFL.com is the following account:

Washington lost three offensive linemen in the game, nearly causing it to use emergency lineman Lorenzo Alexander on the final drive. Stephon Heyer, Todd Wade and Casey Rabach all left with injuries.... For the Packers, tight end Bubba Franks was carted off in the fourth quarter.... Brett Favre broke the all-time interceptions record with his 278th. Washington was also the team Favre had his first two career interceptions against.

(nfl.com/gamecenter/2007101403/2007/REG6/redskins@packers%23tab=recap)

In 2005, the Redskins had a 10–6 record, made the playoffs, and then won their wild-card game against the Tampa Bay Buccaneers, 17-10. The Redskins season ended with a 20-10 loss to the Seattle Seahawks in their division playoff game.

23

The '06–'07 Redskins Seasons

"[ONE TIME DURING THE 2006 SEASON] SEAN TOOK ME TO THE FACILITY so we could work out together," said Pete Taylor. "There was a special-teams and offensive-line coach in there working out too. They saw us working out, and they said, 'We see young blood working out over there,' and it just sent a message that Sean was there to put his work in. They knew Sean wanted to play hard for the Redskins."

Sean just liked playing and getting the win. He cared about his team. In one of the few interviews he gave, he said, "It's all about the rings and championships. It's also about giving the fans what they want," Pete Taylor said.

Lorenzo Alexander

One of the new players who joined the Redskins in 2006 was Lorenzo John Alexander, who was born May 31, 1983, making him two months younger than Sean. Alexander played his college ball at the University of California–Berkeley, and as of this writing is with his third NFL team, the Arizona Cardinals.

He originally signed as an undrafted free agent with the Carolina Panthers in 2005. In 2006 he signed a contract to join the Baltimore Ravens practice squad but was released five days later. In October 2006, Alexander joined the Washington Redskins first as a member of the practice squad. By week five of the 2007 season, Lorenzo was a full-fledged member of the Skins, playing primarily on special teams and as a reserve defensive tackle.

♦

"I met Sean Taylor back in 2006, when I was a member of the practice squad and I had to try and block him," Lorenzo Alexander began. "That was the first time I got to meet Sean face-to-face. I would like to remember that as 'I hit him first,' so let's just say it was a good competition that ended in a tie. But you know how competitive Sean was. Once we did that, I think he respected me," Alexander said.

Sean and Lorenzo weren't particularly close off the field. They didn't hang out or go to lunch. But Lorenzo did say, "Just being in the locker room with him gave me a unique perspective—just being able to see him—because when you see a lot of guys on television, you get a certain perception of who they are, and it's not really them."

Sean used every weapon he could think of to get under his opponents' skin on the field. "But being able to come to this team [the Redskins] and see what type of person he was, type of father, type of friend, how down and humble he was, and how hard he worked—it really changed my perception of him, and it taught me a lesson on how not to judge a person based on what other people say."

Like so many, Lorenzo saw Sean grow and develop over the short time they were together with the Redskins. "We're the same age—that's to say we were born in the same year—and we both matured a lot," Alexander said. Sean recognized where he fell short and constantly worked on those shortcomings. "It made him a greater person on and off the field."

Since Lorenzo Alexander was also on the defensive side of the ball, he and Sean saw each other in defensive meetings. Alexander remembers Sean as a very quiet guy. "He was humble, chill, laid back, took good notes, and he did what he had to do to go out there and play the game. He never was a rah-rah type of guy, and I actually respected him a lot for that. He went out there and showed them on the field, and I tried to image myself on his type of demeanor. I was never the athlete that he was, but I carried everything he did and respected him and tried to make that a part of me as well."

Lorenzo clearly saw the spiritual side of Sean Taylor. "He'd meet with the pastor every week, sitting down and talking to him, so I knew it was something important to him. Some guys looked for an excuse not to do it, or they'd speak to the pastor once in a while, but with Sean, he would meet with him week in and week out for thirty or forty minutes."

On the Redskins, James Thrash and Renaldo "the Rev" Wynn were the "resident Christians," and some of the players looked to them for spiritual guidance.

🏈

When Lorenzo Alexander left Washington for Phoenix to join the Cardinals in 2013, he left behind a legacy of charitable foundations and giving. His Aces Foundation supports children in need.

Alexander, along with Redskins Ryan Kerrigan, Kai Forbath, and Kedric Golston, and former Redskin Antwaan Randle El, organized the events Ride to Provide, Dare2Tri Para Triathlon, and Ride 2 Recovery, all of which support wounded warriors. Since Lorenzo still calls Northern Virginia home, his foundations are still active in the area.

More information on Ride to Provide is available at http://www.ridetoprovide.org/page.asp?id=28

Pete Taylor

Pete Taylor remembers 2006 as a monster season for his son, with eighty-nine tackles and twenty-five assisted tackles. "It was his best year of his first three," Pete said. On the other hand, Sean's Redskins team did not fare as well, going 5–11, thereby missing the postseason.

So in January 2007, with the Redskins' season over, Sean took a brief mind-clearing trip to Costa Rica with his friends. Early one morning after they returned, he got a call inviting him to the Pro Bowl as an alternate. (That's when the Pro Bowl actually meant something, before many rule changes softened the game.) So he called his father at work to give him the news.

Revelation

"'Dad, I just got a call inviting me to the Pro Bowl in Honolulu, Hawaii,' Sean said. 'But I'm not going.'"

Astounded, Pete asked, "Why?" Before Sean could answer, Pete said, "I'll come by the house later, and we'll talk."

As promised, after work Sean's father headed to Sean's house. After saying their hellos, Pete's first question of his son was this: "What do you mean you're not going to the Pro Bowl?"

Sean said, "I just don't want to go."

After a few seconds of shaking his head, Pete said, "Look, Sean, you don't get that many great opportunities in life, but when one comes your way, you just have to take it because you may never see that opportunity again."

Sean actually had a legitimate reason for not wanting to go. The Redskins had already lost their last game of the season, and Sean had stopped his heavy workouts. He had just gotten back from vacation and felt like he was no longer in game shape, mentally or physically.

Sean's in-season morning routine called for running two miles and doing three to four hundred push-ups and the same number of sit-ups, but he had cut back considerably to give his body a little break.

The NFL doesn't announce its Pro Bowl selections until the regular season is over. Some of these elite players picked for the Pro Bowl may not actually make the trip to Hawaii (or wherever the Pro Bowl is being played) because they are practicing with their respective teams for the Super Bowl. On the other hand, injuries may also prevent a player from attending the Pro Bowl. In either case, alternates are chosen. Sean was one of those alternates..

Sean reconsidered and said, "'Well, I'll tell you what, Dad. I can take four people and fly coach, or I can take two people and fly first-class. Because you've been instrumental in my life, I want to make sure you go with me. So what do you think? Do you want to go?'

"I said, 'Son, I would love to go with you, and I would love for you to play.'"

Still unsure if he wanted to attend the Pro Bowl, Sean said, "But Dad, I already quit working out."

Sean's committed father then made this deal with his reluctant son: "I'll tell you what I'm going to do. I'll pick you up before I have to be at work every morning between five fifteen and five forty-five, and I'll take you to work out at Chris Carter's [speed camp near Ft. Lauderdale, Florida]. I'll even work out with you if you want, to help you get back into game shape." Sean agreed to the conditions set forth.

Pete wanted to make sure someone was going to be at Chris Carter's that early, so he called to ensure someone would be. He said they'd get there around six and asked if that would be okay. It was fine.

"I ended up driving Sean from Miami to Ft. Lauderdale just so we could work out together," Pete said. "The workout was to end at seven forty-five so I could drive him back.

"The first morning of Sean's new workout schedule, I go by his house to pick him up. No problem. He's ready. The second day, I show up, knock on his door—no answer. It turns out, Sean is sleeping and he doesn't want to get up. I'm outside knocking on the door and he says, 'Dad, I'm sleeping.'

"I go in and I say, 'Hey, youngblood, grab your stuff, you're going to work out, *now!*' Reluctantly, he gets up, gets his stuff, and gets in the car. Then he goes right back to sleep. But you know what? That's okay. I was kinda expecting that. I used to make this drive up to the camps in Boca even when Sean was young, so we were used to this."

Sean got in four or five sessions before he had to leave for Hawaii. In the meantime, the Redskins shipped Sean's and fellow Pro Bowl alternate Chris Samuels's gear out to the facilities in Honolulu.

"So he flies out first. I fly out the following day. When I get in the next evening, I don't see Sean. Turns out he was trying to track me down to see if I had made it in yet. I get to the hotel, get my room, and get situated." Eventually they found each other.

"The next morning, I jump out of bed and go down to the weight room so we could work out together. Sean oversleeps. So he calls me and says, 'Dad, where are you at?'

"I say, 'The weight room.'

Sean the competitor was pissed. "Dammit! How did you get up before me? Oh man. You beat me today, but you're not going to beat me tomorrow," he grumbled.

"That, my friends, was a testament to Sean's competitive nature. He never liked losing to anyone over anything. So eventually he comes down to the weight room so we could work out."

The NFL gives players about a week to both practice and enjoy the island prior to the Pro Bowl. "I actually got to see three team practices," Pete said. "Sean and I were also busy working out on our own."

Training Tip

"We went to the beach and got some sand work and water work in. [Sand work is designed to strengthen leg muscles, while water work is designed to work upper- and lower-body muscles.] We rode stationary bikes and lifted together. Then we hit the sauna and sweated in preparation for the hot and humid Honolulu weather. Sean wanted to be ready for that."

The two worked out mornings and evenings. It wasn't all work and no play, however. In their rented car, the father-and-son team rode around town and the rest of the island, seeing the sights. They even got to the beach to enjoy the Hawaiian scenery, surf, and sun.

The next morning, Sean got out of bed early and beat his father to the gym. "I said, 'You son of gun, you beat me this time.' And Sean had a big smile on his face."

After working out some more, they once again went out in their rented car to go exploring. When they got back that evening, Sean said, "'Dad, let's go jogging.' So while everyone else was out enjoying the nightlife, we went out and jogged," the elder Taylor said.

"I'll never forget this. So we're jogging around our hotel, and as we turned the corner, the late, great Gene Upshaw, God bless his soul, the then-president of the NFLPA [National Football League Players Association] sees us jogging and pulls up next to us in his car. He says, 'Hey, young man, this is why you're at this Pro Bowl. You are a true professional because of what you are doing right now—preparing yourself to play.' He went on to say, 'The rest of the guys are out having fun, but I see now you truly deserve to be here.'

"What a compliment! Gene went on about his business, and we continued to jog back to the hotel.

"The next day, there was a walk-through, so Sean says, 'Dad, come by the field today.'

"I asked, 'Why?'

"He said, 'Steve Smith of the Carolina Panthers threw down a little challenge, and I want you to be there.'"

Daniel Snyder

Dan Snyder recalled what Chris Samuels told him about Pro Bowl practice: According to Samuels, "Steve Smith [of the Carolina Panthers] said, 'I could catch touchdowns and run by that guy [Sean] all day.'

"Samuels said, 'Hey, don't start no shit.'

"Smith says, 'Why?'

"'Hey, man, I'm telling you, stop bullshitting! It's gonna get crazy out here in a minute,' Samuels said."

Snyder continued, "The next play, they back up, and Samuels says, 'Stop playing around, 'cause it's gonna get very aggressive and shit's gonna get crazy, and you better tone it down.' Smith backs off." And that was just practice.

●

So on Saturday, February 10, 2007, at Aloha Stadium in Honolulu, Hawaii, before a crowd of 50,410, Sean Taylor took the field in lieu of injured Dallas Cowboys safety Roy Williams.

Sean's friend and former University of Miami teammate Andre Johnson was playing against Sean for the AFC. A couple of plays into the game, during Sean's first play on defense, the ball was coming to Andre, but he let the ball go and stepped to the side when he saw Sean barreling in to make a play. Sean turned away from him.

"I don't know if he let the ball go on purpose or not, but trust me, if Dre had grabbed the ball, there would have been a massive collision," said Pete Taylor, smiling.

The game continued, and before long Sean made one of the most famous hits in Pro Bowl history. That was the hit heard round the NFL, and there are some who are still talking about it.

Sean laid out Buffalo Bills punter Brian Moorman, who came out of formation to try to run for a first down. Sean stopped him cold with what some considered a vicious hit. You see, when they remain in their position and just kick the ball, punters DO NOT GET HIT! In fact, if they do, the penalty for roughing the kicker is called. Since punters are generally slight of frame, anytime they get hit, it's a big deal.

Daniel Snyder

Snyder continued, "Sean hit that punter during the Pro Bowl, and I called him up when he got back, because the media went crazy; they said Sean wasn't a gentleman for putting that hit on him. You weren't supposed to hit anyone like that. I called him and said, 'You did the right thing. The guy took off, and you prevented him from getting the first down.'"

Sean said, "Thanks." And that was that.

The 2007 Season

In the 2007 season, Sean was on his way to having another great year. Through the first ten games, Sean had five interceptions for ninety-eight yards. He had a total of forty-two tackles, plus tackle assists on ten passes.

In game ten of the 2007 season, the Philadelphia Eagles came to FedEx Field to play the Washington Redskins. In that game Sean suffered a knee injury that essentially took him out of commission for the next two games versus the Dallas Cowboys and the Tampa Bay Buccaneers. As it turned out, the eventual 33-25 loss to the Eagles would be the last game Taylor would ever play.

24

Three Claps and a Snap

"HE NEVER WANTED TO BE KNOWN AS JUST A FOOTBALL PLAYER," SEAN'S friend Mike said.

"T. J.," Pete said interrupting. "My little boy [Gabe] is good in sports too, but he had this goal to be an artist. It was just about having fun doing whatever."

T. J. said, "Yeah, no matter what. Even the workouts turned into fun."

At that very moment, Pete's youngest, Gabriel Taylor, fresh off the basketball practice court, popped into the Kendall Ale House, where this part of our story was unfolding.

"Hey, good to see you, Gabe," I said. "Are you hungry?"

In the next few minutes, we all spent a little time catching up with Sean's youngest sibling. We talked about basketball, football, and school.

The Sean conversation picked up again when T. J. brought up "The tattoos!" He said, "There is not one day since the day he [Sean] passed away when I look in the mirror or take a shower I say I know he got that, Mike got that, and I got that. Nobody else can say that. We all got the same tattoo at the same time...."

"What did you call yourselves? The three what?" I asked.

Mike and T. J. did their signature hand slap for me.

T. J. continued. "Like when we meet each other, it was like three peas in a pod. So we give each other three claps...."

Mike piped in. "We didn't want to call ourselves the three stooges, because we didn't look at ourselves like that."

"Yes, but what was the name you gave yourselves?" I asked again.

Instead of answering, Mike showed me where on their bodies each one of them had that same tattoo. Then T. J. said, "We were the three claps and a snap!"

Pete practiced the three claps and a snap on me. We all laughed because I didn't quite catch on, as I am rather uncoordinated.

T. J. commented, "It went from us three doing it to now anybody that know us is doing it. It's socially acceptable. Anytime people approach me, they do the three claps and a snap just out of respect. We get that everywhere we go. So even that is a reminder of my homie.

"I have so many reminders, so many ... just in my life when you walk in my house, I got a portrait, a painting of him hanging. It was always, that was my brother. I would do anything for him, and he would do anything for me. And that was instilled from his father—to be a man. Some things you can never take away, like, we always used to tell each other you could go buy good credit, but you can't buy a good name. Once you screw up your name, you're done. So that's what we lived on as friends and why we stayed so true.

"That's why I do little things for his cousins, his mom, his brother," T. J. said. "We love them to death. We tell him we gonna watch him play as if it's my little brother. Anything I can do to help out, like with Gabe.

"Pete played a big part in my life as a father figure to me growing up as far as just understanding what it took to be better. But one summer of me running a post 4.7 [seconds], to the next summer, to working out with Pete, to running a 4.5 wasn't a coincidence. The fact is, whatever I was doing, I wasn't doing it right. Once I make all this money and become this entrepreneur, I want to retire as a coach. I want to give back all the stuff that Pete showed me and learned and done, with ups and downs. I want to give back to the community. I want to give another little kid or anybody else that needs help ... because of my experience, not that I saw something on TV or read it or heard about it ... no ... I have actually been there. I've done it. I know what it takes. I know that if you're working when another person is sleeping, you are winning. You have to put forth maximum effort each and every day. So I feel like I am privileged for just being part of this."

T. J. said, "Sean lived the true underdog story, but coming out on top. Kids in high school used to say he was never that good [because of the 'inferior' competition he was up against at Gulliver]. But every time they closed their eyes, he was wide awake, working to get bigger, faster, and stronger while everyone else was being normal, going to practice then going home. After practice he's still working, doing all the extracurricular things to make sure he was extra huge to put himself over the top. He wanted to separate himself from the next guy.

"At the end of the day I don't want anything negative to spoil his legacy."

And with that, my time with T. J., Mike, Pete, and little Gabe was over. At least it was over inside the Kendall Ale House. You see, we spent another twenty-five minutes outside the restaurant just talking and carrying on, all in good fun.

25

Santana Moss Knew

"WE SAT BY EACH OTHER IN THE BIG TV ROOM; WE SAT NEXT TO EACH other on the plane," former Washington Redskins teammate Santana Moss said. "So we always found a way to be around each other when we were in the same area. Our lockers were even right next to each other.

"There's this thing I remember; it's crazy, but prior to Sean's passing, we shared a little time inside the training room together.

Revelation

"So the week leading up to us going to Tampa to play that game and him going home, it's crazy, man, because we talked about someone breaking into his house earlier that week. I'm sitting there, and he told me about it, and I'm like, 'Naw,' and he was like, 'Yeah, someone tried to break in.' He wasn't sure if they broke in or not, and I'm like, 'Naw, man, don't worry about it.' (According to Pete Taylor, it may have been Sean's mother Donna who alerted him to the first break-in. The entire Junor family were frequent visitors to the home and on a visit, Donna may have found the back door pried open.)

"He said, 'Well, I gotta go home anyway, so I want to make sure everything is good.'

"So I was like, 'Okay, cool.'" Moss said.

It turns out Santana Moss was the only one on the team who knew Sean was heading to Miami on the weekend of his death.

When team owner Daniel Snyder ran into Sean as he was boarding the team bus that was about to take everyone to Dulles for the flight to Tampa Bay, he said to Sean, "Go home and rest." But when Snyder said that, he was referring to Sean's Virginia home. But what Sean was planning was a trip to his Miami home with what he thought was the team owner's advice and blessing.

"Another thing—I think it was Thanksgiving morning—Sean came in, and it was crazy because … this is what my grandma said … it was always … I don't know how to word it … she said uh … when it's time for somebody to go, or if they are on their last couple of days, they have a different kind of glow about them. I don't know if y'all had heard that, but it's something my grandma said.

"So Thanksgiving morning: it was strange how Sean came in and addressed every single coach. He went to every man as a man and said, 'Happy Thanksgiving. Happy Thanksgiving. Hey, coach, Happy Thanksgiving.' I was just getting over my injury, and I hadn't been there for weeks, but you know, it was just strange. I was like, 'Sean, man …'

"And he said, 'You have to be thankful for the day.' And I said, 'Yeah man, you right. You're absolutely right.'

"He asked, 'You not thankful for the day?'

"I said, 'Yeah man, I'm thankful.'

"Well, he wanted to tell everybody Happy Thanksgiving, 'cause everybody's not thankful. 'Not everybody feels the way we do, Tana,' Sean said. 'Some of these guys are clearly not thankful. Some of these guys are just not thankful for being here today.' So I was like, 'Yeah. You right, man.' That was that day.

"Two days later, we were about to go on the trip to Tampa Bay. We're sitting around, and there's this big lightning storm and Sean was like, 'Oh man, what's up, Portis? You look kinda like Santana." Moss laughed. "You look like Tana a little bit.' Me and Portis … that was like the laugh we had together. Then he wished us well and said to Portis, 'Man, I hope you run for two hundred yards.' Portis said something like 'Yeah, that would be money.'

"It was crazy. I thought there was something different about him. We had been sitting in the training room a lot, and we were talking about—well, you name it. Thanksgiving was that day, but he seemed like he was a whole different person. Sure, he always said hi to everyone, as he was that kind of person, but that day he went out of his way to say hello to everybody. It was crazy, because that was the last thing I remember, those last few moments. It wasn't something I could say joking wise, but it was just crazy, because to be honest with you, when everything went down, it was that, that kept coming into my mind. It was those couple of days of just talking and joking, you name it."

So Moss knew Sean was going to Miami. Mr. Snyder and his coaches unequivocally made the absolute point of saying they had no idea he was going there.

"I don't think they would have known that," Moss said. "Most guys spend their time off the way they want and don't broadcast it. I knew he wasn't going on that trip [to Tampa Bay], so it was the perfect time to go down to Miami. He had a weekend longer than most weekends. He was thinking he had a little time off, so he wanted to shoot down there real quick, take care of his business, then come back."

PART V

26

Pete's Premonition

"WITHOUT A SHADOW OF A DOUBT, IT WAS MY FAITH IN GOD THAT GOT me through all this. If it wasn't for the good Lord above, I have to be honest, I wouldn't be here today," Pete Taylor said.

"So, let's talk about Thanksgiving. That morning when we got up, we said a little prayer thanking God for everything and then we just went on about our business.

"I work in law enforcement. As part of my job, nearly every weekend I would work escorting funerals from the city.

"Sometimes Sean would call me and say, 'Dad, what are you doing?'

"I said, 'I'm doing an escort for somebody's funeral.'

"He'd say, 'Man, you're doing another funeral?'

"I'd say, 'Yeah.'

"One night something came to me. I heard a voice. Something or someone was speaking to me. I heard this: 'Something is going to happen in your life that is going to be so devastating that you're going to have to be strong to survive.'

"At the time I really didn't know what that meant. How could I? As part of my job and even sometimes for friends and family, I found myself going to a lot of funerals. I kept having to deal with the death issue, and because of that, I found myself in church even more than normal. When I told Sean about this, I said, 'Man, I've been going to church a lot lately. I don't know what this is all about.'

"I might go to a prayer meeting on a Wednesday or for some special program on a Saturday, and of course I went every Sunday, too. I didn't know what had come over me. What is going on? But I'll never forget waking up on Thanksgiving morning and all the kids called me but I didn't hear from Sean because he had practice. I was sitting around the table with [my wife] Simone, and I remember telling her, 'It's going to be different this morning.'

"She said, 'Why?'

"All I could say was, 'Today as we go around the table, we are all going to say what we appreciate about life. How much we love each other. But that's not all. You can talk about whatever is going on in your life and what you are going to do to make it better. Or if things are going wrong for you, what are you going to do to come out of it?' Odd, huh? Then everybody had to pray. We were going to give our thanks to God.

"Simone, Simone's daughter Brooke and son Patrick, and my son Gabe were all sitting around the breakfast table. We talked and we prayed.

"Later on that night we were all at my aunt Merryl and uncle Joseph's house for Thanksgiving dinner, and Sean called me about nine p.m. During the call, Sean said his knee was still bothering him and he was going to speak to the trainers about it. I advised him to go to the next game versus Tampa Bay even if they didn't play him."

Pete thought that if Sean was on the sidelines, he'd see the game close up. If he didn't play, then perhaps he could help out the other players. It couldn't hurt just being around the team.

"I told him how much I appreciated him and how proud I was of him, and that by God's grace, I couldn't believe how much he'd accomplished till then.

"So Sean said, 'Okay, Dad. Love you.' He was in very good spirits.

"I said, 'Be good, and we'll talk later.'"

When the team decided he was not cleared to play and didn't put him on the plane, he came to Miami Saturday morning as the Redskins flew to Tampa.

Saturday came and went, and everything was fine. "As far as I knew, the team flew to Tampa on Saturday morning and Sean was on the plane," said Pete.

27

November 25-27, 2007

"On Sunday I was in front of the television in Homestead, Florida, watching the Redskins play the Tampa Bay Bucs," said Pete Taylor. "I was looking for Sean on the field, and it didn't take me long to realize that Sean wasn't playing. So now I'm scanning the sideline when they showed it to see if I could see him. I never did. Little did I know Sean had flown to visit Jackie and their eighteen-month-old daughter, Baby Jackie, in Miami on Saturday morning instead of recouping at home in Ashburn, Virginia. I can tell you the Redskins ended up losing that game 19–13.

"So I headed north, and by the time I got to the house, it was late and I went to bed."

The Break-In

On Monday, November 26, 2007, at approximately 1:30 a.m., Sean Taylor awoke to loud noises emanating from somewhere in his four-bedroom, four-bath home with private fenced-in pool, sitting on three-fourths of an acre on Old Cutler Road in Palmetto Bay, Florida.

"Jackie ... wake up! I think I hear noises, and there may be someone in the house," Sean Taylor said to Jackie Garcia, his then girlfriend and mother of their eighteen-month-old baby daughter, also named Jackie. "Jackie, where's the machete?"

Half asleep, Jackie responded, "By the bed."

"I want you and Baby Jackie to stay hidden under the covers while I check this out," Sean said urgently. Jackie agreed and pulled the bed sheets over her and their child's head.

Sean found the machete he used mostly as a gardening tool and "for protection [as his girlfriend Jackie stated at the trial of convicted killer Eric Rivera Jr.]." He picked it up and headed for the locked bedroom door so he could survey the house and quite possibly use it to defend his family.

As Sean approached the door, seventeen-year-old Eric Rivera, Jr., kicked it open. Rivera and three accomplices (Jason Mitchell, who was convicted of second-degree murder and masterminding the burglary, and two alleged cohorts, Charles Wardlow and Timothy Brown, who still await trial) were rummaging through the house. They were searching for what they believed was a large sum of cash they had heard Taylor kept in his safe, sometimes upwards of one hundred thousand dollars. Why so much cash? One of Sean's half sisters testified during the trial that it was easily accessible gambling money.

The fourth accomplice, Venjah Hunte, who was the proverbial "getaway driver," remained inside the vehicle just outside of Sean's home. Hunte eventually plea-bargained for a twenty-nine-year sentence in exchange for his testimony against the others. So far his testimony has not been needed.

So when the bedroom door flew open from the force of Rivera's kick and Eric saw the massive 6'2", 212-pound Sean Taylor standing there, he panicked and shot Sean in the upper leg. The bullet hit the femoral artery, and with a loud grunt, gasping for air, Sean Taylor collapsed, falling face first to the floor.

As Taylor lay there in a pool of his own blood, Eric Rivera likely screamed for his companions in the house to abort the heist and quickly make their exit.

According to the report filed by the Miami-Dade Police, when Rivera got to the rear glass patio door, he shot at it so he and his cohorts could escape unimpeded.

When they emerged, they ran toward the front of the home and scaled the cement-and-iron fence, racing for their rented black Toyota Highlander SUV with coconspirator Venjah Hunte waiting inside.

The five then sped off into the wee hours of the morning, heading northwest toward Alligator Alley and eventually ending up in Ft. Myers, Florida, where they all lived.

On police videotape Rivera not only confessed to shooting Taylor but also said he got out of the SUV to dispose of the murder weapon—a 9 mm handgun. He maintained that he stuffed the gun into a sock and then threw it into the Everglades. No more murder weapon, and no more "smoking gun."

What the assailants did not know was that on the way back to Ft. Myers, they had left a trail of mobile cell tower pings from Miami all the way home as they made several calls to friends, setting up their alibis; they also called one of the assailants to locate his phone, which he thought he had left at the scene. These pings were used as evidence in the Rivera trial.

After feeling safe enough to come out of hiding, Jackie emerged from under the covers. She saw Sean lying just outside the threshold of the bedroom and ran to him. Her boyfriend was bleeding profusely. Before calling 911, she wrapped towels around his bleeding leg. Within minutes, first responders from the Miami-Dade Police Department and emergency rescue services arrived at the scene, where they tried in vain to stop the bleeding from his leg. When that didn't work, Sean was medevacked to the Jackson Memorial Trauma Center, where he underwent emergency surgery.

The news was out on the police band. Next, one of the on-duty Florida City Police Department (FCPD) officers got a call stating that the son of their chief had been shot and taken to the hospital. The officer forwarded the gruesome information to Major Steven Taylor and Sgt. Rocquel McCray, whose job it was to deliver the horrible news to Sean's father, Chief of Police Pedro "Pete" Taylor.

Pete Taylor

"During the first part of the sleep cycle, you're knocked out a little bit, so I didn't realize my phone was ringing. I was in such a deep sleep I couldn't even get up to answer it.

"After the third call I looked at my cell and I noticed I missed two calls from a number I recognized and one from a number I didn't. So now I'm thinking, *'Who is calling me in the middle of the night? What is so important?'*

I'm also thinking, *'Damn, something must have happened in the city* [and the calls were police business].'"

Pete's major, Steven Taylor, called twice. There was no answer when Pete called him back. Then Pete listened to the message from the number he didn't recognize; it was from Mommy Jackie.

"'Pete, it's Jackie. Call me right away.' So I called the number that Jackie was calling from, and it turned out to be a police officer's cell phone. The officer picks up and lets me talk to Jackie, who was standing nearby.

"'Pete, you got to come quick. Sean's been shot!' Jackie screamed into the phone. 'He's lost a lot of blood. Come quick.'"

"So I asked Jackie, 'Where are you?'

"'I'm at the house,' Jackie said.

"All I could get out was 'Okay,' and I hang up. Now my major, Steven Taylor, is calling me again.

"'Pete, where are you at?' he asks.

"'Home! I'm at the house.'

"'Well, I'm on my way,' Major Taylor says. 'We just heard over the radio that Sean's been shot.'

"At first I'm thinking this is just a fucking dream. This is a bunch of bullshit going on. I'm slowly coming to and I'm thinking, *'What is going on?'* I didn't see Sean on TV in Tampa, so my first reaction was to say, 'What happened in Washington? How did he get shot?' I didn't have a clue he was here in Miami.

"'We don't know anything,' Major Taylor said.

"I'm still thinking I was dreaming this whole thing. In my half-daze I walk on over to my front door, and there's nobody standing out there. *'Oh shit. This is a damn dream,'* I thought again. So I went back to lie down, and I thought, *'What the hell just happened?'*

"I get back into the bedroom, and I pick up my cell to call the major back. 'Steve, did you just call me?'

"'Yeah, man. I'm right around the corner from your house. I'll be there in a minute.'"

"So I'm like, 'Okay.' It wasn't a dream. It was my worst nightmare.

"I was still on the phone with my major when he said he was pulling up to the front of the house. He walks up and through the door; he yells, 'We have to go to the hospital. Sean was shot in Miami. They flew him up to the hospital by air ambulance. Sean's been shot in the leg.'

"'Miami?' I asked. 'What was he doing in Miami?'"

"So I asked him if he was sure. He said it was for sure. Next thing I did was to go get my keys to open the door. I couldn't get it to open. I asked myself again, what did he just say?"

Pete eventually managed to get the door open.

"I tell him, 'I guess I'll drive over to the hospital to see what's going on.'"

"He says, 'No. I'll drive you.'"

"I thought, '*Oh man, I don't like that kind of driving because it's always serious.*' So I get dressed again. I close the door and I guess I was a little discombobulated and I still can't figure out what's going on. We start out to drive over to the hospital. I ask, 'Is everything okay? Is everything all right?'"

"The major says, 'We ain't heard nothing.'"

"So I say, 'What the hell happened? How did he get here?'"

"The major says, 'I don't know.'"

"So I'm thinking, '*Damn, Sean isn't supposed to be here. He's supposed to be in Washington.*' Now I'm sitting in the backseat of the cruiser completely dumbfounded. '*Shit,*' I keep saying to myself. I'm sitting back there hoping and praying to God that everything is going to be all right."

On the way to the hospital, Pete called his mother to let her know what happened. He also called his soon-to-be ex-wife, Josephine Taylor, who was staying with her mother since they had recently separated. "Sean's been shot," Pete told Josie. "Let the kids [Joseph and Jazmin] know; tell them I love them and I'm on my way to the hospital [the Jackson Memorial Hospital Trauma Unit]." He wanted them to hear about it from him before they heard it on the news.

"Finally Steve [Taylor] and I get to the hospital, where I see some other cops I know. I'm just looking for a sign—something ... anything. I want them to say something bad or good. I want them to give me a thumbs up or down. Just something. You know things are bad especially when no one says anything to you."

When Pete Taylor got to the emergency room, the first order of business was to meet with one of Sean's doctors to get an update on his son's condition. Things were not looking good for Sean, who had already lost massive amounts of blood. He was in the operating room, where the doctors were attempting surgery to repair his femoral artery. After the meeting with the doctor, Pete called Sean's agent, Drew Rosenhaus, and Washington Redskins coach Joe Gibbs to alert them to the developments of the moment.

"So they have Sean in the ER, and the doctors are working on him. He's in surgery. By that time I guess the word had gotten out, because other family members began to arrive at the hospital.

"I'm still trying to figure out what happened. I'm in a daze. I'm so lost!

"I called Simone and told her to give Gabe a hug and to tell him I loved him. I said, 'Sean's been shot; I'm at the hospital; I don't know what's going on; and we'll see what happens.'"

At the hospital, the Taylors were kept in the dark for several hours. Finally Pete got a chance to go up and see Sean. "I knew it was serious. I spoke to him for a moment, and just then the machines he was hooked up to started acting crazy. The doctor was in the room, and we spoke for a moment. When the numbers on the machines started changing, I was asked to leave.

"Later that morning, team owner Daniel Snyder, General Manager Vinny Cerrato, and Clinton Portis arrived at the hospital. So much was going on. They were there to lend their support in any way they could.

"They moved us all to the family room. I remember it was dark in the room. Now more and more people are coming to be with us.

"The first twenty-four to thirty-six hours were critical, so we're just praying for the best. The doctor comes back out to talk to me. He said some of the other family members can now go up and see Sean. In the meantime, I was getting more updates. I know people that were shot ten times and made it. So I thought he'd be fine. He'd miss a little time off work, but that would be it.

"During the surgery, one of the doctors told me Sean was responding a little, because when prompted, he squeezed the doctor's hand. The positive news was short-lived.

"It was a revolving door with family members coming and going. Once again I get a private moment with the doctor and he says that Sean is not going to make it.

"My cousin Anthony McCabe and I slipped out of the hospital and drove down to Sean's house so I can check out the scene. While we were driving over, I was visualizing how the crime took place.

"When we get to the house, it's about four thirty in the morning and it's still being secured by Miami-Dade police. So I asked them if it would be possible to check out the crime scene if I promised not to contaminate it. The CSI [crime scene investigation] was completed, so at that point all they were doing was protecting the home from looters and curiosity seekers. I wanted to peek inside so I could see firsthand what the hell had happened.

"I came around back through the pool area and saw the back door was jimmied open and was broken out of the frame. I look to the right and saw the porch glass door had been shot out. I walk down the hallway toward the bedroom, and I remember Jackie saying something about there being a lot of blood on the floor. I make the turn toward the bedroom, and sure enough, there was blood everywhere. My heart dropped, and all I could say was 'My God.' I didn't want to believe it, but it was then when I realized just how serious this was. I went back outside and thanked the police officer for allowing me access.

"I thought my cousin had to go to work, so I asked if we needed to go back to the hospital so he could drop me off. He said he didn't and he'd rather stay with me and take me back to my house. When we got there, I ran in and I brushed my teeth and changed real quick because I had been in the same clothes for nearly two days. Then we drove back to the hospital."

The rest of the family got to the hospital in time for the doctors to make the announcement: "Sean Taylor has passed away."

"After the doctor gave everyone the horrible news, the media went nuts. It was a whirlwind of questions I didn't have the wherewithal to answer. Luckily I escaped with my cousin, who drove me back to my house again."

Sean Taylor Loses the Battle

On November 27, 2007, Sean Taylor was pronounced dead at Jackson Memorial Hospital.

"At the time," said Taylor, "I coached basketball at Florida Memorial University, so Coach Bellinger and some of the other coaches came by after they got the news. The year prior, we won the Florida Sunshine Conference Basketball Championship. My son Joey was playing basketball there with them at the time.

Revelation

"After I met with them for a moment, I said my good-byes and I returned to Sean's house. I put on my gloves, and I went to work. I mopped up all the blood on the floor. So, yes, I had my son's blood on my hands. I did that because I didn't want anyone else to be walking through my son's blood. I put everything on my shoulders."

It was a great burden that only a special man and father could endure.

"My cousins Andre and Yolanda came over to the house and helped procure some things. When we looked outside, we noticed cameras and uplink trucks were everywhere.

"After a while I left Sean's house and went back to mine. That's where a lot of the family was gathering. I was trying to be careful when cleaning up Sean's house, but apparently one of my relatives noticed the bloodstains on my shirt. So I went off to my bedroom to shower and change again.

"My aunt reached out to the pastor at her church. His name was Pastor Jackson. So he came over and prayed for the family. Later on that day, we started receiving calls from Jackie's uncle, actor Andy Garcia. He came over to the house. He did leave Miami but returned for the funeral the next week.

"Reverend Jesse Jackson called and said he wanted to be with the family as well. He flew in the day before the funeral and stopped at the house. He came because this was just another senseless killing of a young person, and I guess that was one of his big things at the Rainbow Coalition. He went to the funeral and was even part of the funeral procession. In fact, if you look at some of the pictures, you can see him sitting next to me at the service along with my boss, Mayor Wallace and Vice Mayor Jane Barry, and all of the city's commissioners."

Pete instinctively knew that a lot of people would come to the service for Sean and that they needed to find a very large place in which to hold it. "I called Major Taylor, who, along with my assistant Michelle Ramirez, helped with the enormous task of coordinating the funeral service at FIU and the funeral procession from the Second Baptist Church with the Miami-Dade Police Department.

"They did all of this while I flew into and back from Washington, D.C. where I had to take care of some Redskins paperwork.

"When I got back to Miami, we reached out to the funeral home we were using for Sean's first service. We talked to some people that were going to help us out with the funeral. Next the morgue called me to come identify the body. This was one of the hardest things I had ever done. As a father, you raise a child knowing pretty much he or she is going to outlive the parents. You know, it's just not supposed to work this way when the child dies first. It's crazy. Trust me. I never in my life would have dreamed this.

"The next day, Jackie, her father, and I went to pick out a suit for Sean and a casket. Oh man. It was just one thing after another.

"You can imagine … it's Thanksgiving … there are football games going on, and traffic is a nightmare. So the only way we could get to the funeral home by eight thirty a.m. was with a police escort. This was something I coordinated in Florida City many, many times for others, but never in my wildest dreams did I think I'd be coordinating one for my son.

"Because so many arrangements had to be made, we were going to do the funeral service on a different day. But in speaking with Mr. Snyder, he offered to fly the team—the entire organization—down to Miami. He thought everybody should be there, so I pushed the funeral to the following Monday, because that was the team's off day.

"The team was going to fly into the private Tamiami Airport, while the coaches were going to fly into Miami International Airport. So we had to set up escort teams at both airports for the buses. FYI, the coaches were flying in separately because they were still planning for the next game. Everything worked out perfectly, and I thanked Mr. Snyder from the bottom of my heart for everything that he did for me and the family.

"While all that was going on, the family was being escorted by about thirty to forty motorcycle officers. Altogether there must have been three hundred fifty police officers with escort duties, including blocking off roads for the team buses and the family.

"FIU's athletic director, Pete Garcia, my major [Major Taylor], my admin Michelle, and I all had a hand in this massive operation. Being on the phone the whole time certainly allowed me to take my mind off things. People said I was crazy, but it kept me busy as well, also making sure everything was right.

"Gulliver Prep had a candlelight vigil for Sean on Friday morning, the day we returned from Washington. This event and the candlelight vigil held at the University of Miami really warmed my heart. The UM event actually went off at eight p.m. the following Sunday night. But we had a conflict. The viewing began at six p.m., so we had to leave at five p.m. to get there. Now, as you got to the church, you saw the fans with flags flying from their vehicles. People showed up in football shirts and jerseys. I looked over to my left and said to myself, 'Wow, how amazing.' It was almost like a football tailgate or pep rally.

"We left the church after the viewing and went over to UM for the vigil, getting there about eight thirty p.m. Coach Randy Shannon came out and spoke and gave me a picture of Sean that's still at my home today.

"We finally got back to the house around eleven p.m. after a whirlwind day. The next day was the funeral."

28

The Rush to Judgment

It's no secret that after Sean passed, many in the local and national press were not kind to him. They reported on the death of the former Miami Hurricanes and Washington Redskins superstar dragging up past indiscretions, as well as unfounded rumors, innuendo, accusations, but rarely his acquittals.

No, Sean Taylor was not a saint, but as per usual, some in the press reported on his past without all the facts; according to the family, there wasn't much fact-checking going on when it came to Sean Taylor.

Some blog posts even raised allegations of racism to explain why he was being treated with such disdain. To some bloggers, the mere fact that Sean was an African American was the reason a few press outlets reported his death the way they did.

The widely read blogs *Outside the Beltway* and *ESPN.com* (among others) couldn't report on the death of Sean Taylor without dragging up past infractions. Those include, but are not limited to, the DUI incident (in which he was cleared of all charges), the two missed mandatory rookie symposiums, his seven fines for late hits (what player doesn't get fined for late hits?), even the fine he received for a uniform violation for mismatched socks. Then there was the incident of the stolen all-terrain vehicles (ATVs), where Sean was accused of brandishing a gun. The truth is— HE NEVER EVEN OWNED A GUN! Most of these incidents have already been addressed in this book.

(http://www.outsidethebeltway.com/sean_taylor_redskins_
safety_murdered/; http://sports.espn.go.com/nfl/news/story?id=3129406)

In Leonard Shapiro's article in the *Washington Post* entitled "Taylor's Death is Tragic, but Not Surprising," in part he questions whether anyone could "honestly say they never saw this coming" considering "Taylor's checkered past." Are you kidding? His insinuations could not have been further from the truth. Mr. Shapiro, in the same article, goes on to quote noted media sports journalist Michael Wilbon, who made the following assumption: "Taylor grew up in a violent world, embraced it, claimed it, loved to run in it and refused to divorce himself from it" (http://www.washingtonpost.com/wp-dyn/content/article/2007/11/27/AR2007112701111.html).

In the blog *Edge of Sports*, the writer takes on many in the mainstream sports press, accusing them of racism in a piece entitled "Kicking a Man When He's Dead: To Slander Sean Taylor." Writer Dave Zirin cites others calling Taylor out as a "thug" who got what he deserved. In his piece, he points to this as "yet another example of how sports has become an absolute trash receptacle of racism over the past several years" (http://www.edgeofsports.com/2007-12-04-299/).

Further, in the November 29, 2007, *Washington Post DC Sports Bog*, Dan Steinberg called out Colin Cowherd for jumping to conclusions as to the hows and whys of Sean's murder. Steinberg wrote, "If you actually want to have a serious discussion, this has immediately disqualified you. This is pure drivel, meant to do nothing but incite."

Cowherd said, "Sean Taylor, great player, has a history of really, really bad judgment; really, really bad judgment. Cops, assault, spitting, DUI. I'm supposed to believe his judgment got significantly better in two years, from horrible to fantastic? 'But Colin he cleaned up his act.' Well yeah, just because you clean the rug doesn't mean you got everything out. Sometimes you've got stains, stuff so deep it never ever leaves."

Steinberg goes on to say, "I suppose this is true enough, in general. How it relates to this case, neither I nor Colin Cowherd has any idea, since we have absolutely no idea how Taylor's judgment related to what happened to him. Cowherd is just throwing stuff like that out there to stir passions among his listeners. It's nasty stuff. There is no possible justification for using 'stains you can't get out' in what you're claiming is 'serious, grown-up talk.' That's media jackal talk."

"I want to know the truth," Cowherd said. "I want to know the details. It's not pretty? I don't care, I'm a grown-up. I can handle not pretty. A lot of people can't in the media, a lot of people can't. 'Oh, wah wah wah, sensitivity, he's a great person, wah wah wah.' Hey, I don't care, that's fine, he died, let's get to the truth. We're all about the truth. We always say on this show, we're not always good, we're always honest. Just give me honesty." (http://voices.washingtonpost.com/dcsportsbog/2007/11/colin_ cowherd_on_sean_taylor.html)

Why all the negative reporting? It's been speculated that the press didn't know Sean, due in part to his reluctance to speak with them. So they reported—or should I say misreported—events over the years in a rush to get a story out and many times made Sean look like a malcontent, thug and common criminal. For the most part, because of how he was treated, Sean stayed away from reporters, saying to his friends that they always misquoted him anyway, so why should he talk to them? In fact, out of sheer shyness, if he didn't know a person, he'd probably avoid him or her regardless of the person's position in life. Unless of course you were a fan seeking an autograph or to engage in light conversation. Sean loved his fans.

To be fair, it wasn't all bad press, as evidenced by the November 28, 2007, Washington Post article by Mike Wise. He refrained from dwelling on Taylor's past; rather Wise focused on the impact Sean made on his team and his fans. Wise got it right when he said, "Though he rarely opened himself up publicly and was easily one of the NFL's least-known players with such star status, Taylor's reclusiveness played right into the cult worship that began to grow with each violent tackle. It almost contributed to the mystique, that of the young, misunderstood man who put all his angst into his profession." Wise also pointed out, "Outside the team's training facilities, more than 200 fans paid their respects in front of his No. 21, painted in large, white letters, outlined in gold, on a grassy field a few hundred yards from where he practiced." (http://www.washingtonpost.com/wp-dyn/content/article/2007/11/27/ AR2007112702775.html?sid=ST2007112702001)

The Team and the Fans Mourn

On December 2, 2007, at FedEx Field in RalJon, MD—a mere five days after Sean's death—the visiting Buffalo Bills were in town to play the Washington Redskins. Before a single down was played that afternoon, the home team ran a video tribute to Sean Taylor's career. The video can be found on YouTube.

Needless to say, emotions were running extremely high that day. The grief-stricken team took the field in front of 85,000 heartbroken fans who were given Sean Taylor commemorative towels.

The NFL even got into the act by mandating that all teams place a "21" sticker on the backs of all players' helmets in tribute to the fallen Redskin.

As the game began, the fans waved their towels as the Redskins went on offense first. After Rock Cartwright's twenty-seven yard return of a sixty-five-yard Rian Lindell kickoff to begin the game, Jason Campbell guided the Redskins down the field for seven minutes, forty-four seconds, at which point Shaun Suisham banged a twenty-seven-yard field goal and gave the Redskins a 3–0 lead.

When it was time for the Washington defense to take the field for the first time, some realized they sent out only ten of the eleven men required to play the down. The Redskins ran the "missing-man formation" with the free safety position left open to honor their fallen teammate. Unfortunately the play resulted in a twenty-two-yard run by Bills rookie Fred Jackson. Reed Doughty, who replaced Sean in the starting lineup, entered the game on the next defensive play.

When Santana Moss caught his first pass of the day, he displayed the 21 sign with his index, middle, and pinky fingers held skyward. He continued that practice for the rest of the game. When Clinton Portis scored on a three-yard run, making it 16–5 Redskins, he lifted his uniform jersey and revealed his T-shirt, which read, "In Memory of Sean Taylor."

The Bills started their final drive of the game on their own twenty-two with all of fifty-six seconds left and no time-outs. When it was time for Coach Gibbs to "freeze kicker Rian Lindell," who was going for a long fifty-one-yard field goal, Gibbs, letting his emotions get the better of him, called for two timeouts in a row. Doing so is against the rules, so the Skins were called for a fifteen-yard unsportsmanlike conduct penalty, giving the Bills' kicker an easier shot by reducing the field goal distance to 36 yards. The Bills made their play with four seconds remaining. Their three-pointer was good, and the Redskins lost the game 17–16, destroying the possibility of winning one for their fallen superstar.

There was enough blame to go around, but essentially Coach Joe Gibbs put the loss on himself. In the postgame presser, Gibbs said, "There is no one to blame but myself. I should have known the rule."

If there was to be a bright note concerning the game, the Skins' defense managed to hold the Bills to zero touchdowns, with all of their points being scored on a first-quarter safety sack of quarterback Jason Campbell and five subsequent field goals.

●

The team finished the year 9–7 after winning four of their last five games, thus winning their division and making the postseason. On January 5, 2008, the season came to an abrupt end when they lost to the Seattle Seahawks in the first round of the playoffs.

29

Where Were They When ...?

EVERYBODY OF AGE REMEMBERS WHERE HE OR SHE WAS WHEN PRESIDENT John F. Kennedy was shot, when the USA put a man on the moon, or when the World Trade Center buildings fell in New York City. If you were a Sean Taylor fan, you may remember where you were and how you felt when you heard he was shot and went to football heaven.

Please note: I would never dare suggest the death of an outstanding athlete is on par with any of the events mentioned above; however, if you were a fan of the man and of his teams, it may have been devastating in your world. Every life is precious, whether it is one of a police officer, firefighter, construction worker, or student, and it is of no matter if the person reached maturity or was a mere babe in the woods; all life is precious.

We asked a few of the people closest to Sean where they were when they received the news of what had happened to him and what their initial reactions to the event were. None had any problem remembering.

Josephine Taylor

"We had no clue he was in town. In fact, Pete called at four o'clock in the morning. We were separated in July of 2007, and Jazmin and I went to live with my mother, who lived two and a half miles away from Sean's house. So whenever Sean came into town, being that I wasn't too far from him, he would always come visit. This is how family oriented Sean was.

304

"One night he came and knocked on my bedroom window, and I opened it and said, 'What are you doing here this time of night?' He said, 'You know I have to come check on you and Jazmin.' That's how I knew he was in town that particular night. That happened two, three weeks prior to Sean's passing.

"The night Pete called, I'm thinking, *'Since Sean got shot, I gotta get on a flight to Washington.'* So then I asked him what hospital Sean was at, and he said Jackson [Memorial Hospital]. Surprised, I said, 'Jackson?' I had no clue Sean was here [in Miami].

"I think I was in a daze for a couple of weeks," Josephine said. "I was so concerned for [my other children] Joey and Jazmin. I had to make sure they were okay. Joey was in college. When I got the news, Jazmin and I went to get Joey from Florida Memorial University and then go to the hospital. Joey and Jazmin were so angry, and since I could no longer help Sean, I had to focus on the two I had here and make sure they were okay. You know, Joey and Sean shared a bedroom to the end! Even when Sean was with the Redskins and he would come visit, he slept in the bedroom with Joey. At that time, they were both not there, because Joey was away at school and Sean was with the Redskins. But the bedroom never changed."

Half Sister Jazmin Taylor

"I was at my grandmother's house. I was actually sleeping, as it was very early in the morning. I got a text from my dad. It was brief and right to the point: 'SEAN HAS BEEN SHOT. EVERYTHING WILL BE OK.' So I find my mom, and she's on the phone with my dad.

"'Jazmin, get your clothes on,' My mother told me. I thought she meant get dressed to go to school. Then I thought he got grazed on the arm or something, like, whatever. Instead of driving me to my school, we drive all the way to Florida Memorial [University in Miami Gardens] to get Joey from college, and that's when I got scared. We had to go in to get him, and Joey was just crying. That's when I knew this was something serious. This isn't just a graze on the arm. It's serious.

"Joey was crying uncontrollably. I'm in the front seat. My mom is driving, and she told us to calm down. 'We don't know anything yet. Just stop. Don't worry about it.'"

They all arrived at the hospital, and the next thing they knew, they were ushered into a little waiting room. "I saw my aunt, Sean's mom, Jackie, and some police officers. The doctor is now talking to us, but I can't tell you what he was saying, as my mind was just blank. In the ER there's a small waiting area for families and a larger waiting area [for the general public].

"I never told anyone this story. I only kept this to myself. Well, there was a family in the larger room. When the doctor finished talking to them, they came storming out of the room crying … 'They shot her, and now she's dead,' said one of the family members. That's all I heard, and they went running down the hall crying. So I got freaked out, and I told myself I was never going in that room. 'If I go in that room, something bad is going to happen to Sean.' A few hours later, the nurses moved the family to the big room because everyone was coming in left and right. It took me about three hours after my family was moved to even go near that room.

"Then they let us upstairs to see Sean. I'm not going to speak on what I saw or what I said in his room. So then someone said, 'We are going to pray; everybody come in the big room.' I told them I wasn't going in. That's when my mom told me, 'Come on, Jazmin. We have to go in the room and pray together.' So I went in."

Daniel Snyder

"I was the last guy in the parking lot to see him when we left that weekend," reflected Snyder. "We did not know he was going to Florida. I remember him [Sean] jumping up and down. 'Look, look' he said [showing the boss he was ready to play]. And that's the last time I saw him."

Following a long pause, Snyder continued. "It's fun for me here because I do get to see young men grow up. I really do. I was looking forward to spending fifteen years with him, but he got taken from us.

"This is how I found out what happened to Sean. I received a phone call from security at about five in the morning, and he told me Sean Taylor has been shot in his leg. I said, 'What are you talking about?' So [in a daze] I got up, threw on sweatpants and told my wife what happened, and I drove to Redskin Park at around one hundred miles per hour. I called Gibbs and woke him up, and I said, 'Meet me at the park. Something happened.' We got here, but the news was so scarce from down there in terms of what was really going on.

"I got here around six. It was still dark out. Me and Joe [Gibbs] sat in his office and waited a little bit to see what was going on. It was obvious he was in critical condition in the hospital after he had been airlifted.

"When the team arrived for work, I addressed them and said, 'I'm going down [to Miami], and I will let everyone know shortly what was going on.' We were all basically in the dark. No one was answering any phones. Clinton wanted to go, so I took Portis and my general manager at the time, Vinny Cerrato. We flew down and went straight to the hospital."

Snyder looked at Pete, who was sitting diagonally across from him at his conference room table, and said, "You were there. It was so awful. I guess we stayed most of the day.

"We were all crying. It was pretty emotional. The surgeons came in and said he gripped their hand; in other words, he responded, which was a tremendous accomplishment, and they were optimistic.

"I remember going back to the Mandarin Oriental hotel. I used to stay there all the time; the food was great, but I haven't been back since 2007. I will never stay at that hotel ever again—too painful. Anyway, my sister was in town for a business meeting in Miami, and she met us at the hotel."

After dinner, Snyder, Cerrato, and Portis retired to their respective rooms at the hotel. A few hours later, "Drew [Rosenhaus] called me to tell me we lost him. I had to go across the hall and tell Portis. It was [one of] the hardest things I ever had to do. We were all on the same floor. I didn't want to do it over the phone, so I walked across the hall and knocked on his door. When I was inside the room, I couldn't say it. I couldn't talk. But he just knew. I was not doing well. He wasn't either. Eventually C. P. came to my suite, and he stood on the balcony for thirty minutes by himself."

Clinton Portis

"I mean, the same person who called me to tell me about the Banshee situation was the person that called me and told me that Sean got shot. I remember jumping up that morning, and she like yellin' 'Sean got shot.' I'm like, 'Naw!'

"It was Lex Rolle, Antrel's sister … she was the one who told me that Sean got shot. I was like, 'Naw, uh-uh.'"

Portis dressed quickly that day and raced for the practice facility. "When I get to the building, I go straight to Vinny. Vinny and Coach Gibbs were waitin' on the information."

C. P. grew quiet, pensive, speaking more deliberately. "In the building, it was kinda like everyone was on pause. I guess they had heard about it, but they were trying to figure out more information on the situation. They called a team meetin' to inform everybody they was waitin' on the word.

"Mr. Snyder, Vinny, and myself got on the same plane and flew down and came straight to the hospital off the plane. We get over to Jackson and it was like, yeah, he's stable, everything cool. He gonna pull through.

"I remember leavin' the hospital. We stayed at the Mandarin Oriental. We went to dinner at the Mandarin with Mr. Snyder. Mr. Snyder gives a toast. I think the docs was callin' and informin' him. They had just called and informed him of good news. Mr. Snyder gave a toast and shared the news with everybody that he was pullin' through. I remember we was all happy, sittin' inside the Mandarin. Everybody had dinner, and everybody upbeat.

"When we left dinner, I just had a weird feeling like I wanted to go back to the hospital. I was thinkin' about just jumpin' in a cab and goin' back, and not sayin' anything. Mr. Snyder asked me what was I gonna do, and I told him, 'You know, I think I'm gonna go back and see him.' Mr. Snyder said, 'Oh, rest up. He's okay and he needs to get the rest. We're gonna go first thing in the mornin'. We'll go see him before we leave.'

"I was like, 'Cool.' So I went back to the room and [was] kinda relaxin'. But I couldn't sleep. I think I fell asleep probably about one thirty or two in the mornin'. I was just sittin' up thinkin', *I should go back. I should go back.* I finally end up fallin' asleep, and I hear a *boom boom boom!* at the door. I rolled over, and it was kinda like knowin' it was bad news. But it was that hard knock. And I rolled over and grabbed my phone. When I grabbed my phone, I think it said like four something in the morning. As soon as I looked at my phone, I was like, 'No!'"

C. P. began reflecting and spoke very softly. "Man, I went to the door. I looked through the peephole, and I saw Mr. Snyder. So I opened the door, and he was standin' outside cryin'. He [entered my room and] just said, 'He gone!'

"I was like, 'No, no.'

"He was like, 'He didn't make it through the night.'

"I just wanted to be like, he's all right. [After Snyder left and I was alone] I shut the door, and I don't know if I prayed. I got back into bed, and it was just like a reflection. 'This cain't be real,' you know.

"Then we went over … I think we came down to you [Pete]."

Pete said, "Yeah. You came to my house."

"We also went over to the hospital, did some runnin' around, and then we came down to your house.

"I remember when we got back, havin' to speak to the team. Man, I hadn't cried up to that point. I don't think I cried in probably … it probably had been ten years since I can recall cryin'. So I spoke to the team. I remember everybody in the room really just breakin' down and boo-hoo cryin'. Tryin' to figure out … you know, nobody was thinkin' about football; it was like how suddenly we lost a piece of us. *At that very moment, Sean became bigger than life.*

"It just goes to show you, like, the appreciation for Sean [while] livin' was not the appreciation for Sean gone. I think there was so much negativity with Sean, and every time he did something good, they brought up the DUI, they brought up bein' in [and walking out of and being fined for] the rookie symposium, and they brought up the shoot-out [over his stolen ATVs]. They brought up [the spitting] any incident that he was involved with.

"I remember when he stopped talkin' to the media, you know, just kinda stepped away, and that's why he said, 'No matter what I do, C. P., like, these people write what they wanna write. So I just don't say nothing.'

"I think instantly we realized what we had, and I think at that moment— you know, you don't go through life tellin' people you appreciate 'em; you don't go through life tellin' people you look up to 'em, or you respect 'em, or— you know, I mean, you just don't. That's human nature. I mean, everybody idolize you when you're gone, and you don't get to hear it. It is through passin' along your story to someone else. I think that's what happened with Sean. Nobody knew the effect Sean had in households until he was gone. All of a sudden when you seen everything in transition to 21 … I remember the S-dot … man … me and Santana was the only person, well, Smoot, Sean's friends, me, Santana. Marcus Washington is the one who started callin' Sean S-dot. And it stuck. Like, S-dot, but if you look at S.21 [pronounced 'ess dot twenty-one'], it's everywhere, and it's crazy … hype … how much, or how big Sean became, life after death, you know.

"In my eyes it's like a Tupac or Biggie situation. I tell people all the time Sean was the best player I ever seen play the game. I've been a football fan. I can't go back to Jack Tatum and talk about days of old. I didn't live that game.

But with my own eyes, like the stuff that I seen Sean do was spectacular and unreal. That's from me seein' Sean punk T.O., from me seein' Sean try to knock Andre Johnson head off (who went to college with us) to knockin' Reggie Wayne head off (that went to college with us), after we all done sat and had a conversation: 'How's your mama doin'? How's the family? What's goin' on? Yeah, good seein' you.' And [as] soon as he fastened that chin strap, it wasn't no, 'I didn't go to college with you, me and you not friends ...'"

Connie Dingle

Sean's grandmother, Connie Dingle, said, "I cut my phone off; they had been trying to call me. I didn't know nothing. I was sitting up in a meeting, and one of the workers came to me and beckoned to me to call the hotel because I [had] an emergency.

"I was in Tampa at the Buccaneers and Redskins game. I was going to be at a meeting the next day at Disney World anyway, and Tampa isn't that far. It was a nurses' meeting. So somebody beckoned to me to adjourn the meeting around midday and told me to call the hotel. I tried to call the hotel, but the line was busy.

"I cut the phone back on and saw my niece called me and said, 'Are you sitting down?'

"I thought something happen to my daddy because he's ninety-something years old. I said, 'Yeah,' and she say, 'Pete need you in Miami.'

"I had knee surgery, so my niece said, 'Don't try to drive back; go catch a plane.'

"She say, 'Sean been shot; Pete needs you.' Then my sister called, and she told me the same thing. 'Don't drive; catch a plane back. Hurry, catch a plane.'

"I didn't know what to do. I had another girlfriend of mine who had driven up there with me. She called me. It was all over the news. Everybody knew, and I didn't know anything. She called me and told me, 'I'm going to the hotel to get your things. Where are you?'

"I gave her my location, so she came and left her car there and drove mine back to Miami. And when we got to Miami, man, the paparazzi and all them was all around the hospital. I couldn't see Sean then, because they were still working on him.

"I saw Coach Joe Gibbs and Dan Snyder talking. Gibbs said, 'I let him go home so he could rest his knee for Thursday's Buffalo game.' (It was probably Dan Snyder who said that.) Even though when they are hurt they are supposed to be at the game. They all loved Sean, you know. I know Snyder loved Sean.

"By me being a nurse when I saw him, I just … just went to him and told him I loved him. That was it.

"But you know Sean died in November, and in April someone had sent his father a video. They had done an interview with Sean, and in it Sean says he doesn't mind dying, God has been good to him, he doesn't mind dying, and that made his father feel … he said he made peace with the Lord, and that made his dad feel so good."

Buck Ortega

"I was in Delray Beach, Florida. Drew Rosenhaus was my agent, and I was a free agent at the time. I'd been 'on the street' for maybe two weeks. I'd been with the Dolphins for a short time. Drew called me that morning and said, 'The New Orleans Saints are going to sign you, and here's your flight information.' I know I was supposed to fly out that night. Well, right after that call, he calls back and asked, 'Did you hear about Sean?' He was the first one to call me. Obviously the high that I was on from being signed with a team quickly evaporated because of what happened to Sean. So I immediately jumped in the car and drove down to Jackson and met my father there. It makes me sick to this day to be in that situation and to know it was very, very bleak for him with little chance of survival."

Renaldo Wynn

"I got cut that year by Coach. I spoke with Coach Blache, and he said the Redskins were moving on—time to get a little younger. Hey, I had already played ten years, and I was on the [New Orleans] Saints in 2007 [the same year one of Sean's high school buddies, Buck Ortega, got picked up by the Saints].

"Being recently removed from the Redskins, I still kept in touch with a lot of the guys and felt like I was still understanding what they were going through as a team. Phillip Daniels kept me posted when it first happened.

At first we heard it was a flesh wound, and we were like, 'Okay, he'll make it. He'll be fine. It looks pretty good.' I'm sure everybody thought the same thing. Then obviously nobody knew about him getting hit in the artery with so much bleeding he didn't make it out.

"Being close to home, being in that locker room probably was one thing, but I got a chance to see a different perspective on how guys that didn't play with Sean, didn't know Sean, how they responded to that news. They were all very much in shock in the Saints locker room. They couldn't believe it. They respected him even though they didn't know him as a person. They respected his game. They respected him as a player. When Eugene Upshaw made the announcement with Roger Goodell to put the 21 … on the backs of everybody's helmet [as a tribute], everybody in my locker room did it. I think the only guy who questioned it was [Head Coach] Sean Payton, and he wanted to see how his players felt about it. All of our leaders, from Drew Brees to Will Smith to Reggie Bush, all those guys were on board with it. We all kept the 21 on the backs of our helmets for the rest of the year.

"I got the helmet sitting here in my office. I'm sitting here looking at it. All my helmets are on my desk here at Joe Gibbs Racing. They are all facing forward except for that one Saints helmet. I have that one facing back. There's a story behind it. I'll take a picture of it and text it. I have all my helmets up top, and what you'll see is my Jacksonville helmet, my Redskins helmet, then the Saints, then the Giants helmet. After I played with the Giants, I came back to the Redskins. I'll take them in order, and then I'll take a close-up of the Saints helmet."

Lorenzo Alexander

"There were six or seven news vans parked out front [of the facility], but I really didn't think too much of it, because there's always something going on at Redskins Park," said Lorenzo Alexander. "It wasn't until I got inside the building and I saw Miss B. J. [the receptionist], and she was the one who told me.

"My immediate reaction was it was surreal. I had feelings of disbelief because as athletes we think we are indestructible and nothing is ever going to happen to us. For this to happen to a player and a friend, someone you admire, I really had a sense of uh, uh … I was soul searching.

Revelation

"*This incident was the eye-opener that made me give my life to Christ. I was twenty-four at the time—same age as Sean—and kept thinking, 'What have I done in my life [that] if I was to pass right now … ?' If there was a positive in any of this senselessness, this was it. It put my life on the right path because I didn't want to be one of those guys that waited for something to happen, and then where is your legacy?*

"He had created something great for himself, was doing great things, moving forward. I was a guy in transition, so this really helped me as far as being a believer in Christ."

At the funeral Lorenzo did get a chance to speak to a few of the guys. "We talked about what a great athlete he was, what a great person he turned out to be, especially being a great father.

"This event really brought us together as a team, as far as relationships. People take those for granted, so when you lose somebody like that, you know, people generally get closer, because you never know when your time is up.

"The Redskins did go on that great run at the end of 2007 and made it to the playoffs, so a team *was* brought together."

Santana Moss

"I recall being home [on my day off] when I heard about it. It was very early Monday morning. All I heard was, he was shot. We didn't have any of the details. We knew nothing. I was like, 'Wow, what happened?' Finally we heard that someone broke into his house. And that almost slapped me in my face, because we had just talked about this. So it was like, 'Okay, boom!'

"I went to sleep Sunday night and I got another call later on from Drew Rosenhaus telling me that it was not okay and he was fighting for his life. I was like, 'I thought he got shot in the leg and he was going to be all right.' I later woke up out of my sleep because now I was worried. It was like one, maybe two o'clock in the morning.

"I remember I had my guy up there who was with me since 2005. It's a guy I use outside of the team that helps me take care of my body. So the next morning I was at his house, not too far from my house, and I was on the table and we were talking about it, and he was like, 'For real?' So we were just talking, hoping that he was all right, and that's when I got another call saying he was gone.

"So I was on that table and crying. I was still trying to get healthy, and I never kinda thought that, you know … I was bawlin', man; I just couldn't believe it. They told me he was going to be all right … not okay, but he should pull through. You know what I'm saying?

"Like I told people, guys that played with Sean for no matter how many years, we all took something from his presence. I felt like there was something special about that guy from day one. It was crazy being around him for the two years we shared together because it seemed like we shared a lot more than just a normal person that hangs out with him every day shared. So I got to know him a little different than … and that's why it hurt so much.

"I felt like there were people who knew him all his life who probably felt worse than I felt because he was such a special person. But just to see how Sean carried himself, to see how he acted, you know, how he spoke about his daughter; how he prepared himself [for field battle]. So the things I learned about him daily … it was just amazing to me that he was living that life the way he was living it.

"So he was betrayed by some vicious thugs or whatever you call them. You know what I'm saying? That's another reason it hurt so much, because I was like, there was so much more I could have learned from him and how much more we had to talk about. There was so much more I wanted to share with him, because like I said with all the guys, there was no one I opened up to like I did with him. So the way I feel and the way I am going to try and remember him [will be by] the things I do. That's why I said as long as I am on that field I will always try my best to keep his memory … because you have to know his dad, his relatives, to share and know how special he was. You know what I'm saying? I appreciate it. I felt like I was that close. He was a teammate first and then a friend."

Moss and Taylor never dwelled on the media much, "but I did address the media on his behalf when he passed, because … it was ludicrous … here's a guy who you don't know, and you don't know what he's been through in his life … no one knows … all you can do is go on assumptions of what you think you know or what you've heard. You remember something that happened to him in the past instead of mourning the guy that was taken from us. I was pissed off about it because I just felt like they were looking for somebody to jump on when it came down to it ... something negative because of the way he played. Sean was fierce playing the game, so the media took that and tried to pin that on him as an individual. He wasn't like that at all. Sean was a great guy. If I was the father of a girl around Sean's age, I would want her to date him, because that's the kind of guy he was outside the game, outside of football. I feel like the stuff I did was way worse than what Sean was about. The way I lived my life at the time? Sean wasn't that type of guy."

Drew Rosenhaus

"I was at home, and I got a call early in the morning notifying me that Sean had been shot. I believe I was in bed at the time. No one knew of the severity of his injuries at the time, so the first thing I did was race over to the hospital. When I got there, that's when I realized it was a life-threatening situation.

"We were all hoping and praying he would make it. I was part of the vigil the family went through over the entire time Sean was in the hospital. It was round-the-clock prayers hoping he'd pull through. He held on as much as he could. We were all so devastated when his life ended. I think it saddened a lot of people, and I was one of them. So many were absolutely crushed by his loss.

"Sean touched a lot of people—his teammates Santana Moss and Clinton Portis. He touched a lot of people at the University of Miami. He had a big impact on his family, and it was truly a tragic loss for them and the community. It's one of those things in life that leaves you scratching your head."

Struggling for the right words, Rosenhaus continued. "It just doesn't make any sense. What a waste. What a loss. This was a guy that had his whole life ahead of him and *so much* to give and *so much* promise. What a terrible, terrible loss ... just an absolute tragedy. 'Tragedy' is a very strong word, but it absolutely applies here.

"This was a devastating part of my life, but it only made me a lot stronger. I had not been exposed to that type of tragedy in my lifetime, and it was a real eye-opener for me because I had been very blessed up until that point with my family, friends, and clients. This was just a tremendous pain in my heart for sure. To this day I don't think a day goes by where I don't have a thought about Sean. You know? I think about him very often. So when I just chatted with his dad, it seemed like it was only yesterday that his dad and I spoke on a daily basis. During Sean's playing days, we talked almost every day.

"So my heart continues to go out to all the people that loved Sean, and he'll always mean a lot to me, and I'll think of him only in the most positive ways. I'll miss him for a long time."

Gregg Williams

"I was the very first person they called from the organization. They called and woke me up that night. In fact, they weren't able to get a hold of anyone else. So I got a hold of Vinny [Cerrato].

"When he passed that morning, I cried like a little baby. While I was sitting in the corner of my room, I couldn't help but to think about one of the famous sayings Sean used when he and I would have our moments of controversy or confrontation on the sidelines.

"'Hey coach. Hey. Get on to the next play. Get on to the next play. Get off my back and get on to the next play.'

"When he passed and I was in mourning, I heard him say, 'Hey coach; get on to the next play. I will always be there with you.' The next morning, when we had our press conference, I mentioned that to the media. While I'm telling you this, I have goose bumps because I know he's in the office with me listening to me talking about him right now. He is my angel in life, and I care for him dearly."

Struggling a bit, Williams adds, "I wanted to see him. I wanted to touch him, and I wanted to be with him until the final end."

Williams mentions "a really neat memento" given to him that sits on his desk. It's a tombstone of Sean Taylor in crystal with a lighted base. "His image is sitting here on my desk every single day with a framed certificate a fan sent me. I know he watches over me; he's with me at every decision, and I think about him daily. And I'll text a picture of it."

Another memento given to Williams was the one Dan Snyder made—a Hall of Fame–type coin cast with Sean's image. "I gave one of them to every player who played with him and every coach that coached him. We are the only ones who have those, and I have it in my pocket every single second of every single day. When I bump into [Sean's agent] Drew Rosenhaus, we kind of compete to see who will say, 'Okay, let me see the coin,' because he knows I have it in my pocket and it travels with me everywhere I go.

"Well, when we [finish talking], I'm going to send a picture of the special Sean Taylor coin I keep in my pocket and a picture of the crystal piece with Sean's image in it that sits on my desk. There's also a picture of him sitting on my desk. He does watch over me, and when I send it, you'll see that I'm not bullshitting."

Coach Williams said, "I didn't realize until after he passed how close he was with my own three children, especially my two sons. They called themselves the three amigos, and Sean used to tell them, 'I know you took the ass chewing at home from your dad at night, but I took the ass chewing from him during the day!'"

Finally Williams said, "Someday I would love to work with Pete Taylor. He's a great guy and great coach, and he's passionate about what he does. I would be open at some point in time to make it work."

True to his word, Coach Gregg Williams texted me the pictures of the Sean Taylor coin and the lit crystal holographic image statue that sits on his desk.

Coach Steve Jackson

Jackson gave a long, deep sigh. "Oh man ... well ... here's an interesting story. We were playing Tampa Bay that weekend. I was on the sideline, just enjoying the sunshine, waiting for the guys to come out. I try to get to the field early to get a feel for the stadium, the weather, the wind, the game, etc. It was a little chilly when we left Virginia, and it was sunny in Tampa, so I decided to also work on my tan a little bit. Just then a security guy comes running out toward me. 'Coach Jackson. Coach Jackson. We have an emergency at your house.'

"So I take off running behind our security guy. Since he used the word 'emergency,' the first things I thought of was my kids but they weren't supposed to be at home. So I'm running across the field behind him. Now, I am old and fat, so I get about halfway across the field ... and I'm huffing and puffing, and I ask, 'What's ... the ... emergency?' He says, 'your townhouse is on fire.' I said, 'Oh, that's it?' I walk the rest of the way across the field and I see one of our trainers who is a volunteer EMT, so she tells me, 'Yeah, Coach. Something caught fire in your house, and your third floor is all burnt.'

"I don't remember if we won or lost the game, but when we got back to Virginia, I go to my townhouse and everything I have in there is gone. Things either smelled like smoke or was burnt or was drenched from being sprayed with the hose. So I said, 'Damn. We got practice tomorrow, and I have to deal with this,' and it was just me. I am a divorced dad … it was just me.

"The next day, I get to the office about five-something in the morning. As I am walking to go get some coffee I see Vinny and Dan walking to the coach's side of the building. They have this look on their faces … they're never there that early in the morning. So I said, 'What's going on?' They say … 'Sean's been shot.' I said, 'What?'

"'That's right. Sean's been shot.' At that moment, I'm thinking it's okay … Sean being the superhuman guy that he is, he's going to be all right. So I asked, 'Is he going to be okay? What happened?'

"As I'm saying those things, I'm thinking in my mind how insignificant all those material things were that I just lost in the fire. These things meant everything to me. It was all that I had in the world, but I have a player that's just been shot and is holding on to dear life.

"It's just ironic that both of those things happened at the exact same time. My townhouse catches fire and Sean gets shot on the same day."

After a very long pause, Coach Jackson continued. "I was broken at that point. We were all in a daze and in a funk. Everyone kept saying, 'I think he's going to be okay. He's going to fight through it. He'll be all right.' I think that was on a Monday, so only the coaches were in there. I think that Tuesday he passed.

"At that next meeting, I had to give a presentation on an aspect of the game plan. So there I was, in front of the room, in front of the defense, and I look back…. At that point I had been in Washington for four years, and I had never been in a meeting without Sean. So I look back there at his seat, and it was empty. LaRon [Landry] was sitting in the room with his head down, and he knew where I was going. LaRon and Sean. Those were my two guys, and I always looked at them before I started anything to make sure they were paying attention … and the seat was empty. As far as I was concerned, that seat would never be filled again. Literally. And then tears started streaming down my face, and I couldn't finish. Somebody else had to finish the meeting. I tried. I just couldn't. That's how that meeting went.

"It still chokes me up thinking about that. Just like that, he's gone. Someone that special, that talented, and that gifted … gone. Never to be seen, spoken to, or told 'I love you' ever again. This incident really changed my coaching approach."

In his Jerry McGuire moment, Coach Jackson said, "[From that moment on] I never left a meeting; I never left a practice without letting the guys know how I felt about them. I coached them on how they could get better as men, on how they could become better players, and even how they could get better as teammates; because I may never get the opportunity to coach them tomorrow. I mean, you never know what's going to happen in this world. We get so caught up in wins and losses we forget sometimes it's about people. All it takes is for one incident to happen and that person can be gone forever. We think just because we are in the NFL it's not going to happen to us. We're just going to go home to our big homes and our big cars and we are immune from all the craziness in the world, and we're not. It just helped me to appreciate the guys, the games, and life more.

"During the season, I'm sure I spent more time with Sean than he would have liked. So as a coach, when you spend that much time with your players … like when a guy is a free agent at the end of the year, that's one thing. But when you draft a guy, he's your guy, and whatever happens in the relationship, he becomes like a son. Just by the amount of time I spent with Sean, I can only imagine what it was like and what his dad went through. Every time I think about it, it makes me swell up. I knew Sean outside of number 36 or number 21. Then just watching him grow from being a rookie hotshot, a guy who didn't know anything about the league, turn into the man he became."

Jazmin Taylor

"About eleven o'clock at night, my mom said we're all going home. We heard Sean was doing better and he was moving a tiny bit. 'Sean is going to be okay, so let's go home and get some sleep,' my mom said. So we all went home.

"I woke up to my mom screaming. She was on the phone. I looked at my phone, and I had a missed call from my dad. Mom said, 'I left my glasses at the hospital. I'm going to go get them.' She said it again: 'I left my glasses at the hospital. I'm going to go get them.' I heard my parents speaking, and I heard my mom say, 'Why can't I come to the hospital?' My dad said, 'Because we lost Sean.'

"So we drove to my dad's house, but nobody was there. I had to use my house keys to get in. When we got inside, my mom said, 'This is a lie. Someone is lying about this. This isn't true. This didn't happen.'"

As Jazmin recalled the events of that morning, she began to cry. I felt myself tearing up as well as I sat listening in silence. "My mom calls my aunt and asks her if it was true. She just hung up the phone. I asked, 'Mom, what's going on?' All she could say was that 'it was true.' I had my keys and my phone in my hand, and I just dropped everything on the floor. I ran into Sean's room, and I got on his bed and I just laid there and cried.

"Ten to fifteen minutes later, that's when everybody started coming over. They told me, 'Jazmin, you have to go in your room.' So I did. I couldn't get my mind off everything, so I decided to turn on the TV," Jazmin said as she continued to cry while telling this part of her story.

"Just then, on the TV, the news report came on. The crawl read, 'Sean Taylor has died.'

"I started screaming, crying, shaking. From that day until his funeral, it just felt like one long day. It was a week, but it felt like the longest day of my life."

Jazmin said she became very agitated over what seemed to be the simplest things. "I started yelling at people for sitting on his bed."

After a long pause, she continued. "You can't fathom … the thought … of losing a brother you just talked to … a day ago. 'I was just talking to you,' and I kept saying, 'I love you.' And I heard him saying it back to me.

"So who am I supposed to look up to now? Who am I supposed to talk to? Who can take your spot in my heart? And all I could think was, 'No one.' No one will be able to take my brother's spot. I don't care what football player comes along to be the next Sean Taylor, because no one can amount to Sean. No one … can amount to Sean. I'm not just saying that as a football player. I'm saying that as a person," said the very emotional Jazmin Taylor.

"It's just sad because no one knows. No one knows what I went through, you know? All that speculation just because he didn't talk to the media, people assumed the worst about him. I was like, 'Why?' Just because he was quiet? Who can say they never made a mistake in their lives? Who can? I will defend my family until my last days.

"Sean was always religious. He always went to church. He went with his grandma. It never changed. Honestly. You always have a relationship with

God, but as you get older you become more understanding. I grew up in the same house as him, and I love God, but the older one gets, the stronger the connection."

As to doing this interview and the book, Jazmin said, "I'm not going to lie. It's fifty-fifty for me. A part of me says, 'Just leave it alone.' Sean was very shy. He didn't like a lot of people in his business. He didn't like the media much. He just liked to do his job, work out, and go home. So a part of me says just let it be and let him be at rest.

"The other part of me says no. People need to know who Sean was. People need to know what was written about him was seventy-five percent wrong. People need to know he was greater than football. He wasn't just a football player. People need to love Sean because of him, not because of the way he tackled a person or the way he caught a ball. So while I do support this, as you can see, I'm still fifty-fifty."

Jazmin has Sean's picture hanging on her bedroom wall. She said that on her bad days, she'll go on YouTube and look at his videos. "I have my days where I'll wake up in the middle of the night and just talk to him. And I'll have my good days when I say my nightly prayers and just say, 'I love you, Sean, good night.'"

Below are URLs for a few of Jazmin's favorite YouTube videos of Sean:

- http://www.youtube.com/watch?v=4NnvkzDIKuU
- http://www.youtube.com/watch?v=s2VT4JlawAs
- http://www.youtube.com/watch?v=UmqLHY___cfc

30

The Funeral and ...

Daniel Snyder

"I took every single person and their spouses [in the organization] to Miami for the funeral mass. Jeremy Shockey got up and spoke, and at one point he said, 'Would everybody that's here from the Redskins please stand up.' And we had fifteen hundred people standing. It was a lot of people. I was supposed to speak. I couldn't," team owner Daniel Snyder said.

"Joe [Gibbs] said a few words. That was nice of him. He had a hard time. It was very difficult. It's not supposed to happen."

After a long pause, Snyder continued, "At Sean's funeral, Coach Gibbs spoke about their relationship and what kind of athlete and person he was." Since Coach Gibbs is also a very righteous and spiritual person, at the funeral, he also spoke about how one must make things right with God.

Coach Ralph Ortega

Thinking about Sean's funeral, Gulliver coach Ralph Ortega remembered this: "Something interesting happened at the service the Taylors had at FIU. I could tell Coach Gregg Williams was staring at me. I couldn't figure out why. When I got up to leave the auditorium, he came over to me and said, 'I remember the day you told me all those stories about Sean Taylor, how he had the potential to be so great,' and on and on. He said, 'That's the best defensive player I have ever coached.' I don't know if Williams will remember that, if he said this to me, but he said, 'I have no doubt that Sean was on pace to be the greatest safety and possibly the best defensive player to ever play in the NFL.'"

Gulliver Coach McCloskey

"For Steve Howey, [losing Sean] was very emotional," Coach McCloskey said. "He was very close to Sean. When I talked to him at the funeral, he could hardly speak. He was in tears, and so upset at the situation. I remember at the service at FIU, I think everybody had gone [home], but Steve went up by himself to the front and knelt down, and he was just having his private moment. It really hit him hard. He had a very close relationship with Sean and probably went through more with him that senior season because he was coaching him up directly."

Jazmin Taylor

"At the funeral … I'm glad I spoke, because I got to say how I felt about Sean, but a part of me was like, 'Now everybody knows me (because they saw me speak) and everybody wants to be my friend. They all want to talk to me, and I don't want that.' I honestly don't know how Sean dealt with it. He is one of the shyest people, and he had to put up with it."

Sometimes people try to get to Jazmin just because of who she is. "That happened as soon as Sean died. That's one of the reasons I don't even tell people I'm Sean's sister. A lot of people will want to be your friend just to get close to you because of him.

"I went to high school in Broward County, so I had no friends and I didn't know anybody. I ended up taking two weeks off of school when Sean passed away, and when I came back, I had all the so-called friends in the world.

"I got all these questions, like 'How's the family?' 'How's your father?' 'What's new in the case?' I did not like that at all. I have people from high school call me to this day: 'Hey, is your dad still training? Can I train with him?' they'd say. And I'm like, 'Why?' [Because] 'he trained your brother, and I want to be like your brother,' they'd say.

"People are so good at being fakes, and sometimes it's hard to tell who your friends really are. They come to my house and they see pictures of Sean hanging up on my wall and they want to take them, and I'm like, 'Wow.'

Revelation

"When Sean passed away, people that I didn't even know, and I'm pretty sure that Sean didn't know, would come up to me and [tell] me how much they loved Sean and how he was their hero, their role model. At the time, I would say, 'You don't love my brother. You didn't know him.'

"So now you go on YouTube and see some of the stories out there where Sean is referred to as a thug or someone mean spirited or bad tempered," Jazmin said. "And that's not him at all! He was just the sweetest person.

"You just didn't know him. Just because he was into rap music, that makes him a thug? Did you know he listened to gospel music as much as rap music? Did you know that? What about him going to church all the time? Did you know that? What about him being an amazing father, where Baby Jackie got everything she wanted? Did you know about that? It just hurt my heart, because I can only defend him so much. I can't go to the entire world and defend him.

"Sean was just a great person inside and out. There's one thing that no one can deny … that smile of his. To me he was the funniest, most protective, most sincere, genuine person ever.

"Maybe I'm the only one who saw that side? [Lord knows] people speculated about Sean. 'Oh, he has dreads and braids and tattoos, so he must be a thug.' *Um, no!* That's not true at all," Jazmin said, almost scolding no one in particular.

"In my mind, Sean was on top. In my heart and mind, no one can compare to Sean. I don't care what kind of football player you are. I don't care what kind of person you are. If a football player approaches me and asks if they could work out with my dad, if I've seen them in practice, I'll tell them, 'You don't have the talent to work out with my dad.' I'm like, 'Go somewhere else.' No one compares to Sean in my mind.

"Here's the thing. If I were a boy, I'd like to be just like Sean. My dad and mom tell me all the time I have his personality."

Connie Dingle on the Media

"I remember the camera crew was setting up in our yard," said Sean's grandmother. "There was a lot of propaganda going around about where he lived. Sean lived right here, not the slum 'you' reported he lived in; but still you asking me to get the cameras up in my yard?

"I said, 'He had a park close by and a basketball court in the backyard, you know what I mean? This is where he was raised up. Does this look like the slum to you?'

"Some of the things they was saying about him. They was talking about how he was raised, and I said, 'He had plenty to eat because his dad kept the box full of food in the cabinet, and when he didn't have it, I had it in my house next door.'"

31

Pete Returns to Northern Virginia

"I REMEMBER FLYING BACK TO VIRGINIA TO GO OUT TO REDSKINS PARK to do some paperwork a little after Sean got shot. We land, and when we came out of the airport, we saw Sean's car in the valet lot just outside the exit doors of the terminal, but we didn't have the keys to get in it. I did walk over to the car and looked inside."

Revelation

Just like Washington Redskins Coach Joe Gibbs, Sean had given himself to Jesus Christ and "at a very young age he already had a relationship with God and was a regular reader of the Bible," Sean's father said. "I know for a fact that Sean's life was saved through God. Most people don't know that tattooed on Sean's arm was the twenty-third psalm.

"So it was no surprise when I exited the terminal at Dulles Airport and I looked inside the car at valet parking, I saw the Bible open to the twenty-third psalm on the front seat. Sean was reading it just before getting on the plane to Miami. He never made it back. It was like the car was saying to us, 'Here I am, right here.' If it wasn't in plain view, we'd have never seen it.

> *Psalm 23*
> *A Psalm of David.*
> *The Lord is my shepherd; I shall not want.*

He maketh me to lie down in green pastures: he leadeth me beside the still waters.

He restoreth my soul: he leadeth me in the paths of righteousness for his name's sake.

Yea, though I walk through the valley of the shadow of death, I will fear no evil: for thou art with me; thy rod and thy staff they comfort me.

Thou preparest a table before me in the presence of mine enemies: thou anointest my head with oil; my cup runneth over.

Surely goodness and mercy shall follow me all the days of my life: and I will dwell in the house of the Lord for ever.

"As a father, you look for certain confirmation on things such as, was he 'prayed up?' Was he right [with the Lord]? So when I saw the car and the Bible open, I knew that everything was okay.

"One of the first things I wanted to do was to drive by [the house] where Sean lived. We went over there, and as you came into Ashburn, I saw the footprints in the hills where Sean used to work out. I went back four months later, in March, around the time of the cherry blossoms, and those footprints were still there.

"When I got to Redskins Park, Coach Gibbs asked me to speak to the team. So I got up and thanked them for being great teammates to Sean. I told them to cherish all these moments and never take anything for granted. 'Make sure you tell your loved ones what was on your mind all the time,' I said."

Sean loved the game of football. He loved bringing his passion, intensity, and tenacity. "The main thing is," Taylor told them, "he didn't want to let you guys down." We talked about a few other things, and after that talk, the Redskins went on a huge 2007 run to the playoffs.

"While I was speaking to the team, I saw his locker. It was untouched. I knew how it looked prior to that day, because I used to take stuff up to him in the locker room. I saw it again at the end of the 2012 season while attending the Cowboys–Redskins game. As a special tribute, it is now displayed on the Club Level in FedEx Field. Yes, it was a little emotional. If you see it, know that everything in that locker is real.

"I often wondered if Sean and Coach Gibbs prayed together. What I can tell you is that you didn't play for him unless you were of high moral fiber. That was very important to Gibbs.

"I know Sean's death was very difficult for Coach Gibbs. He gave many interviews where he said this was one of the hardest things he ever had to deal with, in part because he never had to deal with anything like this before. Sean's death impacted him so much, he thought about his own kids and grandkids—he was very close to them. I am sorry to say this, but he had concerns for his own health and all [these] were probably the deciding factors [that led him] to leave coaching. Coach Gibbs was diabetic, and I heard that according to his doctors, the stress was getting to him."

2008–2012

Sean Taylor was posthumously selected to the Pro Bowl played on February 10, 2008.

"In 2012 Sean was inducted into the Gulliver Athletic Hall of Fame. That ceremony was another one of the proudest moments of my life," Taylor said. "You always have dreams for your kids, and you don't know if the dreams will ever come true. When Sean died, they held a memorial service for Sean. Eventually Gulliver also named their high school football field after him: *The Sean Taylor Memorial Field*. I wish he could have been here to see it himself, to see that all the hard work and doing the right thing paid off," Pete Taylor said.

"You tell kids all the time that doing what's right will prevail, but in Sean's case, he never saw it. But I'll see it; his baby will see it; his brothers, sisters, cousins, family, and friends will see that when you do the right thing, it does pay off."

Old friends, even some from college and the NFL who were close to Sean, were there at the dedication ceremony. Some of these friends were Eric Green, Jamal Mashburn, and Mark Strickland. Today, at Gulliver, Sean's little brother Gabriel plays with their kids. He played with LeBron James's kids too before they all moved back to Ohio. There were teachers and those who were inspirations to Sean, fans, and school supporters there, about one thousand people in all that came to the field naming ceremony.

32

What If?

THIS SUBJECT CAME UP OFTEN. WHAT WOULD SEAN BE DOING AFTER HIS playing days were over?

John Krutulis, Coach Steve Howey, Coach Gregg Williams, and Renaldo Wynn all believed Sean would end up mentoring kids. He loved speaking to the kids. They said he might have even been a coach in the NFL one day.

Said Gulliver's John Krutulis, "He'd come back here and speak to the younger kids when he was at the UM. So I think Sean would have done anything that would have involved children. And yes, I'd have hired him in a heartbeat. I was hoping one day he would have wanted to come back here and run our football program, and I would have hired him on as head coach in a minute even if it meant somebody was losing a job.

"He probably would have become an assistant coach right away," said Krutulis. "Sean could have been a motivational speaker; he could have been pretty much anything he wanted, because he just had drive in everything he did."

Coach Steve Howey would have welcomed him on his staff "in a second." According to Howey, "He would have been a great high school coach and mentor for the high school kids. My guess is the University of Miami would have asked him to coach there, and maybe the Redskins too. They probably would have asked him to be a defensive backs coach or something like that."

Coach Gregg Williams said, "After football, I don't know. One of the things I'm most proud of is I have over one hundred former players that have coached with me in high school, college, and the NFL. I don't know if he would have wanted to do that, but it would not have shocked me with his competitive drive. A lot of those players, when they're done playing, continue to compete, and there's no finer stage to compete on than the NFL. I would have hoped he wanted to do that, and if he wanted to, I would have stood side by side with him. If he ever got promoted to head coach, I would have stood by him as an assistant on his staff."

Taking a different approach, Renaldo Wynn thought Sean would have been involved in ministry, but also working with children. "I could see Sean impacting young kids. Kids who resembled him in the same things he went through. He might be coaching or mentoring young people, and I think he would have made such a great impact on those kids because he was so real and had no ego."

Revelation

What most everyone did not know was that Sean had a ten-year plan. That is, he was going to quit football after playing ten years. Josephine Taylor, T. J., and Mike were amongst the few who knew this.

Josephine Taylor

"Sean said, 'When I'm thirty years old, I'm going to retire [from the NFL],'" said Josephine Taylor. "I said, 'Well, Sean … what will you do after that?' He said he may start his own business and take care of his family, his fiancée and his only daughter. He also talked about doing a fast camp so he could work with kids so he could help improve their speed." (Sean went to many of those kinds of camps when he was a child.)

T. J. and Mike

"Whatever business he attacked mentally, he would have succeeded in," Mike said.

T. J. added, "He was always interested in small businesses. Stuff that he could do hands-on."

"Yeah, like franchises," Mike said.

T. J. and Mike spoke about opening car washes—simple things that he could be in on. They once heard Sean talking about opening a couple of Wendy's restaurants. "One morning Sean woke up after playing in the NFL for two years and said, 'Let's fly down to the Bahamas,'" said his friend T. J. "There was a Krispy Kreme convention going on down there." And so they went. However, the news was not good. There were no more Krispy Kreme franchises available in the USA. They could have purchased a few out of the country, such as in France, but that was not on the agenda because Sean wanted to be hands on.

T. J. also said, "His ultimate goal was not to be known as a football player. He'd rather be known for going to college and maybe even [being] a successful businessman. Sean said, 'Football is just something I'm blessed with, and it allows me to provide for my family. I want to be able to take football and build that into another platform in my life as far as business was concerned.' His career would have been like Barry Sanders's. He kept saying, 'I got ten years of this. Ten years. I'm going to go hard for ten years and go out on top.'"

33

The Pete Taylor Message

"When Sean was shot, it really threw me for a loop, and I took a big fall. I always share with people that I don't really know how I made it through. I didn't sleep for a year. When things are on you, that's all you can think about.

"Sean and I did so many things together from the time he came into my home that I can honestly say I have no regrets. I thank God for allowing me to spend those precious moments with my son because I didn't know it was going to be this short. I thank God for my entire family and for the blessing He gave me through them. So the only thing that gets me through is His grace and mercy.

"There's something I want to bring out. You never want to see anyone lose a family member, but when something this tragic happens to you, I can tell you your life becomes slow. Everything you did to raise a kid is like a slow video recorder. You remember every step of his life, and if you miss something, it takes you right back. You're going to remember his first steps, his first words—everything. It's a slow order that eats at you, deteriorates you, wears you down, and the only thing that brings you out of it is God. You have to be very spiritual because so many thoughts go through your mind.

"They say right before someone passes, they see their entire life in the flash of an eye. But when you're the one left behind, you see their life at a snail's pace. This indeed is an interesting dichotomy, and I never thought of it until now. It's exactly the opposite of what you'd expect.

332

"I've seen countless families suffering through the loss of a loved one. I would speak to many families, and they'll tell you everything's okay, but it's not. I know. It's big. It's really big.

"Sean always thought he was just an 'unimportant football player.' He didn't realize how many lives he impacted. People appreciated him as he played for his and their teams. He knew his jerseys were being sold in record numbers. In fact, at one time, his was one of the top-selling jerseys in the NFL. None of that mattered to Sean. He was an ordinary kid playing for the love of the game.

"To this day, the love continues as fans show their appreciation and respect by continuing to wear Sean's jersey, posting pictures and messages on my Facebook wall, keeping his name alive on call-in radio sports talk shows, and even naming their babies after him.

"Many in the media disparaged him for a while regarding his few indiscretions [and non-indiscretions]—all the while misrepresenting his background and where and how he grew up. My daughter Jaz put it best when she said, 'They didn't know his heart. They didn't know who he was or where he really came from.'

"Here's a kid that came up only wishing to be part of a healthy, loving family. He wished the best of the best for everybody, wanting things that anybody else would like to have. Sometimes those things did not happen in Sean's life. Every kid would like to have two parents in their lives living under the same roof. You want to be raised by your mom and pop, but that didn't happen for Sean when he was younger. In fact, for two weeks after Sean moved in with us at ten and a half years old, he was in the bathroom crying. He loved his mom, but he wanted both sides of his family to have a good life."

❦

"To the young men of our society, as a father, I want to say I'm so proud I never became discouraged and let our separation, or Sean's mother not letting me see my child when I wanted to see him, or the court system interfering get to me. I'm proud I made the effort to go by and see him or check on him. My mom and Sean's great-grandmother kept in touch with his mother, so when Sean was at this place or that place, they'd tell me, and I'd show up so I could be with my son. Of course, he was awarded to me by the courts at the age of ten and a half, and I was able to be there for him up until his death.

"So I'd like to say to all devoted fathers, don't give up on your children, and instill the best into them; show them the right way. That's why we're here. There's nothing in life that's easy. It's all hard work. There are disappointments; there's frustration; but at the end of the day, there's satisfaction.

"I don't care if the kids are black, white, green, or yellow. When they don't get what they want, they start pouting; they start showing their butt. But that's what we're here for—to be men, to be leaders of young men because nobody is going to do it for us. Nobody is going to feel sorry for us.

"A lot of times men get frustrated when their women drive them away from their kids. And don't think those kids don't pick up on the bad vibes. 'I don't know my daddy. I don't have a daddy. My mama told me I don't have a daddy.' I didn't want all that for my kids. [Remember. No drama.] I wanted my kids to know all the way through thick and thin, that if I'm man enough to lie down and have a child, I'm going to be man enough to take care of that child.

"And that's just the way it was. That's the relationship we had until the day he died. I hope and pray I was the father he thought I should have been. One of the things I always say is that I wish he was around to see me pass and say, 'Thank God I have a father that made sure he wasn't just a friend but also the guy that took care of business.' I know I was tough—no ifs, ands, or buts. The main thing is that I wish he could have been here to say, 'Dad, thanks for all you've done, sticking with me through thick and thin.'

"I had a father who was tough—an authoritarian—but he made sure what he did was right. I can't complain. It didn't hurt me, so I knew it wasn't going to hurt Sean. And hey, I know some people say, 'Oh, you're too this or too that.' But Sean was told by others many times as a kid that he wasn't going to amount to anything. I heard it. 'Oh, he ain't nothin'.'

"I spent time with my kids going to the parks, being with them and showing them how to keep out of jail, and, above all, making sure they got an education. I called the schools. I got to know the teachers. I made it my business to interact with someone who could give me an update on my child. We have to be more considerate of our kids because they are the future. You don't know how they're going to come out. They may be doctors, lawyers, pro football players, or garbage men. It's important to guide them because we're not going to be here forever and we want them to be the best people they can be. We're going to get old. We're even going to need someone to take care of us one day.

"I know it might sound stupid and redundant, but I was there for my kids. I've seen so many at-risk kids come up, and everybody just throws up their hands. The parents give up and give them up.

"If there wasn't money in my kids' account, I made sure there was. I made it my business to do that because how can I sleep if I don't know if they're sleeping? That's just me. That's how I am."

🏈

"After Sean passed, it took about four years until I started watching football again, sometimes for only ten minutes at a time. I just mentally shut down. I tried to pick up and watch another sport—basketball, something totally different than football. But there were too many football fields we went to games at. There were too many fields where I saw Sean play at since he was a little kid, and every time I passed one, the memories came back.

"We used to break down film together when he was young. I showed him the reads and what to look for. There was just too much of all this, so I had to pull myself away to help control my emotions.

"Now I am once again a fan and a coach, working with the next generation of football-basketball Taylors, my son Gabe."

🏈

Other kids weren't as lucky as the Taylor children. "We were just a loving family, and my kids never wanted for anything. There are, however, players who grew up in poverty. It was sheer determination and great mentors and coaches that pushed them and got them into the league.

"I often think about Pittsburgh Steelers wide receiver Hines Ward's story. He was born in Seoul, South Korea. His dad was African-American and his mom was Korean. When he was just a year old, Hines and his mother moved to Atlanta, Georgia. She, with little English and no friends or family, raised Hines on her own. He made it.

"I think about Shaquille O'Neal—born in Newark, New Jersey—and his dad, who spent most of Shaq's young life behind bars, had no dealings with him even after he got out." Despite Shaq's travails, he became one of basketball's top 50 NBA players of all time, making nearly $200 million in the process. He spent and invested wisely and still has some very lucrative endorsement deals. He also became an actor and NBA analyst.

"I think about Ray Lewis—who was born to a mom of only 16 years old, was ready to retire from the NFL because he never had a father that would come to any of his games and cheer him on. He didn't want that for his own kids. He wanted to go to his son's games and be on the sideline, make all kinds of noise, and yell, 'Come on, boy, run!' He never had that. Despite everything, taken by the Baltimore Ravens in the first round of the 1996 NFL draft out of the University of Miami, he went on to become one of the best NFL safeties to ever play the game, going to the Pro Bowl thirteen times. There are so many athletes going through this struggle today.

"You know, many players who 'made it' despite the odds go broke three to four years after leaving the league. Why? Because they didn't get the proper guidance. After they make it big and they get a little money, often these athletes are misled. They think a person loves them, but they don't. So many people they know end up just wanting a handout.

"Sometimes athletes squander all of their money on homes too big and cars too many. Sometimes they'll trust people they shouldn't.

"When Sean was coming into the league, there was a situation with a guy called Tank Black, where he supposedly invested money for a group of football players and the whole thing was a scam. These guys all came out of Belle Glades, Florida. One of the player's dads was the mayor. Some of these guys made it with good fathers in their lives. They had good leadership, and they still got taken.

"Then you have the guys who have to buy Escalades, Ferraris, Jags, Maseratis, five houses, bling out the ass, and they wonder why they're broke.

"Everybody has a story, and lots of guys fight the same monsters. Those monsters could include the division of families, who loves who the most, this one or that doesn't care about me, etc. That shouldn't be the point. The point should be to be proud of who helped you and then you opening doors for the next one coming up. It shouldn't be all about money. It should be about getting an education, getting where you want to go, and helping your own self while you're helping others. A lot of the athletes just get caught up in the craziness. I'm talking about the thing they wrestle with. At the end of the day, it's not how much you made; it's how much you've saved and put away.

"Not all African-American professional athletes had their stars burn out after their careers were over. Many have gone on to become successful businessmen [and pitchmen]. Former NBA star Magic Johnson grew up in a large family. Both of his parents worked—his father for General Motors and his mother as a school custodian. From those humble beginnings came a basketball player voted to the top 50 players of all time and a business mogul whose company is worth upwards of $700 million today. For several years Johnson also was a minority owner of the LA Lakers. Today in 2014 he heads the LA Dodgers ownership group, which paid $2 billion for the team.

"Also among the greatest basketball players of all time is Brooklyn, New York–born Michael Jordan. He was one of five children and also came from humble beginnings. Jordan learned the meaning of perseverance. Legend has it that he was cut as a sophomore from his high school varsity basketball team. That only made him practice more and harder and, well, you know the rest of the story. Today he not only has his own brands, he also has lucrative endorsement deals with several companies and is the majority owner of the NBA Charlotte Hornets. Oh, by the way, he's a billionaire."

"When Sean was about to get drafted, we had 'the talk.' I had to make sure he wasn't going to do anything dumb and go broke after his career was over. So we talked a lot about investing and saving. Unfortunately Sean did not get to enjoy his retirement." (Neither did Chris Henry, Junior Seau, Paul Oliver, Dave Duerson, O. J. Murdock, and Jovan Belcher, just to name a few.)

"Learning how money works, how agents work, how the combine and the draft work are all important. And speaking of agents, having a good one with a good reputation is definitely in a player's best interest. But if you don't have a good one, before you know it, agents can steer you away from everybody and isolate you. Pretty soon it's, 'Call my agent for a flight, and call my agent for this or that.' The kid now relies on someone else to organize his life. And after his playing days are over? Guess what: no more agents, and the kid has to do everything on its own, and oh, with no one telling him how great he is anymore.

"A kid about to get drafted needs to learn a lot, and quickly. I never knew that when you go to the combine, you're treated like one of the herd. I was there in Denver. I got a chance to see it happen. You come out in a group like a herd of cattle. You're being measured, you're running for speed, you're jumping … and then they bring the next group out. It's all business. It's very interesting to see how things work.

"Some teams don't draft you on combine numbers alone. That's a good thing. I know Joe Gibbs looked for players with character, drive, and a determination to win. I figured out the young group coming out today don't want to be told what to do. Back in my day if someone told you no, it was no and you accepted that. Today if you tell a kid no, there's pouting, moaning, and groaning.

"These guys don't understand. Who is going to put millions of dollars in their pockets if they can't trust you? If I can't trust you, shame on me. If I knew you were a fool and I gave a fool money, I must be the fool. People don't want to look at a fool. They want to see someone with character, just like Coach Gibbs. When a coach sends a guy out, he wants that guy to represent the organization. You don't send a fool out.

"So now you know why I did this book: so I and the others who knew Sean could speak for him. Sean never liked controversy. He avoided it like the plague. I want people to know that my kid wasn't who you thought he was, but by the same token, other kids are dealing with the same issues and problems Sean did. They are the ones being victimized when they shouldn't be. They should just be allowed to be kids."

34

Gratitude

"THERE ARE SO MANY PEOPLE I WANT TO THANK!" SAID PETE TAYLOR, wrapping up the last of our interview sessions. "From the people who sent prayers ... people that paved the way for Sean and his teammates, his fans, relatives, teachers, teammates and coaches—all of them.

"Trust me, it wasn't just Pete Taylor that made it happen for my son," Sean's father said. "It was hotel owners, doctors, chiropractors, and even our local Greyhound bus company. It was the kind people that gave donations to the kids of Florida City, making it possible for Sean Taylor to do the things he did growing up. For example, Sean couldn't get to San Jose, California, in middle school and compete without these people. These were some great people, and even today they tell me, 'If you ever need something for the kids, come see me.'

"Every day, working the streets, I see those in need, and I'm never afraid to go ask for help. I hear people say, 'Things can't happen for the kids. Nobody cares. Nobody wants to do [anything].' Yes, they would. If you are sincere; if you're not just going to take money and blow it; if you're not going to spend the money on yourself but you're going to ask for the right cause and see the good work in action, see the kids coming out right; and if there is accountability; people will support you.

"I want to thank the city of Florida City; Mayor Wallace; all the commissioners and personnel, and the Florida City Police Department, especially Major Taylor, Lt. Butts, my assistant Michelle Ramirez Gonzalez, who ended her vacation with her family in Miami to be there for me. She and her husband even took turns being at the hospital in case I needed anything. I'd like to thank the hundreds of officers who provided logistical support before, during, and after Sean's funeral. Do you know that while I was flying back and forth from Miami to DC, I was still working the phones, helping to coordinate with fifty people who were meeting at FIU to discuss the massive coordination effort?

"I can't thank the city of Miami, the Florida Highway Patrol, Miami-Dade Police Department, and Sweetwater PD enough for all of their help as well. I need to thank Director Parker, with the homicide unit working on Sean's case, the motorcycle units, and other police agencies for helping all of us get around and through this difficult time. I mentioned traffic was a mess, and if it wasn't for Miami-Dade Police, I don't know what we would have done.

"I'd like to thank my daughter Jaz, Mayor Wallace, Coach Joe Gibbs, Jeremy Shockey, Buck Ortega, and all the others who spoke at the FIU memorial service, I would also like to thank the Reverend Jesse Jackson for coming to the funeral and lending his moral support.

"I'd like to thank former Miami Dolphin and Washington Redskin Jason Taylor for his help and support and for the special gesture he made during the 'Ring of Honor' game. I want to also thank friend of the family Clinton Portis for running the #21 flag full-speed down the field prior to the 'Ring of Honor' game.

"Finding accommodations for the expected huge crowd of well-wishers was a daunting task. So I want to thank Sean's agent Drew Rosenhaus for recommending and speaking to the people at FIU who allowed us to use their facilities. The staff at Rosenhaus Sports Representation came up large for us. Special thanks to Pete Garcia, FIU's athletic director, for helping to get that ball rolling.

"While at FIU, the campus police were instrumental in coordinating bus escorts and parking for the thousands who came to pay their respects. I need to thank the Omega Psi Phi fraternity, Pi Nu Chapter, and Delta Sigma Theta Sorority for assisting the family into the services.

"Here's another thing. I want to thank Golden Beach PD. That department was so brilliant as they filled in for my entire force so all of us could attend Sean's funeral service. That department literally took over Florida City. There are just so many people in law enforcement, fire departments, all over the city, and if I could, I would thank them all personally.

"I'd like to thank Reverend Arthur Jackson, pastor of the Second Baptist Church, for opening his doors on Sunday night for the viewing and moderating at the funeral, and Pastor David Peay for the eulogy at Seventh-Day Adventist.

"Thanks to the many singers and the choir, including Lyn Robinson, who sang "Behold Him"; Eva Bethel; and Ms. Arlene Byrd, who performed at the public service.

"The support our family received even to this day from fans, friends, and relatives was and is overwhelming. These are also the same people who were responsible for sending the truckloads of flowers delivered to the FIU campus for the service. That was just amazing.

"I'd like to thank the coordinators at Gulliver Prep and the University of Miami for holding the candlelight vigils in Sean's honor. We were all truly touched by their efforts. Thanks also to Sean's friends and UM roommates Buck Ortega and Jonathan Vilma for their moral support.

"I especially want to thank every player, coach, roommate, teammate, and family member, as well as Mr. Daniel Snyder, who shared their memories of my son with you all. Special thanks to Santana Moss for throwing the 21 to the heavens after he scores a touchdown.

"I want to thank my friend, business partner, and co-author Steve Rosenberg, who spent countless hours with me and with those he interviewed, to make this book possible. I also wish to thank Patti G! for spending many hours typing and editing the manuscript. It was a daunting task, and trust me when I tell you her help was invaluable. Without Steve and Patti, I don't think this book would ever have gotten finished.

"I want to thank everyone at Killian High School, Mr. John Krutulis, his late mother Marian—Mrs. K—and those at Gulliver Prep and the University of Miami who made sure Sean got a top-notch education, and the Washington Redskins ownership and staff for all the help they gave Sean while he was in the NFL.

"Last but not least, I'd like to thank all of Sean's fans and well wishers for keeping my son's name alive. You have been a blessing and an inspiration to us, Sean's family, even more than you could ever know. So from the bottom of my heart, thank you.

"You know, Sean was a good kid who was taken from us too soon. So I had to realize that it was God's plan and He was still in control. There is nothing I can say after that. And that's my story."

35

The Taylor Family Tree

PEDRO "PETE" TAYLOR WAS SEAN'S FATHER.

Donna Junor was Sean's mother.

Josephine Taylor was Pete Taylor's first wife, Sean's stepmother, and mother to Joseph and Jazmin Taylor.

Simone Taylor is currently married to Pete Taylor and is Gabriel Taylor's mom.

Joseph is second oldest (after Sean). He graduated from Gulliver and went on to Florida Memorial University, where he played basketball and won the Florida Sunshine Conference in his first year (2006–07). There were seventeen years between championships in a national tournament for Florida Memorial. They last won in 1970 as a Division II NAIA school and went to the Sweet Sixteen. Joseph graduated from the police academy in 2011 and currently works full time with the Miami-Dade Police Department.

Jazmin is Pedro Taylor's third oldest. She's currently studying nursing at FAMU. However, her heart is set on becoming a doctor. She always did well in school. She played flag football at Nova Southeastern High School and honored Sean by wearing number 21. She also played soccer at Nova.

Simone Taylor's two older children Brooke and Patrick are Pedro Taylor's stepchildren. Brooke wants to be a nurse, and Pat wants to be an engineer. Pat played football at St. Vincent College near Pittsburgh and later transferred to FIU where he is now finishing his undergraduate degree.

Sean's fiancée's name is Jackie Garcia Haley, and they had a daughter also named (Baby) Jackie. Unfortunately they, along with Sean, were in the house the night of the break-in. Today, Baby Jackie, who's the spitting image of Sean, goes to Gulliver Prep, along with Gabe Taylor. She has her father's smile, and you can see when she runs on those long legs of hers that she is definitely Sean's child. (Baby) Jackie loves to play soccer.

"Nobody has more of Sean's personality than Baby Jackie [Jackie and Sean's daughter]," says Baby Jackie's aunt, Jaz Taylor. "Two days ago I took Baby Jackie and my little brother Gabe water rafting. I swear that little girl is Sean all the way. It turns out that Baby Jackie is the spitting image of Sean. She has his shyness, too.

"I wanted to take pictures of her and Gabe when we were at Rapids Water Park in West Palm Beach. She said, 'I don't want to be videotaped. Don't take my picture. I only want to go into the water.' I said, 'Okay, okay.'

"She came to my mom's house to play with my dog. Baby Jackie was jumping on my mom's bed and flipping up and down on the couch. My mom just sat there and looked at her, and she said, 'You know this is Sean, right?' She was jumping around, hugging my dog … 'I want to hug you,' Baby Jackie said to the dog."

Pedro's mom is Constance "Connie" Mackey Dingle. She's responsible for teaching Sean his alphabet when he was very young. She had the unenviable task of potty training Sean as well. In fact, she taught him to use the bathroom in about ten minutes. She was also one of his biggest fans.

Gabriel Taylor, Pete and Simone Taylor's youngest son, at the time of this writing, is attending Gulliver Prep. Just like Sean, he is a superior athlete. In the fall of 2013, as a sixth grader, he completed his first football season there. Following in his brother's footsteps, he played offense, defense, and on special teams. Gabe even played some quarterback and, believe it or not, throws for distance and accuracy with both hands. On specials he ran back punts and kickoffs, sometimes for touchdowns, just like his brother! Gulliver went undefeated in 2013 and even won its single playoff game. In addition, Gabe is also a truly gifted basketball player for Gulliver—just like his brother.

Pete Taylor already has his youngest son Gabe on a strict workout program of sit-ups and push-ups. As the cooler evenings beckon, the young athlete is outdoors running sprints, working on his craft.

Does the hard work pay off? In December 2013 Gabe was featured as fourth place winner in the *Sports Illustrated Kids* 2013 SportsKid of the Year contest. Look out, world. Just like his older brother, Gabe Taylor is making a name for himself.

For more on the 2013 SportsKid of the Year, visit http://www.sikids. com/photos/56971/the-fab-five/4

Gabe Taylor Pops NBA Threes

"In December 2012, when we went to the DC area for the Redskins Rally hosted by Brian Mitchell and Darrel Young, we had some downtime, and we were getting a little bored. My youngest, Gabriel Taylor, in particular needed to blow off a little steam," Pete Taylor said.

"So me, Patrick [one of Pete's wife Simone's sons] and Gabriel all go to a gym to get a little exercise. We decided to play a little basketball. We were just shooting around and ran into some other guys shooting hoops as well. One of their guys had a pretty decent shot, so we asked if they wanted to play a game. They said sure.

"So we're warming up, just shooting around, and started taking some shots from behind the college three-point line. Those other guys were like, 'Hold up, we count threes from behind the NBA three-point line.'

"They had some pretty big guys, as well as some younger kids who were maybe eleven or twelve years old. I knew Simone's son Patrick was a pretty good basketball player. I could hold my own, but I was a little out of shape. And then there was Gabe.

"They had a couple of good guys who could shoot. So we start playing. One of us shot what we thought was a three, but the guy said, 'No; you have to shoot threes from the NBA three-point line.' So Gabe takes the next shot, and it's an air ball. So I tell him, 'Don't worry about it; you'll get another chance.'

"We're playing and are holding up pretty well until Gaby got hot! My son, who was eleven years old at the time, starts popping NBA threes. We ended up winning the game. I guess they were impressed, and even asked for a rematch.

"So we start playing in another game. They picked up another shooter … a ringer, if you ask me. To look at him you wouldn't think he was a stud, but he was.

"He was half Asian, half something else, and he starts shooting and I go, 'Damn! You got a ringer.' So in this game we actually had to play some defense.

"Anyway, Gaby puts on a crossover move on one of the older guys, and he almost does a split. Then Gaby drops back and hits a three. To close the game out, I ran a pick-and-roll and threw the ball back to Gabe, and he drops a nothing-but-net NBA three. And then … we were out of there! It's nice to know we can come out there to DC and take care of business!"

36

Players Are Only Human

IT'S BEEN SAID THAT WITH THE ADVENT OF FREE AGENCY, PLAYERS AND coaches no longer stay loyal to their teams. For both it's a business. As far as the players go, if they are lucky enough to last past their rookie contracts and become free agents, they get to negotiate with whoever will have them, and sometimes they move on. Fans invest millions in jerseys with players' names on the backs, only to see their favorite players leave. Would Sean T. have stayed with the Redskins for ten years? Probably, but we'll never know for sure. Regardless of the team Sean T. would have ended up with, remember to respect the man.

Pro players were once high school and college players with coaches, teammates, and roommates. More often than not, those friends and teammates go off in hundreds of different directions, but some stay in touch once they are out of college (regardless of whether they go pro or not). In fact, some even start businesses with each other despite not being teammates anymore. Some become godfathers to their friends' children and, whether the fans like it or not, have dinner with each other when they are done battling on the playing field. So please keep one thing in mind. When you loudly boo and curse at a player on the other team, remember that he may be best friends with your favorite player on your favorite team. *Respect the man.*

Fans need to be mindful that pro football players are human and are not perfect. Some come to the league very young and inexperienced. Please treat them with respect and common decency. It's okay to cheer for your team, but if someone from that team has a bad day, please show him a little human kindness. These players take losing just as hard as you do, if not harder. *Respect the man.*

Jazmin Taylor, Sean's youngest sister, told me how hard Sean took losing. I'm sure you read somewhere in this book that Sean hated to lose more than he loved to win. Rides home with Sean were never pleasant after a loss. I was told that he kept reviewing the game in his head over and over, thinking what he could have done to make plays he didn't make; and believe it or not, he blamed himself for his team's losses. He was just as hard on himself as you were on him when you cursed him for dropping a ball or missing a tackle. So too are most members of your favorite team hard on themselves. So please, *respect the man.*

Epilogue

Wednesday, January 22, 2014

THE SECOND PART OF A MORE-THAN-SIX-YEAR-LONG ORDEAL FOR THE Taylor, Garcia, and Junor families came to a close when self-proclaimed shooter Eric Rivera, Jr., was sentenced to 57½ years in prison on the charges of second-degree murder and assault with a deadly weapon in the killing of son, father, brother, student, football player, teammate, and fiancé Sean Taylor.

As the writer of the Sean Taylor stories, I have become intimately involved with the Taylor family in just over three years. Being in the courtroom, I felt as though I was more than just a casual courtroom observer; I felt a part of the process and the family. I can only imagine what the "real" families went through. I felt as if I were taking part in a movie, with its last scenes playing out in court before and after Rivera's sentence was imposed. But it was no movie. It was all too real.

Simone Taylor, Pete Taylor's current wife, said to me after the sentencing, "Nobody won today." Both families suffered the loss of a son. The Taylor/ Junor family lost their son Sean, and the Riveras lost their son too, but not quite in the same way. The Garcias lost a potential son-in-law, and Jackie Garcia lost a fiancé and the father of her daughter.

Eric Rivera, Jr., stoically sat shackled in the courtroom, garbed in his red prison jumpsuit next to his two lawyers for the nearly two-hour procedure. He sat motionless and expressionless, as both the accusations and pleading for his leniency echoed through the courtroom. This was in sharp contrast to the jovial Eric Rivera, Jr., we had observed in the courtroom during the trial—a trial in which his defense team must have convinced him he'd win and be set free because of technicalities.

Both sets of lawyers addressed Judge Dennis Murphy, the judge who had been presiding over the case for more than six years. The State (prosecution) presented its case and then asked for Rivera to be sentenced to sixty years in prison. The defense presented its case for leniency rather than acquittal.

The State read three affidavits: from Jackie Garcia (Sean's fiancée and the mother of their child, Baby Jackie); Jackie's father, Rene Garcia; and Sean's mother, Donna Junor. Sean's father, Pedro "Pete" Taylor, then addressed the court in person.

Jackie's letter dealt with how difficult it was to put into words what she was feeling at the present time. She wrote about the loss of the love of her life, her high school sweetheart, Sean Taylor. She wrote of her sleepless nights and not having him around for their daughter's sporting events and birthday parties. Baby Jackie knows her father is in heaven now, but there's something unfair about all of her friends jumping into their fathers' arms at those events and special occasions. Jackie wrote, "I went to bed with a fiancé and our daughter's father and woke up the next morning without him."

In the letter from Sean's fiancée's father, Mr. Rene Garcia mentioned watching his daughter fighting through the effects of post-traumatic stress disorder (PTSD) and how her life was changed forever. Both daughter and father were in the courtroom and in their letters asked Judge Murphy to impose the maximum sentence. Sean's mother Donna Junor's letter was also read in court, and it described how Sean said he would always be there for her, his brother, and his two sisters, but because of the actions of Eric Rivera, that would never be possible.

Then Sean's father, Pedro "Pete" Taylor, addressed the court. Looking directly at Rivera, he spoke about the loss of his son. He also said he was the one who returned to Sean's house, the crime scene, and cleaned up every last drop of blood on his own. Taylor, who is well versed in the law, also brought up Florida's 10-20-Life rule. Since Rivera was convicted of assault with a deadly weapon and second-degree murder, Taylor asked the judge to impose the maximum penalty—life in prison. Taylor also spoke of God—and how Rivera would one day have to answer to a higher authority. After those letters were read and Mr. Taylor spoke, there wasn't a dry eye in the house (at least on our side of the courtroom).

When it was time to recommend a sentence, the prosecuting attorney addressed the court. State's Attorney Reid Rubin spoke about a lying, manipulative, self-serving convicted felon who with his friends senselessly took the life of a son, father, fiancé, and hero to many. Rubin could have asked for life in prison but instead asked for sixty years, which is a little more than twice the sentence received by Venjah Hunte, the getaway driver who plea-bargained for a twenty-nine-year sentence earlier in the process in exchange for his testimony, which in the end was never requested in the Rivera case. (During Rivera's trial, the defense team often stated he knew nothing about the knee injury Sean had sustained two weeks prior or that the football player had chosen to rest his knee at his Florida residence instead of his Northern Virginia townhouse. So Rivera could not have known Sean was at home in Florida, where he could also spend some quality time with his girlfriend and baby daughter. This thereby eliminated the possibility of premeditation.)

At this juncture I'd like to point out what was stated by the prosecution during the Rivera trial: the convicted shooter was arrested two other times in 2007 for possession of a firearm but was never prosecuted. It was important to note those arrests because when it was time for the defense team to address the court, the letters written by Eric's pastor and two teachers described a churchgoing, polite, great, salt-of-the-earth kid, and how his actions were very unlike him. That may be so—but his past did not reflect that image, especially the part where Rivera, Jr., participated in a burglary and murder.

Rivera's grandmother and his father, Eric Rivera, Sr., also addressed the court and talked about bad decisions by a youthful offender, peer pressure, and the possibility of rehabilitation. They talked about how mature he had become in the six years since the crime—all of which Rivera, Jr., had spent behind bars. They also apologized to the Taylors and said how sorry they were for their loss. All pleaded for mercy and the minimum sentence.

When it came time for Eric Rivera, Jr., to address the court, the shackles around his ankles slowed his walk to the podium. Facing the judge and looking quite nervous and confused, he began.

In his own way, Rivera first apologized to the judge for his crime: "My words may not mean much, but over these past six years I learned that Mr. Taylor was a good man, and I'm not making any excuses for my decisions or my actions." He continued, "But I just want to say that I live with it every

351

day and I'm going to have to live with the consequences, [turning his head to address the Taylors, he added] and I'm truly sorry for your loss."

Sitting in the courtroom, I thought about Rivera's words. To me, they appeared to be a poorly rehearsed, forced statement with a lack of conviction. What was also curious to me was the brevity of Rivera's statement, the omission of a request for leniency or an apology for lying under oath—or at least an explanation thereof, especially when his life was on the line.

When it was time to pronounce sentence, Judge Dennis Murphy said, "And here's the hardest part of being a judge. I am not here to make friends; I am here to interpret the law."

With that, Eric Rivera, Jr., received a sentence of 57½ years in prison. With six years of time served, that knocked the sentence down to 51½ years. He'd have to serve at least 85 percent of the sentence, which would make him eligible for parole in 43¾ years, or when he's 66¾. In other words, he's going to be a much older man when he next sees the outside of those prison walls.

Immediately after the sentence was handed down, Rivera's legal team asked for an appeal, which, I was told, is quite normal. It's also quite normal for appeals to last years.

Eric Rivera, Jr., confessed on videotape and in the courtroom apologized for his actions, saying he had to live with the consequences. So what's there to appeal? I heard him confess. Everyone heard him confess.

So the appeals process has already begun. Unfortunately the Taylor, Garcia, and Junor families cannot appeal the ultimate and untimely loss of Sean Taylor.

From the Associated Press: "Jury Convicts Suspect in Sean Taylor Slaying Trial," *USA Today*, June 10, 2014 (http://www.usatoday.com/story/sports/nfl/2014/06/10/jury-convicts-suspect-in-sean-taylor-slaying-trial/10269371/):

> A man identified by prosecutors as the greedy organizer of a bungled 2007 Miami-Area burglary that ended with the fatal shooting of Washington Redskins star Sean Taylor, was convicted Tuesday of murder and burglary, and immediately sentenced to life in prison without parole. A

12-person jury deliberated nearly four hours before finding Jason Mitchell, 25, guilty of first-degree felony murder and armed burglary. Miami-Dade Circuit Judge Dennis Murphy swiftly imposed the mandatory life sentence for murder, plus 40 more years for the burglary conviction.

So now the Taylor, Garcia, and Junor families patiently await the trials of the remaining two alleged assailants, Charles Wardlow and Timothy Brown.

One Final Note

PETE AND I HOPE THAT YOU ENJOYED READING THE STORIES ABOUT HIS son Sean. For this book, Sean's family, friends, teammates, coaches, Pete's assistant, and even a team owner—forty-four people in all (thirty-three included in this book)—were interviewed. Had Pete and I included all of the interviews in this book, it would have been over 700 pages long.

So that all of the people we interviewed can have a chance to share their stories, a second volume of *Going Full Speed* is planned.

Appendix A

2001 Season Recap

Led by quarterback Ken Dorsey, running back Clinton Portis, free safety Ed Reed, wide receiver Andre Johnson, tight ends Jeremy Shockey and Kellen Winslow, Jr., offensive tackle Bryant McKinnie, and strong safety Sean Taylor, Miami won the 2001 national championship.

The Hurricanes began the season with a nationally televised primetime win over Penn State in Beaver Stadium. With a 30-0 halftime Miami lead, Coker pulled his starters and Miami cruised in the second half to a 33–7 victory. The 26-point margin tied for Penn State's worst home loss under Joe Paterno. Miami followed up the victory with wins over Rutgers, Pitt, and Troy State. After building up a 4–0 record, Miami won over Florida State in Doak Campbell Stadium, 49–27, ending the Seminoles' 37-game home unbeaten streak. The Hurricanes then defeated West Virginia, 45–3, and Temple, 38–0, before heading to Chestnut Hill to take on Boston College (BC).

Miami started with a 9–0 lead over the Boston College Eagles, but Miami's offense began to sputter as Dorsey struggled with the swirling winds, throwing four interceptions. The Hurricane defense picked up the slack by limiting BC to just seven points. However, in the final minute of the fourth quarter, with Miami clinging to a 12–7 lead, BC quarterback Brian St. Pierre led the Eagles from their own 30-yard line all the way down to the Hurricanes' 9-yard line. With BC on the verge of a momentous upset, St. Pierre attempted to pass to receiver Ryan Read at the Miami 2-yard line. However, the ball ricocheted off the leg of Miami cornerback Mike Rumph, landing in the hands of defensive end Matt Walters. Walters ran ten yards with the ball before teammate Ed Reed grabbed the ball out of his hands at around the Miami 20-yard line and raced the remaining 80 -yards for a touchdown. Miami won 18–7.

After the close win over Boston College, Miami went on to win over #14 Syracuse, 59–0, and #12 Washington, 65–7, in consecutive weeks in the Orange Bowl. The combined 124–7 score is an NCAA record for largest margin of victory over consecutive ranked opponents.

The final hurdle to the Rose Bowl BCS National Championship Game was at Virginia Tech. Miami jumped on Virginia Tech early, leading 20–3 at halftime, and 26–10 in the fourth quarter. But despite being outgained by the Hurricanes by 134 yards and being dominated in time-of-possession, the Hokies never quit. After a Virginia Tech touchdown and two-point conversion cut Miami's lead to 26–18, the Hokies blocked a Miami punt and returned it for another score, cutting Miami's lead to just two points. But with a chance to tie the game with another two-point conversion, Virginia Tech sophomore Ernest Wilford dropped a pass in the end zone. Still, the resilient Hokies had one more chance to win the game late, taking possession of the ball at midfield and needing only a field goal to take the lead. But a diving, game-saving interception by Ed Reed sealed the Miami victory, 26–24. Defeating Virginia Tech earned the top-ranked Hurricanes an invitation to the Rose Bowl to take on BCS #2 Nebraska for the national championship.

Nebraska proved to be no competition for Miami, which opened up a 34–0 halftime lead en route to a 37–14 final score. Miami won its fifth national championship in the last 18 years, and put the finishing touches on a perfect 12–0 season. Dorsey passed for 362 yards and 3 touchdowns, while wide receiver Andre Johnson caught 7 passes for 199 yards and 2 touchdowns. Meanwhile, the stifling Miami defense shut down Heisman-winner Eric Crouch and the Huskers' vaunted option offense, holding Nebraska 200 yards below its season average. Dorsey and Johnson were named Rose Bowl co-Most Valuable Players. ("2001 Miami Hurricanes Football Team," *Wikipedia*, last modified July 10, 2014, http://en.wikipedia.org/wiki/2001_Miami_Hurricanes_football_team.)

Appendix B

Jim Thorpe Award

Each year, a committee from the NCAA (not affiliated with the Heisman Award) chooses the best players in different categories. If you fit the criteria, you're invited to this meeting.

2003 Home Depot College Football Awards

Maxwell Award, Best All-Around Player
Larry Fitzgerald, Pittsburgh
Eli Manning, Mississippi
Jason White, Oklahoma
Chuck Bednarik Trophy, Best Defensive Player
Michael Boulware, Florida State
Tommie Harris, Oklahoma
Teddy Lehman, Oklahoma
Outland Trophy, Best Interior Lineman
Shawn Andrews, Arkansas
Robert Gallery, Iowa
Chad Lavalais, LSU
Davey O'Brien National Quarterback Award
Eli Manning, Ole Miss
Philip Rivers, N.C. State
Jason White, Oklahoma
Doak Walker Award, Best Running Back
Kevin Jones, Virginia Tech
Chris Perry, Michigan
Darren Sproles, Kansas State

Biletnikoff Award, Best Wide Receiver
Mark Clayton, Oklahoma
Larry Fitzgerald, Pittsburgh
Mike Williams, USC
Jim Thorpe Award, Best Defensive Back
Keiwan Ratliff, Florida
Derrick Strait, Oklahoma
Sean Taylor, Miami
Lou Groza Collegiate Place Kicker Award
Nate Kaeding, Iowa
Jonathan Nichols, Mississippi
Trey DiCarlo, Oklahoma
Ray Guy Award, Best Punter
Dustin Colquitt, Tennessee
Kyle Larson, Nebraska
BJ Sander, Ohio State
Disney's Wide World of Sports Spirit Award
Neil Parry, San Jose State
Home Depot Coach of the Year
Pete Carroll, USC
NCFA Contributions to Football Award
Keith Jackson, ABC Sports

Appendix C

Cover images

Front cover:
Sean Taylor
(Photo courtesy of the Washington Redskins)

Back cover:
Sean making a tackle as a Miami Hurricane: "It's all about THE U!"
(Photo courtesy of The University of Miami and JC Ridley)

Steven Rosenberg and Pedro "Pete" Taylor
(Photo by P. Rosenberg)

Pedro "Pete" Taylor, a South Florida native, is currently
the Chief of Police of Florida City, FL. That's his job. His other passion is football. In 30 years Pete has coached football players of all ages and stages. However, it's one thing to coach someone else's children but an entirely different "ballgame" coaching one's own. Pete began training his son at the age of 11, and that was the foundation for Sean's stellar football career.

Steven M. Rosenberg, a Brooklyn, NY native, moved
to the Washington, DC area in 1983. By 1988, he had established his own advertising, public relations, and event management firm. Over the years, Steven produced, directed and wrote hundreds of print, radio and TV ads. He also created and managed memorable special events that featured many professional athletes. He has since transitioned into a full-time author, playwright, novelist, and screenwriter. Steven splits his time between Washington, DC and South Florida.

Made in the USA
Las Vegas, NV
07 January 2022

40725133R00225